1986

LESOTHO

PROFILES • NATIONS OF CONTEMPORARY AFRICA
Larry W. Bowman, Series Editor

†Available in hardcover and paperback.

ABOUT THE BOOK AND AUTHORS

Wholly surrounded by the Republic of South Africa, the ethnically homogenous state of Lesotho was created in the 1830s by the genius of Moshoeshoe I in the aftermath of the *lifaqane* and owes its independence today to its rugged terrain, the tenacity of its people, and Moshoeshoe's diplomatic skill.

In this introduction, authors Bardill and Cobbe outline the features that make Lesotho unique, tracing its history and discussing the peculiar structure of Lesotho's labor reserve economy and the effects it has on development, politics, society, and culture. They examine Lesotho's fascinating mixture of social and cultural unity and diversity, its problems with rapid social change, the autocratic nature of the government, and sources of political cleavage and constraints on political change. They conclude that despite strong support from the international community since independence, the country has unfortunately been able to do little to promote development, reduce dependence on South Africa, or quell internal dissent. In closing, the authors look at Lesotho's complex international relations—still dominated by South Africa but diversifying in sometimes unexpected ways—and survey the country's prospects for the future.

John E. Bardill has taught at the National University of Lesotho and the University of Manchester. **James H. Cobbe,** currently associate professor of economics and associate dean of the College of Social Sciences at Florida State University, was a research fellow at the Institute of Southern African Studies, National University of Lesotho, in 1981/1982 and has also taught at the London School of Economics and Yale University.

LESOTHO

Dilemmas of Dependence
in Southern Africa

John E. Bardill
and
James H. Cobbe

Westview Press • Boulder, Colorado

Gower • London, England

Profiles/Nations of Contemporary Africa

Copyright © 1985 by Westview Press, Inc.

Published in 1985 in the United States of America by Westview Press, Inc., 5500 Central Avenue, Boulder, Colorado 80301; Frederick A. Praeger, Publisher

Published in 1985 in Great Britain by Gower Publishing Company Limited, Gower House, Croft Road, Aldershot, Hampshire GU11 3HR

ISBN (U.S.) 0-86531-440-3
ISBN (U.K.) 0-566-05159-1

Printed and bound in the United States of America

10   9   8   7   6   5   4   3   2   1

Contents

Tables and Illustrations

ix

Maps

Preface

Lesotho is a beautiful country, but a desperately poor one that has been cursed by geography and history with few resources and many problems. In the chapters that follow, we attempt to give the reader a feeling for the history, economy, social and cultural structure, politics, and international relations of the kingdom. Many of the topics we deal with are open to a variety of interpretations, and some have been the subject of heated debates in the academic literature, reflecting the widely different paradigms of contemporary social science. There are also many issues that, by the nature of things, simply cannot be positively decided one way or the other. To give a simple but illustrative example, there is continuing dispute over whether the country's relatively treeless state is a natural condition or the result of recent deforestation.

Given the introductory nature of this work and the limited space available, we have avoided detailed involvement in academic debates. Instead we have tried to provide a coherent narrative, reflecting our own interpretation of reality and events—an interpretation that owes much to mainstream Anglophone social science, but also much to the Marxist tradition. The resulting eclecticism may well offend purists of all persuasions, but it is unavoidable in a work of this kind, especially when the two authors do not agree on everything. We have tried to note where others have interpreted matters significantly differently from the way we have, but the book is not a survey of points of view on Lesotho. It is our point of view, and if we spur the interests of others sufficiently to generate alternatives, so much the better.

This book has taken us far longer to produce than we originally expected. In the process of writing and revising it, we have accumulated debts to many people, unfortunately far too numerous to mention. Important categories include our colleagues, students, and friends in

Lesotho; library and secretarial staff in Roma, Lesotho, Tallahassee, Florida, and elsewhere; and of course our long-suffering spouses and children. However, a few individuals have helped us so much beyond the calls of either duty or friendship that their efforts should be acknowledged explicitly. These include Colin Murray, who read the whole manuscript in draft, saved us from serious errors, and gave valuable comments; Larry Bowman, series editor, who also made extremely helpful comments on the draft; David Ambrose, who commented on drafts and with his staff in the Documentation Centre of the Institute of Southern African Studies at the National University of Lesotho (NUL), helped us in many other ways; Lucas Smits, for comments; Robert Kukubo, archivist of the NUL Library; Linda Kight and Martha Crow for speeding countless versions of the manuscript through the word processor; and the editorial staff of Westview Press, who were always cheerful and efficient, even when being told another deadline was being missed. None of the above are responsible for the shortcomings of this book, but they share credit for any virtues it possesses.

John E. Bardill
James H. Cobbe

Southern Africa.

LESOTHO

Introduction

The modern Kingdom of Lesotho inherited its boundaries from the British colony of Basutoland. It has a land area of 11,716 square miles (30,350 sq km), slightly larger than the state of Maryland. It is completely surrounded by the Republic of South Africa, filling in the area between the Cape Province, Orange Free State, and Natal in east-central South Africa. Much of the country is mountainous, with elevations above sea level ranging from 5,000 to over 11,000 feet (1,500 to over 3,300 m). No country in the world has a higher lowest point.

The country lies entirely outside the tropics in the Southern Hemisphere. The climate is thus technically temperate but involves great variability in annual, seasonal, daily, and local weather. Four geographic regions are conventionally recognized within the country: the lowlands of the western plateau, the foothills, the Senqu (Orange River) Valley, and the mountains. Four seasons are apparent everywhere, with frost recorded in every month even in the lowlands, but temperatures are normally substantially lower in the mountains than the lowlands, where mean maximum temperatures in January (summer) typically range from 25° to 30° C (77° to 86° F). Absolute minimum temperatures in June and July (winter) may range from −8° C (18° F) in the lowlands to −17° C (1° F) or lower in the mountains. Temperature changes of 50° F (say from 30° to 80°) within twenty-four hours are not unusual. Rainfall is markedly seasonal and variable both from place to place and year to year; Lesotho is in the "summer rain region" of southern Africa, with winters normally dry, although some snow usually falls in the mountains. The average rainfall is *theoretically* adequate for arable agriculture in the lowlands and foothills. However, precipitation most often comes in sudden, violent downpours, frequently in thunderstorms with hail common. Runoff tends to be rapid, and soil erosion (both sheet and gully) is a widespread

Senqu River Valley. Photo courtesy of L.G.A. Smits.

and serious problem. Crop damage from hail and storms is frequent; so are drought, which can be local or nationwide, and frost, which damages maize (corn), the most widely grown crop.

Although the population is predominantly rural, with only 10 percent living in towns, the country is not well suited for arable agriculture. Only about 13 percent of the land area is suitable for cultivation, which implies much less than an acre of cultivable land per rural person. Historically and potentially, pasture for livestock is excellent in much of the foothills and mountains, but the quality of pasture has been seriously degraded by overstocking and poor management. The estimated size of the national livestock herd in 1981/ 1982 included 560,000 cattle, 1,330,000 sheep, 930,000 goats (mohair-producing), over 100,000 horses, 97,000 donkeys, and 60,000 pigs. Horses and donkeys are important means of transport for both goods and people in much of the country; most ploughing is done with oxen, and the ox-drawn cart is common.

The common root *Sotho* is found in the name of the country, *Lesotho*, the language, *Sesotho*, and the words for a person, a *Mosotho*, and the people, *Basotho*. Because many adult Basotho males temporarily migrate to South Africa to live and work, it is customary to distinguish between the de facto population, those physically present in the country, and the de jure population, those who are legal permanent residents. In mid-1985 the de jure population was a little more than 1.5 million and relatively homogeneous ethnically. Sesotho is the

Semonkong Falls. Photo courtesy of L.G.A. Smits.

Lesotho.

mother tongue of more than 85 percent of the population; the small minority that speaks Xhosa live mostly in the south.

The 1976 census enumerated 1,211,923 Lesotho citizens in the de jure population and only 4,892 resident foreigners. Of the latter there were 2,901 South Africans (mostly Black), 863 Europeans, 579 from the Americas, and 83 Asians; 258 were from elsewhere in Africa and 208 were of other or unidentified nationality. During the colonial period, Lesotho's customary land tenure was largely respected by the British authorities; thus, settlement by foreign farmers was prevented, with the result that the only Lesotho citizens who are not Black are a very few missionary and trading families of European or Asian descent. The official languages of government are English and Sesotho, with the former predominant in technical and legal uses, but Sesotho becoming more widely used within government. Legislation and public documents are normally issued in English and often never officially

translated into Sesotho, but important policy and political pronouncements are often made in Sesotho. Spoken Sesotho lends itself
to figurative and colorful expression, and it is widely agreed that
many political speeches lose a great deal on translation into English.[1]

Lesotho used South African currency (initially the pound, later
the rand [R]) exclusively until 1980. Now Lesotho maloti (plural;
singular loti) circulate alongside and at par with the South African
rand. The rand exchanged for half a pound sterling until 1967; one
rand was worth approximately $1.40 from 1967 to 1971; and since
then the exchange rate has fluctuated, reaching a high of $1.49 in
1973 and a low of under $0.40 in August 1985.

Most administrative, legal, educational, medical, and other technical practices and institutions in Lesotho are clearly recognizable as
strongly influenced by British traditions, but often with important
South African and local overlays. The legal system, for example, is
highly complex, having inherited substantial Roman-Dutch elements
from the brief period of Cape administration in the nineteenth century,
a corpus of statutory and common law from the British, and an
important role for customary law.[2] South African influence is highly
pervasive, a result of location and history. During most of the period
of British administration, Lesotho was treated for most purposes as
part of South Africa (and most of the personnel for the administration
were locally recruited in South Africa). Basotho have been migrating
to work or to settle in South Africa for more than a century, and
for more than fifty years it has been normal for as much as half of
Lesotho's adult male population to be in South Africa.

Lesotho's dependence on South Africa is obvious and extreme.
Both the country as an entity and its people as families and individuals
are subject to violent disruption and instability in politics, economics,
and almost every aspect of daily life as a result of decisions taken
outside the country's borders. In what follows, we seek to explain
how this situation came about, describe the dimensions of this
dependence and the vulnerability it causes, and explore the dilemmas
it poses for the government and people of Lesotho.

NOTES

1. There are two rival orthographies of the Sesotho language. One,
derived from that devised by nineteenth-century missionaries, is used in
Lesotho and in this book, despite some anomalies of pronunciation (e.g., h
in th and ph is usually silent; single l before i or u is pronounced as d). The
alternative orthography is arguably more consistent, having been developed
in this century in South Africa, where it is regarded as orthodox, but it is

not accepted in Lesotho as correct. A good brief guide to Sesotho pronunciation in the official Lesotho orthography is found in Leonard Thompson, *Survival in Two Worlds: Moshoeshoe of Lesotho 1786–1870* (Oxford: Oxford University Press, 1975). With the exceptions of Basotho, Lesotho, and Sesotho, we have followed Thompson's practice of using only the stems of proper nouns: e.g., Koena rather than Bakoena.

2. See, for example, Sebastian Poulter, *Legal Dualism in Lesotho* (Morija, Lesotho: Morija Sesuto Book Depot, 1981).

1

The Historical Setting

MOSHOESHOE AND THE RISE OF THE BASOTHO KINGDOM TO 1840

Although radiocarbon dating has shown that people were using rock shelters in Lesotho 50,000 years ago, the first inhabitants of whom we know much were the San, or Bushmen. They were primarily a hunting and gathering culture, using stone tools, and lived in Lesotho for many hundreds, if not thousands, of years. Their rock paintings are found throughout modern Lesotho. By the sixteenth century, if not much earlier, they had been joined by iron-working cultivators and herders. These were members of the two main branches, Sotho and Nguni, of the Bantu-speaking peoples who had begun their migration into Southern Africa over a thousand years earlier. By the late eighteenth century Sotho groups predominated throughout most of this area, except for its southeastern fringes, where Nguni-speakers were prominent. The San, users of a simpler technology, came under increasing pressure from both groups. Although they bequeathed to these groups vestiges of their culture, particularly through intermarriage, they were forced into local extinction by the late nineteenth century.

Socially and culturally, these Sotho and Nguni groups were divided into clans such as the Fokeng, Koena, and Tlokoa (Sotho) and the Phuthi and Polane (Nguni); each clan traced its common descent from a distant ancestor and preserved its distinctiveness through reverence for a common totem—the crocodile in the case of the Koena. Clans were further subdivided into lineage groups, frequently named after a recent ancestor. Politically they were organized into chiefdoms, which largely comprised people from the same lineage group but frequently included some non-kin members as well. Chiefly succession was patrilineal. Although contested on occasion, it normally passed to the first son of the chief's senior wife.

7

By 1820 the majority of chiefdoms were small, consisting of three hundred or four hundred people at most. In a situation in which land for expansion was still available, this small size reflected the tendency for individuals to strike out with their supporters and establish autonomous chiefdoms of their own. Over the next two decades, however, this division and segmentation gave way to a process of amalgamation from which the powerful Basotho kingdom emerged. In explaining this phenomenon, attention has largely been focused on the abilities of Moshoeshoe and the repercussions of the *lifaqane.*

Born in 1786[1] and originally named Lepoqo, Moshoeshoe was the first son of Mokhachane, chief of the Mokoteli, a relatively junior lineage of the Koena. Lepoqo grew up in his father's village of Menkhoaneng, situated in the north of modern-day Lesotho. In about 1804 he was initiated into adulthood, and soon afterward he set out to establish his claim to manhood by leading his initiation age-mates in a series of successful cattle raids. To commemorate one of these he composed a praise-poem to the effect that he had shaved his unfortunate victim's beard, i.e., his cattle. From this time onward he assumed the name under which he was to become famous throughout Southern Africa, that of Moshoeshoe—pronounced Moshweshweh—which was derived from the sound made by a razor shaving.

In 1820 Moshoeshoe left Menkhoaneng with his family and followers and established himself as a village headman, under the overall authority of his father, some miles to the north at the foot of Botha-Bothe Mountain (now Butha-Buthe). It seems clear that by this stage he had become an ambitious and talented leader, and his talents were soon put to the test by a series of conflicts and upheavals that swept the highveld in the 1820s. Known collectively as the *lifaqane,* these events threatened the very existence of all the highveld peoples.

When Moshoeshoe was establishing himself at Botha-Bothe, his contemporary Shaka had already embarked on a process of territorial expansion that led to the creation of the powerful Zulu empire east of the Drakensberg Mountains. Clan after clan of Nguni people was subordinated to Zulu hegemony. Not all succumbed without a fight, however, and some preferred flight to subjugation. Three such clans migrated across the Drakensberg in the early 1820s: the Hlubi, Ngwane, and Ndebele. Trained in the superior tactics of the Zulu army, these groups launched a trail of death and destruction throughout the highveld in the 1820s.

Moshoeshoe's people were soon engulfed by the *lifaqane.* Although securing temporary immunity from attack by the Hlubi and

Ngwane through the payment of tribute, Moshoeshoe was unable to forestall attacks by other groups. Foremost among these were the Tlokoa of Sekonyela. The first Sotho community to be displaced by the Hlubi onslaught of 1822, the Tlokoa engaged Moshoeshoe in a number of skirmishes in 1822 and 1823, culminating in an all-out siege of Botha-Bothe in March 1824. Although defeat was narrowly averted, Moshoeshoe decided to seek a more secure refuge for his followers, who by this time included his father and brothers. The site finally selected was Thaba-Bosiu, 50 miles (80 km) to the south of Botha-Bothe. Thaba-Bosiu is a mesa rising 350 feet (100 m) from the fertile valley of the Southern Phuthiatsana River. The flat-topped summit, about 2 square miles (5 sq km) in area, afforded good pasturage and contained a number of springs. Furthermore, its steep uppermost cliffs and the passes in them could be readily defended.

Thaba-Bosiu's defensive properties were put to good use over the next few years, particularly against attacks by the Ngwane in 1828, Sekonyela's Tlokoa in 1829, and the Ndebele in 1831. This last raid, however, marked in many ways the end of the *lifaqane* for Moshoeshoe's followers. The Ngwane left the area in 1828. Sekonyela was sufficiently impressed by the growing size and power of Moshoeshoe's following to refrain from launching any further direct assaults, and the Ndebele confined their operations in the future to their home base north of the Vaal River.

A more permanent source of concern was the arrival in the late 1820s of armed horsemen from the southwest. These were the Kora, descendants of the Khoi, or Hottentot, people, who were being pushed into Moshoeshoe's territory by expansionary forces in the Cape. Their superior weapons and mobility initially enabled them to inflict serious damage on the outlying communities of Moshoeshoe's steadily growing kingdom. But by the mid-1830s, Moshoeshoe's supporters, equipped with guns and horses, were better able to contain them.

The Kora were not the only new immigrants to the area. In 1833 and 1834 about 8,000 Rolong, coming from the northwest, settled at Thaba 'Nchu, 50 miles (80 km) to the west of Thaba-Bosiu. The Rolong were a Tswana-speaking group, seeking a permanent home after the turmoil of the *lifaqane*. Traveling with them were a number of European missionaries and several hundred Griqua and Newlanders. The latter were "colored" émigrés from the Cape, descendants of marriages between Khoi and Europeans. Despite opposition from some of his subordinates, Moshoeshoe originally welcomed these newcomers for the protection they afforded his western flank, and for a while relations between them and his own followers were peaceful.

Moshoeshoe's chiefdom not only managed to survive the *lifaqane* and to contain the threat of newcomers to the region; it also expanded rapidly. In 1824, when he moved to Thaba-Bosiu, his following numbered several hundred people. Ten years later it was estimated by missionaries to be about 25,000 people who were spread over a wide area surrounding Thaba-Bosiu. By the mid-1830s, therefore, Moshoeshoe's small and insignificant Mokoteli chiefdom had been transformed into a kingdom, the largest and most powerful in the region. His own preeminence was increasingly recognized through the titles by which he was now commonly addressed: *Morena oa Basotho*, Chief of the Basotho, rather than merely of the Mokoteli or the Koena; and *Morena e Moholo*, Great Chief or King.

In accounting for the rise of the Basotho kingdom most studies have emphasized the character and skills of Moshoeshoe that enabled him, to a far greater extent than any of his contemporaries, to take advantage of the uncertainty occasioned by the *lifaqane* to attract and maintain a rapidly growing following.[2] Of particular importance were the protection and material benefits he provided and the fair and tolerant justice he dispensed.

Protection was ensured, however tenuously at times, by his military strategy, adopted during the *lifaqane* and pursued until the end of his reign. He correctly concluded that tenacious defense coupled with conciliatory gestures toward his foes offered the best chance of survival. In the early 1830s Moshoeshoe's ability to protect his followers was enhanced by his decision to seek the assistance of European missionaries. Informed that they were proving helpful in bringing peace to neighboring Rolong and Griqua settlements, he sent an invitation to them to come and do the same for his people. In response to this, three young Frenchmen of the Paris Evangelical Missionary Society (PEMS) arrived at Thaba-Bosiu in June 1833. Other PEMS missionaries were soon to follow, and by 1847 nine mission stations had been opened. These missionaries were to have important long-term effects on the social, economic, and political life of the Basotho. In the beginning, however, they were valued for the protection they afforded against groups such as the Kora, who could ill afford to antagonize White opinion in the Cape and to jeopardize their supplies of weapons and ammunition by willful attacks on missionary settlements.

Many of those who sought Moshoeshoe's protection were destitute on arrival. To these he offered support, especially through the loan of *mafisa* cattle. Under the *mafisa* system cattle could be used by the recipients for milk and draft power but remained the property of the owner. In welcoming new adherents and providing them with material support, Moshoeshoe demonstrated a high degree of impartiality. Some of his new subjects were former adversaries, and his tolerance toward them never ceased to surprise his less-forbearing advisers. To his administrative and legal duties he devoted himself assiduously and fairly. Although resolute when necessary, he was rarely dictatorial; he preferred to consult the views of his councillors and less frequently those of all his adult male followers at a general meeting (*pitso*), where opinions could be expressed freely and critically.

Moshoeshoe's growing following came from diverse ethnic and cultural backgrounds. To attract people was one thing. To weld them into an embryonic Basotho nation was another. This he tried to do by initiating policies designed to strengthen not only his personal control but also that of his Koena lineage over the disparate elements that were increasingly coming to make up his kingdom. One of these was the *mafisa* system, which was used far more extensively by Moshoeshoe and his senior Koena relatives than by rival chiefs such as Sekonyela. While conferring benefits on the recipients of the *mafisa* cattle, the system also served to strengthen the dependence of such recipients on Moshoeshoe and his senior chiefs, as the cattle could be repossessed. Other policies included the placing of relatives as subordinate chiefs, forging alliances and creating obligations through judiciously arranged marriages, and controlling trade.

Although Moshoeshoe was prepared, and to some extent forced by circumstances, to exercise a loose rein over his most powerful non-Koena subordinates, such as the Phuthi of Moorosi, he tried to place his brothers and senior sons in positions of authority over the weaker communities in the kingdom. He also encouraged his chiefly relatives to marry on a scale hitherto unprecedented for the Koena and set a prodigious example by marrying more than a hundred wives himself. As women were primarily responsible for cultivation, this policy served to expand the productive capacity of the chiefly homesteads. This capacity was increased in addition by the extension of tribute-labor obligations (*matsema*), under which the chiefs could call upon the unpaid labor of their male followers for work in the fields of their senior wives. As the price of *bohali* (bridewealth paid in cattle) was rising at this time, it was only the chiefs, and especially the senior chiefs, who could afford to marry on an extensive scale, thus widening the gap between rich and poor. Intermarriage between cross-cousins (children of opposite-sex siblings) was also encouraged and served to retain cattle wealth within the lineage.

The increasing wealth enjoyed by Moshoeshoe and the senior members of his lineage gave them lucrative opportunities for trade, particularly with the expanding mercantilist nexus in the Cape. Initially,

Basotho grain was exchanged for cattle to replenish stocks depleted by the *lifaqane*. Later, both grain and cattle were traded not only for items of consumption, but also for implements such as plows that facilitated even greater agricultural productivity. Of special importance were the guns and horses that were acquired through trade and used to enhance Moshoeshoe's position as protector of his people.

To create and consolidate a powerful kingdom from the turmoil of the *lifaqane* was a considerable achievement. But by the 1830s the kingdom was still a loose confederation rather than a tightly knit unitary state. Many of Moshoeshoe's brothers and sons, now stationed throughout the territory, were showing ambition for greater autonomy and became frustrated when autonomy was denied them. So too were powerful non-Koena subordinates such as Moorosi. To contain these pressures, Moshoeshoe was forced to exercise all his diplomatic skill. Even so, had the *lifaqane* and its Kora aftermath ended in peace, the tendency toward fission might once again have become dominant. That it did not was largely the result of pressure in the late 1830s from large numbers of Dutch farmers, or Boers, fleeing the Cape Colony in the wake of the Great Trek of 1835.

THE BASOTHO KINGDOM UNDER PRESSURE, 1840–1871

External Challenges

The White frontier had reached Moshoeshoe's kingdom in the early 1830s in the form of Dutch pioneers, or trekboers. These were descendants of the settlers who had occupied the Cape peninsula in 1652 under the auspices of the Dutch East India Company. Over time they had spread out from the Cape in search of land and greater autonomy from company rule. Their resentment against government interference from Cape Town was intensified after the imposition of British rule in 1806, and in 1835 it culminated in the Great Trek. Over the next ten years the original trekboers were joined by about 14,000 voortrekkers, migrating to areas outside immediate British control. Passing close to Moshoeshoe's kingdom, some continued to a new life north of the Vaal River. Others, however, settled in the southeastern highveld, where their appetite for land (6,000 acres [2,400 ha] was a normal Boer farm) brought them into increasing conflict with Moshoeshoe and posed the most serious challenge yet to the Basotho kingdom.

In responding to this challenge, Moshoeshoe appealed as early as 1841 for the protection and support of the strongest power in the subcontinent—the British. His continuing efforts to align himself with the British and to forestall a potentially disastrous British-Boer alliance against his people formed a major part of his strategy throughout the period. In the 1840s this strategy met with some initial success. In 1843 he entered into a treaty with Sir George Napier, the governor of the Cape, which recognized a considerable portion of his territorial claims. In an 1845 agreement with Napier's successor, Sir Peregrine Maitland, Moshoeshoe accepted a reduction in the southwest part of his kingdom, to appease White claims, in return for the promise of stricter British control over Boer encroachment elsewhere. Such controls were also enshrined in the Orange River Sovereignty, which was proclaimed by the British in 1848 over all the lands between the Orange and Vaal rivers.

For the most part, however, Moshoeshoe was to be disillusioned by British policy. Having established the sovereignty, the British were too parsimonious to provide sufficient funds and personnel to enable it to fulfill its tasks effectively. Moreover, its administrator, Henry Warden, was far from impartial. He increasingly accepted the view of the Boers and of Moshoeshoe's African adversaries[3] that the Basotho were the major threat to stability in the region. In 1849 he enforced an unpopular and vastly reduced boundary on Moshoeshoe, and in 1851 he led a force to chastise the Basotho; however, the attack was easily repulsed. Although British humiliation at this defeat was partially avenged a year later by Governor Sir George Cathcart, the Colonial Office in London became more and more disenchanted by the sovereignty's inability to bring peace to the area. In February 1854 the British withdrew from the sovereignty, and at a convention in Bloemfontein they transferred the government of the area to what became the Boer Republic of the Orange Free State.

The convention was ominously silent on the crucial question of the boundary between Basotho and Boer. With the dissolution of the sovereignty, Moshoeshoe argued that the boundary should revert to the Napier and Maitland lines. The Orange Free State rejected this and pressed, ultimately with British support, for the recognition of the Warden line of 1849.

The tension mounted and finally erupted in the wars of 1865–1868. As the fighting progressed, the unequal arms provisions of the Bloemfontein Convention, that allowed the Boers but not the Basotho to obtain weapons and ammunition from the British colonies, tilted the balance decisively in favor of the Free State forces. By late 1867 nearly all of Moshoeshoe's territorial chiefs had been forced to capitulate, and although Moshoeshoe himself remained defiant on Thaba-Bosiu, it seemed only a matter of time before the kingdom

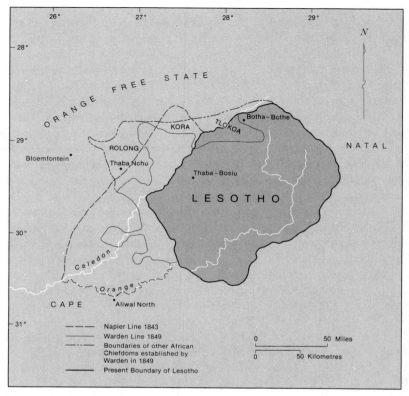

Moshoeshoe's Shrinking Kingdom.

that he had struggled so long to build would finally disappear. That it did not was largely the result of British intervention.

Moshoeshoe's overtures for British protection were stepped up after the outbreak of hostilities in 1865. Although initially rejected, these appeals finally bore fruit, and in March 1868 the kingdom was annexed to the British Crown under the name of Basutoland. One obvious reason for this action was the genuine sympathy for the Basotho cause shown by the governor and high commissioner in the Cape, Sir Philip Wodehouse, whose dispatches to London were so important in securing British intervention.

It is unlikely, however, that the compassionate appeals alone would have been sufficient to reverse Britain's reluctance to expand its imperial commitments in Southern Africa. Additional factors were clearly involved. The wars of 1865–1868 sent a disturbing influx of Basotho refugees into the Cape and Natal. There was also the possibility

MORENA MOSHOESHOE

Moshoeshoe I, photographed in 1860. Photo courtesy of David Ambrose.

that the Free State might attempt to sever its former economic dependence upon the British colonies by using its conquest of Lesotho as a basis for expansion toward the coast through the independent Xhosa chiefdoms that lay between the Cape and Natal. Equally if not more important were the damaging consequences of the wars for the lucrative trade that had long been established between British merchants and Basotho grain producers. Commercial groups in the colonies, as well as in the Free State, were loud in their protest. So too was Wodehouse. In a dispatch to the colonial secretary, for example, he explained, "I was most desirous of bringing to a close war which had ruined our commerce with the interior, and caused destructive losses to the merchants of the colony."[4]

In February 1869 Wodehouse met with a Free State delegation and agreed on a boundary between Basutoland and the Free State. Despite Wodehouse's sympathy for the Basotho, this agreement resulted in the loss of much of the arable territory claimed by them, including all their lands to the west of the Caledon River. Only a few minor alterations in Lesotho's borders have taken place since then.

Having assumed overall control, the Colonial Office in London was reluctant to assume direct responsibility and the costs that responsibility entailed. Instead it favored annexation by a neighboring British colony. Initially the preference was for Natal, but in the face of opposition to this idea from both Wodehouse and Moshoeshoe, it was finally agreed in 1871 that the Cape Colony would take charge. Moshoeshoe did not live long enough to witness this. He died in March 1870. But he was laid to rest secure in the knowledge that his life's work had not been completely in vain.

The Internal Cohesion of the Kingdom

The external threats to the integrity of the Basotho kingdom between 1840 and 1871 were accompanied by the emergence of important domestic contradictions. Although the kingdom still tended to become more consolidated under the authority of Moshoeshoe, his Koena lineage, and the chieftainship in general, it encountered a number of challenges to its internal cohesion.

The consolidation of the kingdom was fostered by increasing land pressure and by a sense of national unity aroused by the wars with the Free State. It was further enhanced by the growing privileged position of the chiefs with respect to commodity production and exchange, which saw remarkable growth despite the conflicts that frequently disrupted them. The kingdom's principal export was grain. Sorghum and maize were produced for both consumption and exchange; wheat almost exclusively for sale. Although no reliable statistics exist for exports during the period, the frequent references made at the time to the kingdom's position as the "granary" of the Free State, and indeed of the Cape, attest to the size and significance of Basotho exports. The majority of commoner homesteads were unable to produce sufficient surplus to permit anything other than a marginal participation in the expanding commercial nexus. The chiefs, however, did have a surplus to exchange; and with their greater land, their more extensive use of tribute-labor, and their increasing use of the imported plow, this surplus rose rapidly over time. In return for their grain they were able to acquire horses, cattle, guns, and manufactures; this material accumulation bolstered their economic and political power. Such imports could also be obtained by encouraging their followers to seek temporary work on European farms outside the kingdom; thus began what has become the dominant feature of Lesotho's economy—its dependence on migrant labor.

The cohesion of the kingdom did not go unchallenged, however. First, the divisive tendencies of the pre-*lifaqane* period were by no means eradicated. By necessity, as well as by temperament, Moshoeshoe was compelled to exercise a loose rein over the activities of his outlying subordinates. In addition, his reliance on his personal authority and his failure to create institutions that might have complemented and outlived him served, to some extent, to perpetuate divisions in the chieftainship rather than to eliminate them. This was particularly the case when the succession issue became vital. Because of the coolness that marked his relations with his eldest son and chosen successor, Letsie, Moshoeshoe did little to prepare him for his future role. As a result, Letsie enjoyed no more power and respect than many of the other territorial chiefs, a situation that had obvious implications for the future unity of the kingdom.

Second, the power of the chiefs came under increasing attack from the PEMS missionaries. At first they had tried, with some success, to convert chiefs and through them reach their followers. By the early 1850s, however, nearly all the converted chiefs had reverted to their customary beliefs and had rejoined the vast majority who had always regarded the missionary presence as a serious challenge to their power. Practices condemned by the missionaries, such as polygyny and tribute-labor, were so inextricably linked to the perpetuation of chiefly preeminence that they could not be curtailed, let alone abolished.

Over time, therefore, the missionaries came to see the chieftainship as an obstacle rather than an ally in their work. Instead they turned their attention to the commoners. To attract commoners to the mission stations, it was necessary to sever the ties that bound them to their chiefs and to replace those bonds with an alternative economic base. Although small in number and thinly dispersed, the mission stations soon became thriving entrepôts of commercial activity and posed a growing challenge to the economic and political domination of the chiefs.

Finally, although many chiefs and Christian converts prospered as a result of the economic transformations taking place, this was far less true of a growing number of commoner homesteads, especially during the drought and famine of the early 1860s and during the devastation and displacement of the wars that followed. The hardships experienced by such families were aggravated by the failure of many chiefs to fulfill their traditional redistributive functions. During the wars, such chiefs frequently protected their own stores of wealth while leaving their followers to bear the brunt of the suffering. This stimulated popular grievances against the chieftainship that were to grow and to be articulated more frequently in the years to follow.

PEACE AND WAR: CAPE RULE, 1871–1884

The Attack on the Chiefs

In his appeals for British assistance, Moshoeshoe had envisaged a loose form of protection under which the domestic affairs of the country would have remained under the control of the chiefs. When the Cape Colony assumed responsibility for Basutoland in 1871, the structures introduced for its administration were based on radically different premises. These were embodied in the regulations proclaimed by the governor of the Cape in October 1871. Basutoland was to be ruled directly by resident magistrates stationed in four newly created districts. These magistrates were responsible to the governor's agent based in Maseru, the new capital, and through him to the governor in Cape Town. Lawmaking powers were vested in the governor, subject to final ratification by the Cape Parliament. Finance for the administration of Basutoland was to be raised internally, largely through the collection of hut tax (a fixed annual payment levied on each dwelling unit).

These regulations signaled a major challenge to the power of the chiefs, since many of their powers, notably land allocation, were transferred to the Cape administration. For most of the 1870s, however, the actual strategy followed by the Cape government and its officials in Basutoland was one of gradual erosion rather than total onslaught. By exploiting the divisions that existed within the chieftainship, which had increased since Moshoeshoe's death, the magistrates attempted a divide-and-rule policy, whereby cooperative chiefs were rewarded with official support in their rivalry with their opponents. Collaboration was also encouraged by allowing the chiefs to retain 10 percent of the hut tax collected from their followers, a privilege that could be withdrawn if they proved recalcitrant. In addition, officials were frequently prepared to turn a blind eye to some of the practices of which they disapproved.

The gradualist approach, by its very nature, did not anticipate spectacular results. But successive reports by the governor's agent expressed increasing satisfaction with the progress being made. The administration could count on the support of Letsie, the paramount chief, and, after some initial reluctance, that of Molapo, Moshoeshoe's second son and principal chief of the northern Leribe District. Revenue was rising, law and order had been secured, and missionary penetration (by Catholics and Anglicans, as well as the PEMS) was steadily expanding.[5]

Opposition from many chiefs was still present, however, and in the case of the fiercely independent Moorosi and his Phuthi followers in the southern part of Basutoland, this opposition culminated in 1879 in open rebellion, suppressed by Cape forces with much loss of life. Although the Moorosi Rebellion did not spread to other parts of the country, it did reinforce the imperatives of the gradualist approach if similar incidents were to be avoided in the future. However, to the alarm of the Basotho, local officials, and missionaries, the Cape government shifted from gradualism to a policy of direct confrontation. Early in 1880 a number of provocative measures were introduced: an unnecessary doubling of the hut tax (revenue already exceeded expenditure), a proposal to auction land to White settlers, and most important, an order for the Basotho to surrender their firearms. These measures alarmed and divided the Basotho and led ultimately to a nationwide rebellion (the Gun War of 1880–1881). The Cape government lost the war despite the expenditure of more than £3 million.

The disarmament proclamation was repealed, and hostilities between Cape forces and Basotho ended, but a bitter civil war within Lesotho continued between followers of chiefs who had remained loyal to the government during the Gun War and those who had rebelled. The Cape government realized its inability to control the situation and moved to "disannex" Basutoland. The British government in London, having convinced itself that the territory could pay for itself and that its rule, rather than the Cape's, would be acceptable to most of the population, assumed direct responsibility for Basutoland in March 1884.

By their resistance in the Gun War and their unwillingness to accept the continuation of Cape rule, the Basotho avoided the fate of many other Southern African kingdoms, whose powers were broken and whose people became later the exploited victims of segregation and apartheid. Direct British rule also led to Lesotho's ultimate political independence in 1966. The kingdom's economic independence was a different question, however.

The Origins of Economic Dependency

South Africa, it has been suggested, "advanced politically by disasters and economically by windfalls."[6] The period of Cape rule coincided with the first such windfall, the discovery of diamonds. Alluvial deposits were found in 1867, but it was the discovery three years later of the rare and extensive underground deposits in what was to become Kimberley that resulted in the mining revolution and dramatic transformation of the South African economy. Exports of diamonds soon exceeded those of other commodities. Kimberley developed almost overnight into South Africa's second largest town. An ambitious program of railway and harbor construction began. With the growth of infrastructure and towns, the demand for foodstuffs and labor-power rose rapidly; it was to supply these two commodities that African societies were progressively integrated into South Africa's nascent capitalist economy.

There was a remarkable growth both in commodity production in, and in migrant labor from, Basutoland between 1871 and 1874. Grain production recovered rapidly from the ravages of the wars with the Free State, and exports increased fourfold during the 1870s. Wool production also grew. The chiefs and the Christian converts were largely responsible for this expansion, as they had been in earlier years. After 1871 production of goods explicitly for sale, most notably wheat, became far more common throughout the country, facilitated in part by the increasing use of the imported plow.[7] One immediate consequence was a rapid rise in the amount of land coming under cultivation in the lowlands. Greater pressure was placed on soil fertility and pasturage, and by the late 1870s, missionaries and officials were recording the danger signs. Although the pressure was eased by the spread of cultivation to the mountains in the mid-1880s, it could never be resolved permanently.

The number of migrant laborers also increased markedly during this period. In 1877 about 15,000 passes were issued for work outside the kingdom, and in 1884 more than 20,000 were issued.[8] Migrants worked in almost equal numbers on the diamond fields, on railway works in the Cape, and on farms in the Cape and Free State. External and internal factors propelled them into the labor market. Externally, they were attracted by the relatively high wages that resulted from chronic shortages of labor outside the kingdom. Internally, chiefs, missionaries, and local officials—who were faced with an increasing number of requests for laborers from employers outside the kingdom— also encouraged workers to migrate elsewhere for work.

Migrant labor and commodity production were also stimulated by internal forces, among them the hut tax. From 1872 the tax was paid entirely in cash rather than in kind. To obtain cash, the Basotho could either sell produce in the market or sell their labor power. Cash was also required to buy imported commodities. Chiefs and well-to-do Christians were again the principal consumers, especially of the more expensive items, but dependence on imports became increasingly prevalent throughout Basotho society—a trend reinforced by the decline in local handicraft production.

The growing dependence on commodity production, imports, and migrant labor was to have far-reaching implications. One of these, already noted, was that increases in cultivation and in population were occurring although the land available to the Basotho was now strictly limited by the new borders. Another was the trend toward greater stratification and inequality in society. Accounts by missionaries and officials attest to the growing disparity between chiefs and commoners, and complaints on this issue were aired by the commoners at public gatherings, or *pitsos*. The results of such inequalities were concealed to some extent in the boom years of the 1870s, but with the dislocations of the Gun War and the effects of the depression and drought that followed it, they were to become much more apparent in the 1880s. While the chiefs continued to turn their advantageous position into the private as distinct from communal accumulation of wealth, a growing number of their followers were faced with increasing poverty.[9] Far more vulnerable than the chiefs to the vagaries of climate and market, the poor commoners experienced difficulty in satisfying their needs from agricultural production alone. Frequently in debt and often unable to pay their hut tax, they were coming to depend, therefore, on migrant labor as a necessary rather than discretionary fact of life.

At this stage, the problems of the poor did not stem from inability to produce enough agricultural output in years of normal rainfall. Lesotho still produced a surplus of grain most years. However, the price of grain for export from Lesotho had fallen dramatically, following the completion of railways from South African ports to the mining towns of the interior, and actions by governments elsewhere in Southern Africa to protect their White farmers from Basotho competition.

BASUTOLAND, THE HIGH COMMISSION TERRITORY, 1884–1966

The Administrative Structure: From Parallel to Indirect Rule

With the advent of direct imperial control in March 1884, all legislative and executive powers were vested in the high commissioner in Cape Town and exercised on his behalf in Basutoland by a resident commissioner and a number of district commissioners. For the first fifty years of British rule, however, these powers were used sparingly. In a marked reversal of the Cape's policy of direct rule, the new officials selected the chieftainship as the principal instrument for local administration, reserving for themselves control of external relations, trade, and finance. As long as the chiefs ensured that taxes were collected and that law and order were maintained, the colonial officials were prepared to leave the internal affairs of the territory in chiefly hands. This policy has been described as an exercise in parallel or dual rule.

However, for the British to rule through the chiefs, the divisions among them had to be overcome. The principal British strategy was to bolster the position of the paramount chief. If his preeminence could be restored, there was a good chance that the chiefs and their followers would gradually fall into line. Support was offered, therefore, to successive paramounts—Letsie (1870–1891), Lerotholi (1891–1905), Letsie II (1905–1913), and Griffith (1913–1939)—in their disputes with their major rivals. Such disputes were not resolved overnight, but by the early decades of the twentieth century there was evidence that the paramount's position as the undisputed leader of the nation was being steadily strengthened.

An important development that assisted this process was the establishment of an advisory council for the discussion of the affairs of the kingdom. Originally constituted as the National Council in 1903, this body was given statutory recognition and a new name, the Basutoland Council, in 1910. Over time the council came to replace the *pitso* as the major forum for the airing of national opinion. Unlike the *pitso*, however, to which all adult males were invited, the council had a restricted membership that included the paramount, ninety-four members nominated by him (not all of whom were necessarily chiefs), and five members nominated by the resident commissioner. The paramount's increasing ascendancy was largely due to his powers of nomination to this important body. Although ultimately to become more representative, the council was dominated in its formative years by the chiefs, especially the senior members of Moshoeshoe's lineage. One of the council's first actions was the introduction in 1903 of the Laws of Lerotholi, a codification of customary law that among other things set out the powers and responsibilities of the chieftainship and recognized the preeminent position of the paramount within it.

By the 1920s such developments had certainly helped to promote the cohesion of the chieftainship. They had done very little, however, to equip it with the means to deal effectively with the growing range of problems created by the socioeconomic changes that were rapidly transforming the country. That this was so is evidenced by the growing complaints that were voiced by commoner elements. Although the institution of chieftainship itself continued to be widely respected, individual chiefs were criticized on a number of grounds: for excessive use of tribute-labor, appropriation of stray stock, failure to share their wealth with the people, and the slow and arbitrary justice that was frequently experienced in their courts. Also called into question was the rapid expansion of the placing system, a way of creating new chieftaincies first introduced by Moshoeshoe. This system was now extended to junior as well as senior members of the dominant Koena lineage and led to a rapid growth in the number of chiefs, as existing jurisdictions were progressively subdivided to make way for new incumbents. Despite such criticisms the chiefs continued to use their majority on the Basutoland Council to resist efforts by the council's commoner minority, and belatedly by the British, to introduce reforms.

Change was eventually precipitated by the depression and drought of the late 1920s and early 1930s. These two events had disastrous consequences for the country's economy, and in recognition of this the British government dispatched Sir Alan Pim to inquire into the financial and economic position of the territory. Pim by no means confined his investigation to economic considerations alone because he recognized that these could not be divorced from broader administrative questions. His views on the administrative structure, contained in his 1935 report, were far from deferential. The policy of parallel rule he criticized as "non-interference . . . leaving two parallel Governments to work in a state of detachment unknown in Tropical Africa."[10] Instead, he recommended the introduction of a system of indirect rule, based on British practice elsewhere in Africa, under which native institutions would be "incorporated into a single system of government and subjected to the continuous guidance, supervision and stimulus of European officers."[11]

Pim undoubtedly exaggerated the extent of colonial noninterference in the period before 1930. The British in fact intervened regularly to restructure the chieftainship to serve their colonial objectives. Nevertheless, his report did pinpoint a number of shortcomings in the system of native administration, and during the years 1938–1946 Basutoland officials attempted to rectify some of these by moving toward the creation of an indirect rule framework as suggested by Pim.

The reforms involved statutory recognition of chiefs by announcements in the official *Government Gazette*, reductions in their numbers and powers, and the introduction of official salaries for some of them. By 1950 only 122 chiefs could hold courts, compared to 1,340 earlier, and chiefs had lost rights to tribute-labor, court fines, and the proceeds of sales of stray stock. These reforms, although mostly desirable, were implemented rather arbitrarily and produced much resentment and frustration among both former and more junior chiefs.[12] This resulted in important and divisive effects on politics.

The most serious limitation of the 1938–1946 reforms, however, was the fact that they were obsolete as soon as implemented. In essence the British were attempting to introduce the machinery of indirect rule into Basutoland at the same time as they were beginning to dismantle it in other parts of Africa in response to nationalist pressure for more representative and responsible institutions. The irony of this situation was not lost on the Basotho, who were by no means isolated from the spreading nationalist feelings that followed World War II. "What was needed," argued one authoritative report, "was less emphasis on indirect rule and control from above, and more emphasis on encouraging the growth of responsibility and initiative in the hands of Basotho organs of self-government."[13] Agitation for changes of this kind mounted in the late 1940s and early 1950s, forcing the British to accept a much more rapid process of constitutional change than they had originally envisioned.

The Policy of Social and Economic Neglect

Before the 1930s the British paid almost no attention to social and economic issues. Downing Street's insistence that Basutoland should pay its own way meant that few resources were available for development. Even so, revenue—drawn largely from taxation, from export duties, and following the 1910 Customs Agreement from a share of South Africa's customs and excise duty—almost always exceeded recurrent expenditure. Any surplus that accrued, however, was frequently accumulated or used for purposes other than economic and social development.

The consequences of this neglect were clearly revealed in Pim's report of 1935. Concerning agriculture, for example, Pim observed that "no provision is made for the greatest need of the Territory, the initiation of measures to deal with the erosion which is steadily ruining the country."[14] His report was largely responsible for persuading Britain to reverse its earlier policy of denying external aid to the kingdom. As Chandler Morse's influential report of 1960 observed, however, the assistance provided was too little and too late to do much more than scrape the surface of the problems that beset Basutoland.[15]

Health and nutritional problems remained serious despite increased government spending. The 1956–1960 Nutrition Survey revealed that 75 percent of all Basotho were undernourished and that infant and child mortality rates were rising rather than falling.[16] In particular, the Morse report observed that the antierosion measures initiated by the British after Pim's report were barely containing the situation, which was likely to deteriorate rapidly unless more funds were made available. If problems remained in areas to which funds were directed, the situation was much worse in those to which they were not. Industry, for example, was almost entirely neglected. So, too, was the development of the country's water resources, potentially one of its most valuable assets.

In explaining British neglect, one of the most popular arguments to date has centered on the question of incorporation.[17] If Basutoland, together with Botswana and Swaziland, was ultimately to be incorporated into South Africa—which for many years seemed likely—then it would make little sense for Britain to commit funds and resources for the development of the three territories. Far better to leave development to the South African government when the time came for it to assume responsibility.

That Britain anticipated the transfer of the High Commission Territories can be seen from the inclusion of provisions for this eventuality in the South Africa Act of 1910, which granted self-government to the Union of South Africa. Basing its arguments on these provisions, the South African government pressed steadily and with increasing impatience for transfer over the next forty years. However, during the act's passage through the British Parliament, the British government committed itself to consult the local inhabitants of the territories before any decision on incorporation was taken. It was on this proviso that South African efforts to seek transfer repeatedly foundered. Had the British attempted to test local opinion at any time between 1910 and 1950, there would have been little doubt as to the outcome. The Basotho did not wait to be consulted before expressing their feelings. Antipathy toward transfer was expressed in numerous resolutions of the Basutoland Council and formed a common thread in the otherwise disparate demands of the various political movements that emerged in this period.

Under such circumstances, the British were obviously reluctant to put the matter irrevocably to the test. By encouraging cooperation between the governments of the territories and the Union of South Africa, the British hoped that conditions might be created over time for a more favorable response from the local populations. Such hopes were perhaps never realistic, but they were dashed completely in 1948 when the Nationalist party came to power in South Africa. As the Nationalists steadily erected the machinery of apartheid in South Africa, opposition in the territories to their incorporation increased dramatically. Given this opposition to transfer, it is unrealistic to assume that the British were unaware all along that nonincorporation was as likely an eventuality as incorporation. Had they been unaware, this hardly excuses their failure to assume responsibility for social and economic development in the meantime. The incorporation argument, therefore, smacks of rationalization rather than being an explanation for British neglect.

Perhaps a more useful way of looking at this question would be to dispense with the concept of neglect altogether, since the idea dubiously assumes that Britain failed to fulfill obligations in Basutoland that were discharged elsewhere in the empire. Although Britain may have been unduly remiss in the case of Basutoland, this still represented a difference in degree rather than kind. Nowhere in Africa or elsewhere did Britain embark on social and economic development for its own sake. Rather, officially encouraged or financed development was intended to secure the colonial objectives of law and order, cheap government, and the creation, where possible, of opportunities for British commercial and industrial penetration. The degree of development and the funds committed for this purpose reflect to a considerable extent the nature and viability of the resources to be exploited. In Basutoland such resources were largely lacking, with one notable exception—labor. The British were clearly aware of the great contribution made by Basotho workers to South African industry in general and to mining in particular. They were also aware of the considerable investment of British capital in such industry. In encouraging the flow of Basotho migrants to South Africa, little was required of the British by way of social and economic development. In fact, had social and economic development taken place in such a way as to create alternative sources of income for Basotho, the flow of labor to the Union of South Africa would undoubtedly have been reduced, and this was not what the British had in mind. In a telling example of the logic of this argument, Basutoland's resident commissioner remarked in 1899 that "Basutoland has an industry of great economic value to South Africa, viz. the output of native labour. . . . To those who urge higher education of the natives, it may be pointed out that to educate them above labour would be a mistake."[18]

From Granary to Labor Reserve

The years 1884–1966 witnessed the decline of Basutoland from a prosperous granary to an impoverished and underdeveloped labor reserve. Three related trends were visible in this process: declining self-sufficiency, increasing reliance upon labor migration, and growing dependence on South Africa. The loss of the country's agricultural self-sufficiency is shown by its transformation from a net exporter of grain at the beginning of the period to a major net importer at its close. At independence, more than 90 percent of the population were classed as rural dwellers, and yet less than 5 percent of rural households were able to be adequately self-sustaining from agricultural production alone.[19]

With few local sources of employment to provide the income to pay taxes and to buy imported commodities, labor migration to South Africa became an increasing imperative for the vast majority of households. From 1911 to 1956 the proportion of male migrants to the total male population rose from 10.6 to 29.4 percent. The corresponding figures for females were 1.3 and 10.2 percent.[20] As a proportion of the active adult population, these ratios were far higher, of course, and since the 1930s more than 50 percent of the country's male labor force has been absent at most times, working in South Africa.

The third trend, that of increasing dependence on South Africa, was related to the rise in both migrant labor to and imports of grain and other commodities from South Africa. It was further enhanced by the country's increasing reliance on South Africa for power, communications, transport, banking, currency, and customs revenue. The leverage that such dependence afforded to South Africa and the precarious position in which it placed Basutoland are obvious.

In explaining the underdevelopment and impoverishment of Basutoland and other African societies, the prevailing interpretation for many years was that of dualism, which placed the failure of such societies to "develop" on their inherent traditionalism, backwardness, and inability to adapt to new opportunities and technology. The continuing influence of this explanation is vividly illustrated in the authoritative World Bank report on Lesotho, which stated that at independence Lesotho was "virtually untouched by modern economic development. It was and still is, basically, a traditional subsistence peasant society."[21] Such statements totally overlook the degree of innovation and adaptation that characterized Basutoland and other southern African societies in the mid-nineteenth century and that rapidly transformed their economies from subsistence to commodity production. In recent years, therefore, the dualist thesis has been criticized by scholars who have come to ask not why such societies have remained underdeveloped (the basic dualist question), but why they have become so.[22]

In answering this question in the Basutoland context, attention can be focused on a number of related factors. First, having lost vast tracts of fertile land to the Free State in the years up to 1868, Basutoland was faced with the problem of increasing population pressure on limited productive land, a problem that was accentuated after 1913 by the influx of thousands of Basotho former sharecroppers and tenant farmers evicted from South African farms under the provisions of the 1913 Land Act. Between 1891 and 1921, the population doubled, and to cope with this increase it was necessary to bring all available land in the lowlands under the plow. The resulting decline in soil fertility and the corresponding increase in erosion and overgrazing had serious implications for Basotho agriculture.

One means of relieving the effects of population pressure was permanent migration by whole families to South Africa. In the wake of the depression and drought in the early 1930s, migration of this kind occurred on a large scale and was reflected in the comparatively low rate of population growth in Basutoland between 1936 and 1946. However, the South African government restricted the movement of African families by introducing an extensive array of regulations and controls. These restrictions were intensified by the Nationalist party after its victory in the 1948 election, and with the tightening of border controls in the early 1960s permanent as opposed to temporary migration was precluded as a legal option for the Basotho.

Commercial production in Basutoland came under pressure on a second front. In 1886 the railway reached Kimberley and soon pushed on to Johannesburg. As a result of the railway link between these two mining centers and the coast, the Basotho's grain exports faced competition from cheaper overseas products. Further, protective tariffs against Basotho grain were imposed by the Transvaal in 1887 and the Free State in 1893. These tariffs were designed to strengthen the competitive position of White capitalist agriculture. White farmers were soon to be heavily subsidized and protected by the South African government. African farmers, in contrast, received no such assistance and were placed in a disadvantaged position.

Third, external pressures on commercial production in Basutoland were aggravated by internal constraints. Of particular importance in this respect were the monopolistic pricing policies of the White traders who dominated the country's wholesale and retail trade for much of this period. The low prices offered by such traders, it has been argued, were partly responsible for discouraging the production of goods for sale.[23]

Fourth, the diminishing returns in agricultural production were exacerbated by the extremely low wages paid to migrant workers. Between 1889 and 1966, for example, real wages for Africans at the South African mines actually fell.[24] This made it difficult, if not impossible, for Basotho migrants to invest effectively in agricultural inputs at home, the costs of which rose far more rapidly than wages.

The reasons why an abundant supply of cheap Black labor was necessary to fuel South Africa's industrial revolution have been well documented. So, too, have the techniques used by South African capital interests and the state to control African wages, from the denial of collective bargaining rights to the collusion by employers on pay and recruitment policies. Less well known, perhaps, are the ways in which the British in Basutoland assisted in these processes. The Basutoland Native Labour Proclamation of 1942, for example, made it an offense for Basotho migrants to terminate their contracts without good cause. Turning as it did a civil dispute between worker and employer into a punishable criminal offense, this proclamation severely restricted the ability of Basotho workers to improve their working conditions by changing employers.

Finally, Basutoland's underdevelopment was accelerated by a number of devastating natural events. The outbreak of rinderpest in 1891, which destroyed nearly 90 percent of the country's cattle, and the severe drought and famine of 1932–1933 are just two of the most important examples.

Social Change and the Origins of Protest

Under British rule the national integration begun by Moshoeshoe was completed. At the same time, however, Basutoland experienced rapid social and economic change that placed pressure on the traditional fabric of the society and led, in time, to new forms of cleavage.

During the colonial period the gap between chiefs and commoners progressively widened, as the chiefs took advantage of their traditional privileges and favorable access to the colonial state machinery to distance themselves further from their followers. At the same time, growing divisions emerged within, as well as between, these two groups. Dynastic disputes and personal rivalries continued to characterize the chieftainship, and such cleavages were accentuated following the indirect rule reforms by the increasing disparity between the senior and junior chiefs. The commoner majority was also showing signs of greater heterogeneity. At its apex was a small but developing middle class, emanating largely from the Protestant mission stations, based in and around the urban centers in the lowlands, and engaged in commerce and trade or as teachers, interpreters, and clerical officers for the government and missions. Below these petty-bourgeois elements was the mass of the rural population, but a mass that was itself becoming differentiated according to access to land, livestock, and migrant earnings.

These developing social cleavages were compounded by the influence of the missionaries. From 1904 to 1966 the number of recorded Christians increased from 15 to 82 percent of the population.[25] This growth was accompanied by an intense rivalry between the different churches. At the beginning of the period the PEMS held a virtual monopoly over missionary activity, but this hold was challenged, especially by the Catholic Church, which surpassed the PEMS in membership by the 1940s.[26] Although less intransigent than in the past, the PEMS, as well as the other Protestant churches, continued their campaign to undermine the chieftainship and to eradicate those features of traditional society of which they disapproved. Unable to compete effectively on this terrain, the Catholics turned their attention to the chiefs and through them to their followers, especially those in the more remote mountain areas. Their much more flexible attitude toward practices such as polygyny and bridewealth ensured them success, and in 1913 they made a major breakthrough with the conversion of Griffith who was soon to become paramount chief. By independence, more than two-thirds of the principal and ward chiefs were practicing Catholics. Over time, therefore, the Catholic missionaries came to be associated with the defense of the customary status quo and with strenuous resistance to changes that seemed to threaten it. The resulting conflict with the more radical Protestant churches had a lasting and divisive impact on Basotho society.

One result of missionary competition was the expansion of the educational system. Although narrow in focus and concentrating heavily on the primary level, education provided a degree of literacy to a growing number of people. By so doing, it served to stimulate popular interest in the social and political issues aired in the local press and other publications. Such political awareness was accentuated in particular by the contact of Basotho migrants with nationalist and working class movements in South Africa and by the expanded horizons of those Basotho who saw service overseas with the British in the two world wars (some 22,000 served during 1939–1945).

Early Protest Movements: The Progressive Association and the Lekhotla la Bafo[27]

The first organized political movement to emerge in the period before World War II was the Basutoland Progressive Association (BPA). Founded in 1907 by a group of educated commoners, the BPA sought to articulate the interests of the small but rising middle class from which most of its members were drawn. Through its newspapers and through its representatives and sympathizers on the Basutoland Council, the BPA pressed for reform of the colonial system rather than for its radical change or overthrow. Its leaders agitated for a reduction in chiefly power, the abuses of which they criticized extensively, and for a correspondingly greater role for the educated elite in both the economic and political affairs of the territory. In 1919 they proposed that half the membership of the council should be elected, but this and other proposals were rejected by the council's chiefly majority and ignored by the British.

Following Pim's report the political climate in the 1930s became far more responsive to BPA pressure, and this responsiveness helped to encourge the British to introduce some reforms between 1938 and 1950. The reforms were very limited, however, and the BPA's identification with them seriously compromised its ability to place itself at the forefront of the more militant demands for change that arose after World War II. Nevertheless, the BPA can still lay claim to being a legitimate precursor to the movements that were ultimately to replace it and to steer Basutoland toward the achievement of independence.

A stronger claim in this respect can perhaps be made by a second movement, the Lekhotla la Bafo (LLB). Founded in 1919 by Josiel Lefela, the LLB set out to espouse the interests of the underprivileged commoners against those of the chiefs and the educated elite. Establishing links with South African movements such as the African National Congress (ANC) and drawing inspiration from diverse ideological sources—socialist, nationalist, and pan-African—Lefela and his colleagues, although largely self-educated, bombarded the colonial authorities, the paramount, and the Basutoland Council with a torrent of eloquent complaints concerning the subversive influence of the missions, the malpractices of the chiefs (though not the institution of chieftainship itself), and the injustices of British rule. Although originally regarding the LLB as an irritating but ineffectual nuisance, the British reacted more seriously when it began to publish its attacks in *The Worker*, the organ of the South African Communist party. This choice of publication represented practical necessity more than close ideological affiliation because access to other publications had been progressively withdrawn. Nevertheless, the British labeled the organization Communist and encouraged the chiefs to dissuade their followers from joining it. The Catholic Church needed no such encouragement to discourage its own adherents. Lefela and other LLB leaders were periodically jailed for alleged seditious activities, but on their release they returned to the fray as irrepressibly as ever.

The LLB has frequently been portrayed as an eccentric and extremist appendage to the mainstream of nationalist political protest in Basutoland. In reality it was far more than that. To a much greater extent than their BPA contemporaries, the LLB leaders realized that only through a determined effort to win self-government, in alliance with nationalist forces in South Africa, could an effective beginning be made to advance the economic and political interests of the Basotho people. It is in this that the enduring legacy of the organization lies. For a number of reasons, however, it proved incapable of translating this realization into an effective movement for self-determination. Although defending the rights of the common man, LLB leaders failed to create a mass organization through which they might be articulated. Moreover, through their refusal, whether rightly or wrongly, to enter into discussions of any kind with the British, they ultimately abdicated their claims to the leadership of the postwar nationalist movement to organizations that were prepared to negotiate and compromise over the terms of independence.

Postwar Nationalist Movements: The BCP, BNP, and MFP

The wave of nationalist sentiment that spread through British Africa in the wake of World War II soon embraced Basutoland and challenged the validity of the government's belated efforts at administrative reform. At the same time, it exposed the limitations of the BPA and the LLB. New organizations were needed if momentum was not to be lost, and these organizations were not long in coming. The first was the Basutoland African Congress, formed in 1952 under Ntsu Mokhehle. In composition, its leadership resembled that of the BPA, and most of its membership was drawn from the ranks of the Protestant educated elite. In ideology, however, it was closer to the LLB, and the two parties merged in 1957. Although not neglecting their own class interests, the leaders of the new movement were quick to realize that these interests could only be advanced effectively if incorporated into a comprehensive and radical program for change, in which the interests of the masses were assigned a prominent position. In 1959 the Basutoland African Congress changed its name to the Basutoland Congress party (BCP) in preparation for the 1960 elections.

In addition to attacking the government, White traders, Catholic missionaries, and chiefs, Mokhehle and his colleagues demanded constitutional change leading to responsible government, the rapid Africanization of the public and private sectors, and the introduction of more effective social and economic reforms designed to raise the living standards of the mass of the people. Moreover, they instituted an enthusiastic campaign of mass mobilization in the rural as well as urban areas, enlisting support for the movement's program and encouraging the people to agitate actively for change. Affiliation with existing secular associations was also encouraged, and close ties were established with both the cooperative movement and the Basutoland Federation of Labour, which was formed in 1962 to represent the interests of the majority of the country's trade unions.

External links were developed, particularly with South African nationalist movements, and the BCP stressed the congruity of Basutoland's struggle for emancipation with that of the people of South Africa and of the continent as a whole. Although initially establishing close ties with the ANC, Mokhehle eventually rejected its multiracialism and transferred his support to its more militantly Africanist offshoot, the Pan Africanist Congress (PAC). When both the ANC and PAC were banned by the South African government in 1960, the BCP provided an important focus for anti-South African sentiment, a fact that did little to endear it to the Pretoria regime.

The increasing militancy of the BCP, together with Mokhehle's intolerance of opposition and criticism, ultimately gave rise to dissension, and beginning in the late 1950s a number of members left to form rival organizations. The most important of these was the Basutoland National party (BNP), which was established in 1958 by a group of lesser chiefs and Catholic teachers under the leadership of Leabua Jonathan, a grandson of Moshoeshoe's second son, Molapo, by a junior line. Although advocating constitutional change, nonincorporation into South Africa, and the necessity for social and economic reform, the BNP was far more moderate than the BCP on a number of important issues. This moderate position was reflected in its emphasis on the need for close cooperation with South Africa on matters of mutual interest, for continuing reliance on the skills of expatriates in the public and private sectors, and for an important role for the chieftainship in the future development of the country. The only issue on which the BNP was expressly militant was that of anticommunism, which was felt to be of sufficient importance to be enshrined in the party's constitution.

The moderate tone of the BNP, coupled with its fierce anti-Communist rhetoric, endeared the party to the Catholic Church, White traders and officials, the South African government, and the chiefs, especially the junior ones who saw in the BNP a means for restoring their former status and privileges. These chiefs naturally encouraged their followers to support the BNP. So, too, did the Catholic missionaries, whose extreme sentiments against communism coincided with those of the BNP. Their appeals were particularly successful in the mountain areas and among women, many of whom, it has been argued, were concerned that the BCP's stance against South Africa might result in a retaliatory cutback in migrant labor and a reduction in the remittances on which many were so dependent.

The last of the major parties to emerge in the preindependence period was the Marema-Tlou Freedom party (MFP), which was formed in January 1963 as a result of a merger between two smaller parties. The first of these was the Marema-Tlou party (MTP), which was founded in 1957 by Chief S. S. Matete to defend the principal chiefs against attacks by the BCP. The second was the Freedom party, which was established in 1961 by B. M. Khaketla, after his resignation as deputy leader of the BCP in protest against Mokhehle's dictatorial behavior. Chief Matete became the president of the new party, Khaketla its vice-president, and Dr. Seth Makotoko, a former ANC Youth League activist, its general secretary. Combining as it did both traditional and modern elements, the MFP was less homogeneous in its leadership than the BCP or BNP. In its ideological orientation it was located somewhere between them. The issue to which the MFP devoted most of its attention was the future role of the paramount chief.

In 1960 a new and young paramount, Bereng Seeiso, was inaugurated. When his father, Paramount Seeiso, had died in 1940, Bereng was still an infant. His stepmother, 'Mantŝebo, was appointed regent until he came of age. This occurred in the late 1950s, when he was an undergraduate at Oxford University. Meanwhile, the regent, under the influence of her advisers, including Leabua Jonathan (Chief Jonathan, prime minister, 1965–   ), was involved in an intrigue to block Bereng's accession to the paramountcy. To foil this plot, Bereng cut short his studies, returned to Basutoland, and insisted that he be placed immediately. Chief Matete and the MTP were instrumental in advising him to return, and the support that they were able to mobilize for his succession convinced an originally reluctant high commissioner to invest him as paramount in 1960, under the new name of Moshoeshoe II. Leabua Jonathan's role in the affair did little to improve relations between the country's future king and prime minister. In addition to securing Bereng's succession, the MTP urged that the intelligent and well-educated paramount should have a major executive role to play in any future constitutional dispensation for the country. This issue was taken over by the MFP after its formation in 1963 and came to form the dominant element in the party's platform.

The differences that divided the BCP, BNP, and MFP, although clearly important, must not be exaggerated. The primary aim of all of these parties was to advance the struggle for independence and their own preeminence within it. Confronted as they were by the British with the customary electoral test as a precondition for independence, the leaders of all these parties were frequently pragmatic, if not actually opportunistic, and were prepared when necessary to trade principles for votes. If this diluted the ideological purity of their programs, it did not prevent bitter polarization emerging among their respective supporters, a process that had disturbing consequences for political stability.

The Road to Independence

The late 1940s and early 1950s saw repeated calls for greater representation in the organs of government. Although initially unreceptive, the British government indicated in May 1956 that it was prepared to entertain proposals for representative government. These proposals were embodied in the recommendations of the Constitutional Committee established by the Basutoland Council in 1956. The committee's 1958 report advocated changes at both the local and central levels. The changes in local government, which were implemented in 1959, devolved greater powers to the district councils that had been established in 1944. Such councils, in addition, were to be popularly elected by all taxpayers in the districts, a qualification that disenfranchised almost all women. The changes in central government were incorporated into a new constitution that was framed at a conference in London in 1958 and came into effect in 1960. A legislative council was established, known as the Basutoland National Council (often called the Legislative Council). Forty of its eighty members were indirectly elected by the district councils. The remaining forty included the twenty-two principal and ward chiefs, fourteen members appointed by the high commissioner, and four ex-officio members from the administration. The new council had lawmaking powers over all internal matters. Executive powers were retained by the British, although an executive council, consisting of four British

TABLE 1.1
District Council Elections, 1960

	Number of Votes	Percent of Total Votes	District Council Seats	Basutoland National (Legislative) Council Seats
BCP	12,787	36	73	30
BNP	7,002	20	22	1
MTP	3,043	9	16	5
Independents	12,470	35	51	4
Total	35,302	100	162	40

Note: Registered electorate, 191,663; percentage turnout, 18.42.

Source: Jack Halpern, South Africa's Hostages: Basutoland, Bechuanaland and
          Swaziland (Harmondsworth: Penguin, 1965), pp. 130-131.

and four Basotho representatives, was established to advise the
government.

Elections to the district councils were held in January 1960. The
BCP's attention to grass roots organization paid dividends, and the
distribution of voting patterns in what was a very low turnout enabled
the party to gain control of six of the nine district councils and thirty
of the forty indirectly elected seats on the Legislative Council. The
BCP's elected majority on the council did not give it an overall
majority, however, and together with its lack of representation on
the Executive Council, this meant in effect that the party became the
official opposition. The BCP immediately began to press for a rapid
transition from representative to responsible government. The other
parties echoed this demand, and in 1962 a constitutional commission
was established by the Legislative Council to make proposals for self-
government. Once approved by the council these proposals formed
the basis for the second Constitutional Conference, held in London
in 1964. From this conference emerged the self-government Constitution that was implemented in 1965. Basutoland was to have a
bicameral legislature: the Senate, consisting of the twenty-two principal
and ward chiefs and eleven members nominated by the paramount,
and the National Assembly, consisting of sixty members elected by
universal suffrage in single-member constituencies. In addition, there
was to be an executive cabinet, drawn from members of the Senate
or National Assembly and under the direction of a prime minister
who was leader of the majority party in the National Assembly.

TABLE 1.2
General Election for the National Assembly, 1965

	Number of Votes	Percent of Total Votes	Number of Seats
BNP	108,162	41.6	31
BCP	103,050	39.67	25
MFP	42,837	16.5	4
MTP	5,697	2.2	0
Independents	79	0.03	0
	259,825	100.00	60

Note: Registered electorate, 416,952; percentage turnout, 62.32.

Source: Richard P. Stevens, Lesotho, Botswana and Swaziland: The Former High Commission Territories in Southern Africa (London: Pall Mall Press, 1967), p. 68.

Elections under the new Constitution were held in April 1965 and resulted in a narrow and somewhat surprising victory for the BNP. Chief Jonathan lost his seat, however, and the new government was temporarily led by Chief Sekhonyane 'Maseribane, the deputy leader of the party, until a safe seat could be found for the party leader. This was soon accomplished, and after a by-election victory in July, Chief Jonathan assumed the position of prime minister that he has continued to hold ever since.

A number of factors were important in explaining the reversal of the fortunes of the BNP and BCP in the elections.[28] Weakened by internal dissension and short of funds, the BCP experienced additional difficulty in canvassing in a number of constituencies because of opposition from the chiefs. The BNP experienced no such difficulties. Moreover, unlike the BCP, which relied heavily on membership dues, the BNP received handsome donations from White traders, individual Catholic priests, and the South African government; the donations enabled the party to mount a much more effective election campaign than in 1960. In addition, the extension of the franchise to all women, voting for the first time and constituting 64 percent of the eligible electorate resident in Lesotho,[29] may have advanced the BNP's cause, for reasons mentioned earlier.[30] Of perhaps greater importance, however, was the anti-Communist propaganda spread by both the BNP and the Catholic Church, which tarnished the BCP's image in the eyes of a highly Christian, and by this time Catholic, population. Despite the existence of a small Communist party of Lesotho, founded in 1962, there is little doubt that the BCP was the principal target.

The MFP's performance can be explained largely by its almost exclusive focus on the issue of the paramount. Although attracting considerable support in those constituencies that fell under the paramount's direct influence, the party's lack of attention to other electoral issues prevented it from offering a viable national alternative to the two major parties. The split in the party in 1964, which resulted in Chief Matete resigning to reconstitute the Marema-Tlou party, further weakened its support.

At the London Conference in 1964 it was agreed that one year after the 1965 elections, proposals could be submitted for full independence, providing these were approved by both the Senate and National Assembly, or, in the event of disagreement between them, by the majority of the people voting in a referendum. In March 1966 the BNP government issued a White Paper setting out such proposals. The most contentious item proved to be the future role of the paramount. Before the 1965 elections, which it was by no means confident of winning, the BNP had supported MFP demands that the paramount should be given certain reserve powers, especially over the armed forces and the police, as a check against possible arbitrary action by any future government. The BCP, in contrast, fiercely opposed this proposal. Having won the elections, however, the BNP's enthusiasm for entrusting reserve powers to the country's future king evaporated rapidly. Instead, such powers were to be vested in the prime minister, and Moshoeshoe II's role was to be confined to that of a constitutional head of state. This issue proved the most controversial in the debates in the National Assembly and Senate. MFP pressure for a greater role for the paramount was now supported by the BCP, which had performed a not-surprising volte-face on this question since losing the 1965 elections. However, the BNP's majority in both houses[31] enabled the government to defeat all the opposition's amendments on this issue, and the White Paper was approved on 11 May by the National Assembly and on 27 May by the Senate. Proceedings were delayed in the Senate by the paramount's expulsion of five of the nominated senators for voting with the government. Although they were subsequently reinstated by the High Court, this episode served to further impair relations between the paramount and prime minister.

The stage was now set for the third and final Constitutional Conference, which took place in London in June 1966. The three main parties were represented at the talks, and the MFP and BCP delegates lost little time in putting forward their objections. In addition to pressing for reserve powers for the paramount, they requested that this and other issues that divided the nation should be put to the test through a new election or referendum before independence was granted. In support of their case they pointed to the BNP's narrow victory on a minority vote in the 1965 elections and cited precedents from other parts of British Africa where an additional electoral test prior to independence had been considered essential by the British. The British remained unmoved by such arguments, however, which ultimately led the opposition parties to withdraw from the conference. The British and the BNP delegations were left to conclude the proceedings. The paramount, who was attending as an observer, was invited to add his signature to the final document. He politely refused. On 4 October 1966, however, he did preside at the country's independence celebrations, and as King Moshoeshoe II, he formally accepted the Instruments of Independence from the Queen's representative.

Thousands of people attended the celebrations to witness the consummation of the nation's long and proud struggle to maintain its identity and achieve self-determination. Nevertheless, for many of those present, as well as for those who stayed away, the occasion was undoubtedly marred by reservations concerning the country's future, reservations that had clearly been enhanced by the enactment just a few weeks prior to independence of a number of disturbing measures. These acts included the Emergency Powers Act, the Internal Security Act, the Printing and Publishing Act, and the Societies Act. Giving the BNP government sweeping powers over the declaration of a state of emergency, the holding of public meetings, the censorship of mail, and the proscription of "unlawful" organizations, such measures provided an ominous warning of things to come.

NOTES

1. As no records were kept in this period, there can be no certainty about the precise date of Moshoeshoe's birth, but most authorities place it between 1785 and 1788. Two of the most recent and authoritative accounts of Moshoeshoe estimate 1786 as the most probable date. See Peter Sanders, *Moshoeshoe: Chief of the Sotho* (London: Heinemann, 1975), p. 5; and Leonard Thompson, *Survival in Two Worlds: Moshoeshoe of Lesotho 1786–1870* (Oxford: Oxford University Press, 1975), p. 1. This lack of precision applies to all the dates cited in this work until the 1830s, when missionaries started written records.

2. Sanders and Thompson argue this point persuasively. So too do most of the earlier, and predominantly missionary, accounts of the rise of the Basotho kingdom. For an analysis that locates this rise within the wider context of the social and economic changes transforming Basotho society at this time, see Judy Kimble, "Towards an Understanding of the Political

Economy of Lesotho: The Origins of Commodity Production and Migrant Labour, 1830–1885" (M.A. thesis, National University of Lesotho, 1978), pp. 42–77.

3. Prominent among these were the Rolong, Griqua, and Newlanders. Moshoeshoe's relations with these groups were cordial at first, but turned sour when they came to assert their independence from his tutelage. Despite their small numbers they were able to cause trouble by entering into alliances with the Boers and by attempting to frustrate Moshoeshoe's efforts to win the support and sympathy of the British. Relations with Sekonyela's Tlokoa also deteriorated steadily. Matters came to a head in 1853 when Moshoeshoe led a massive attack on Sekonyela's stronghold and finally broke Tlokoa power in the area.

4. Wodehouse to Buckingham, 2 May 1868, Despatches 23719, *British Parliamentary Papers* 46 (Shannon: Irish University Press, 1971), pp. 57–58.

5. Law and order was maintained in part by the establishment of the Basutoland Mounted Police, into which a number of chiefs were co-opted, including Moshoeshoe's sons George and Sofonia. Growing missionary penetration was evidenced by the rise in the number of people attending the PEMS' weekly religious services from just over 3,000 in 1871 to between 17,000 and 20,000 in 1877, and 3,000 pupils were enrolled in PEMS schools in 1877. J. M. Mohapeloa, *Government by Proxy: Ten Years of Cape Colony Rule in Lesotho* (Morija: Sesuto Book Depot, 1971), p. 96; and Sandra Burman, *The Justice of the Queen's Government: The Cape's Administration of Basutoland, 1871–1884* (Cambridge: African Studies Centre, 1976), p. 71. The Catholic and Anglican churches, which established their first missions in 1862 and 1867, respectively, had made much less of an impact at this time, but they were optimistic about their prospects for the future.

6. C. W. De Kiewiet, *A History of South Africa: Social and Economic* (1941; reprint, London: Oxford University Press, 1972), p. 89.

7. The 1875 census recorded 2,749 plows. In 1878 it was estimated that 3,700 were in use. R. C. Germond, *Chronicles of Basutoland* (Morija: Sesuto Book Depot, 1967), p. 326; and G. Tylden, *The Rise of the Basuto* (Cape Town: Juta, 1950), p. 118.

8. Sandra Burman, *Chiefdom Politics and Alien Law: Basutoland Under Cape Rule, 1871–1884* (London: Macmillan, 1981), p. 83, and Hugh Ashton, *The Basuto: A Social Study of Traditional and Modern Lesotho*, 2nd ed. (London: Oxford University Press, 1967), p. 162.

9. Moshoeshoe's second son, Molapo, for example, received £800 per annum as his share of the hut tax, and a minimum of £1 from the earnings of each migrant worker returning to the Leribe District. "He also possessed large tracts of agricultural land, where immense crops were raised, the proceeds of which went into his coffers." Peter Hadley, *Doctor to Basuto, Boer and Briton, 1877–1906: Memoirs of Dr. Henry Taylor* (Cape Town: David Philip, 1972), p. 44. In contrast, for a discussion of the spread of poverty among the commoners at this time, see Kimble, "Political Economy of Lesotho," pp. 246–248 and 282–284.

10. Sir Alan Pim, *Financial and Economic Position of Basutoland*, Cmd. 4907 (London: His Majesty's Stationery Office, 1935), p. 49.

11. Ibid.

12. Those chiefs who were not officially recognized (gazetted) obviously lost all their former privileges. In addition, many junior chiefs who were gazetted received very little by way of remuneration from the Native Treasury established in 1946. Some received nothing at all. As their traditional sources of income were now terminated, this naturally provoked considerable resentment. Senior chiefs, in contrast, received quite generous salaries from the treasury.

13. The Basutoland Council, *Report on Constitutional Reform and Chieftainship Affairs* (Maseru: Government Printer, 1958), p. 37.

14. Pim, *Position of Basutoland*, p. 134.

15. Lesotho received only negligible amounts of British aid before 1945. The level of assistance under the Colonial Development and Welfare Act of 1940 did increase, however, after World War II. Even so, only £2,157,286 was spent by Britain between 1945 and 1960, which was less than the amounts spent on Botswana (£2,630,708) or Swaziland (£2,759,826), despite the fact that Basutoland's population was larger than that of these two other High Commission territories combined. Chandler Morse, *Basutoland, Bechuanaland Protectorate, and Swaziland: Report of an Economic Survey Mission* (London: Her Majesty's Stationery Office, 1960), pp. 170, 368, and 544. Using a medical metaphor, Morse foresaw Basutoland "lapsing into a state of chronic illness," unless expensive surgery was immediately forthcoming (p. 14). The British did make a greater financial commitment between 1960 and 1966, but a large proportion of the funds went into paying the surgeon rather than into performing the operation. By 1963–1964 more than 50 percent of the country's recurrent budget was spent on public service salaries alone, and the pressure that this placed on fiscal solvency ensured that a considerable amount of the increased British aid was used for balancing the budget rather than for urgent development projects.

16. Cited in Jack Halpern, *South Africa's Hostages: Basutoland, Bechuanaland and Swaziland* (Harmondsworth: Penguin, 1965), p. 173.

17. For two useful accounts of the incorporation issue, see Lord Hailey, *The High Commission Territories and the Union of South Africa* (London: Royal Institute of International Affairs [RIIA], 1957) and Jack Spence, "British Policy Towards the High Commission Territories," *Journal of Modern African Studies* 2, no. 2 (1964).

18. Cited in Kingdom of Lesotho, *Third Five-Year Development Plan, 1980–1985* (Maseru: Government Printer, 1980) p. ii.

19. Gabriele Winai-Strom, *Development and Dependence in Lesotho: The Enclave of South Africa* (Uppsala: The Scandinavian Institute of African Studies, 1978), p. 27.

20. D. H. Taylor, *Basutoland: 1956 Population Census* (Maseru: Basutoland Government, 1958) p. 73.

21. International Bank for Reconstruction and Development, *Lesotho: A Development Challenge* (Washington, D.C.: International Bank for Reconstruction and Development, 1975), p. 1.

22. For examples of dualist interpretations in the Lesotho context, see G.M.E. Leistner, *Lesotho: Economic Structure and Growth* (Pretoria: Africa Institute, 1966); Sandra Wallman, *Take Out Hunger: Two Case Studies of Rural Development in Basutoland* (London: London School of Economics Monographs on Social Anthropology, no. 39, 1969); and J. C. Williams, *Lesotho: Land Tenure and Economic Development* (Pretoria: Africa Institute, 1972). For critiques of dualism and alternative accounts of Lesotho's underdevelopment, see Colin Murray, *Families Divided: The Impact of Migrant Labour in Lesotho* (Johannesburg: Ravan Press; and Cambridge: Cambridge University Press, 1981) and Roger Leys, "Lesotho: Non-Development or Underdevelopment: Towards an Analysis of the Political Economy of the Labour Reserve," in *The Politics of Africa: Dependence and Development*, ed. T. Shaw and K. Heard (Halifax, N.S.: African Studies Series, 1978), pp. 95–129.

23. Halpern, *South Africa's Hostages*, pp. 188–189; Leistner, *Lesotho: Economic Structure*, pp. 18–19.

24. In real rand, wages fell from 84 to 70. See W. R. Bohning, ed., *Black Migration to South Africa* (Geneva: International Labour Office, 1981), p. 15.

25. W. J. Breytenbach, *Crocodiles and Commoners in Lesotho: Continuity and Change in the Rulemaking System of Lesotho* (Pretoria: Africa Institute, 1975), p. 25.

26. The 1946 census recorded 151,312 Catholics, 118, 833 PEMS, 49,432 Anglicans, 24,336 other Christians, and 215,228 non-Christians. Ibid.

27. For a useful analysis of early protest movements in Lesotho, see Richard Weisfelder, "Early Voices of Protest in Basutoland: The Progressive Association and the Lekhotla la Bafo," *African Studies Review* 17, no. 2 (1974).

28. The most detailed and comprehensive analysis to date of the 1965 election can be found in Richard Weisfelder, "Defining National Purpose: The Roots of Factionalism in Lesotho" (Ph.D. thesis, Harvard University, 1974), pp. 256–361.

29. This high percentage is attributable to the fact that no provision was made in the election for postal votes for male Basotho migrants in South Africa. Halpern, *South Africa's Hostages*, p. 255.

30. Frank, for example, has argued that the extension of the franchise to women was the most important factor in explaining the success of the BNP in the election. Lawrence Frank, *The Basutoland National Party: Traditional Authority and Neo-Colonialism in Lesotho* (Denver: Center on International Race Relations, 1971), p. 9. In contrast, Weisfelder found hardly any correlation between female voting patterns and the swing to the BNP. Weisfelder, "Defining National Purpose," pp. 341–343. Macartney did find a positive correlation in his study, but only a fairly weak one. W.J.A. Macartney, "Case Study:

The Lesotho General Election of 1970," *Government and Opposition* 8, no. 4 (1973), p. 478.

31. The BNP had obtained a majority in the Senate by this time because ten MFP members transferred their support to the government. This gave the BNP 18 supporters in the Senate, compared to 13 for the MFP, 1 for the MTP, and 1 for the BCP. Breytenbach, *Crocodiles and Commoners*, p. 89.

2

The Economy

HISTORICAL ORIGINS

The previous chapter described the economic evolution, followed by involution, of Lesotho from its origins up to the 1960s. Changes in what was produced, how it was produced, and in what was consumed occurred throughout the nineteenth century, partly in response to exposure to European influences. There was substantial technical change in agriculture, notably the introduction and rapid spread of the plow and new crops, most obviously wheat. Trade permitted not only the use of the new technologies, but also a substantial increase in the range of goods consumed. Obvious examples include blankets, firearms, tools and implements, household equipment, building materials, clothing, and foodstuffs (e.g., tea and sugar). Artisan and handicraft production within Lesotho previously satisfied the wants now satisfied by cheaper or preferred imported substitutes, and such local production therefore declined.

The majority of Lesotho's households were soon constrained with respect to the opportunities by which they could satisfy their consumption wants. Land was scarce and often of declining fertility. Transport costs were very high, and little or no help was available from the colonial government to facilitate changes in agricultural practices that might increase productivity. Legal and institutional constraints made it almost impossible for a Mosotho to enter commerce or industry in competition with either the established white and Indian traders in the country or the growing established manufacturers in South Africa. For growing numbers of households, this left only temporary or permanent migration to South Africa for employment as the least disadvantageous way to obtain the necessary income for survival.

This does not imply that land ceased to be cultivated or livestock kept. Most land was almost continuously cultivated, although at times the amount left fallow—usually because the household concerned

45

had insufficient resources (draft power, cash, or labor) to cultivate it—caused concern to officialdom. There exists a wide continuum of involvement by households in agricultural activities; many households tend to change position on the continuum with the passage of time and the developmental cycle of the household.[1] At one end are a few households that control sufficient land, cattle, labor, and capital to derive an adequate income from agriculture. At the other end are households with no current access to land and little or no livestock, but who may nevertheless assist in the cultivation of the fields of others for payments in cash or kind. In between are most of the households with some land and some livestock, but not enough to provide for subsistence needs even if optimally used. When migration is possible, the return from migration is usually so much superior to the potential return from agriculture that agricultural assets are not used in such a way as to maximize output.[2] Land is cultivated and livestock kept often more as a store of value, as an insurance against unforeseen income falls, and as a subsidiary source of income from minimal effort.

As a result of this structural situation, which existed for more than half a century before independence and continues to a large extent today, the Lesotho economy ceased to exist as a national economy and developed features very similar to those of the "native reserves" within South Africa proper. The economy became unusually monetized for Africa, and the population heavily dependent on cash earnings from migrant labor and imported commodities. Domestic economic activity came to consist almost entirely of low-productivity agriculture and service and commerce activities that focused not on national markets but on the exchange of cash for goods imported from South African urban centers. Virtually no industry developed, and agriculture tended to become more subsistence oriented and less commercial.

THE ECONOMY AT INDEPENDENCE

The picture that can be drawn of the economy in 1966 is largely a qualitative one, with what quantitative indicators that can be given highly uncertain and unreliable. However, there is no dispute that at independence Lesotho had an extreme labor reserve economy. It was wracked by widespread and extreme poverty and low internal productivity; it had neither the institutions nor the infrastructure of a national economy.

Table 2.1 indicates how stark the picture was in terms of the data available at the time of independence. These data suggest that

TABLE 2.1
Indicators of Lesotho's Economy Around the Time of Independence

A. Structure of GDP in 1965/1966

	Maloti (000)	Percentage
Wages and salaries	10,225	27.4
Gross operating profits	1,454	3.9
Gross income of unincorporated enterprise, total	23,769	63.6
Amount consumed by rural producers	14,338[a]	38.4[a]
Government income from property	151	0.4
Personal income from property	1,781	4.8
Total (GDP, factor cost)	37,381	100.1[b]
GDP per capita, de facto population, in Maloti	M44	

B. Sectoral Origin of GDP in 1967/1968

	Percent
Agriculture	39.0
Mining and quarries	2.0
Manufacturing	0.7
Construction	1.7
Services (including government)	56.6
Total	100.0

C. Labor Force Data

	Male	Female	Total
De facto population age 15 to 64[c]	164,146	263,287	427,433
Working absentees[c]	92,020	12,801	104,821
(Working absentees/de facto population x 100%	56.1%	4.8%	24.5%
[Working absentees/(de facto population + working absentees)] x 100%	35.9%	4.6%	19.7%
Approximate wage and salary employment in Lesotho	14,000	4,000	18,000
Estimated cash earnings of working absentees 1965/1966			M29,429,000

Note: In 1965/1966, M1 = US$1.40. GDP = gross domestic product.

a. Not included in total.
b. Rounding error.
c. 1966 census.

Sources: Derived from data in: Kingdom of Lesotho, Lesotho First Five-Year
Development Plan 1970/71-1974/75. (Maseru: Government Printer,
1970); Michael Ward, "Economic Independence for Lesotho?" Journal
of Modern African Studies 5(3):355-368, September 1967; G.M.E.
Leistner, Lesotho: Economic Structure and Growth (Pretoria: Africa
Institute, 1966).

about 40 percent of total output (gross domestic product, GDP) was
subsistence production consumed by the rural households producing
it; that about 20 percent of the potential labor force was absent from
the country; that about six persons had wage or salary employment
outside the country for each person who had such employment inside

the country; that the cash earnings of these migrants totaled almost three times total wages and salaries paid within the country; and that manufacturing accounted for less than 1 percent of total output.

Imports in 1966 (a bad harvest year) were more than five times exports and included very substantial amounts of food and manufactured consumer goods. Thanks to very substantial foreign transfers to the Lesotho government from the United Kingdom, proceeds from the Customs Union agreement, and substantial remittances from migrant workers, the current accounts of the balance of payments were slightly in surplus. However, under the institutional arrangements of the time, essentially they had to be. Without any formal agreement with South Africa, Lesotho had for many years used South African currency as its only recognized form of money. The only banks were the Maseru branches of the Standard Bank of South Africa and Barclays Bank (DCO), which also operated agencies in some of the districts.[3] The government banked with Standard, from whom it occasionally obtained small and temporary overdrafts. New money could only enter circulation in Lesotho in two ways: (1) via the total of migrants' currency remittances, export earnings, and transfers exceeding payments for imports and other payments to the rest of the world or (2) via the operations of the two commercial banks. But few Basotho had bank accounts, and the banks—operating conservatively in a country where land could not be used as collateral for a loan—typically had fewer assets (i.e., loans extended) in Lesotho than liabilities. Thus, Lesotho was lending abroad through the banks—generally to their Johannesburg or London head offices where they held their excess assets. Increases in the domestic money supply were achieved by foregoing real local production and consumption (e.g., migrant labor that could have been in-country labor and exports that could have been used locally but instead were supplied to South Africa).

Table 2.2 summarizes the Lesotho government's revenue and expenditure accounts for the year before independence, 1965/1966. The two most striking aspects of these data are the astonishing dependence of the government on external sources of revenue and the very low level of real recurrent expenditures. Less than 17 percent of government revenue was derived from local sources, a similar amount came from the Customs Union agreement with South Africa, and over half was due to transfers from the United Kingdom. Total government recurrent expenditures on goods and services (excluding subsidies, debt interest, and transfers) amounted to only M6,660,000 (US$9.3 million)—about M7.81 per annum per person of the 1966 de facto population, or less than $11 per resident citizen per year.

TABLE 2.2
Revenue and Expenditure of Central Government, 1965/1966

A. Revenue

	Maloti (000)	Percentage
Direct taxes	1,084	10.6
Customs Union receipts	1,637	15.9
Other indirect taxes	239	2.3
Other local revenue	406	4.0
UK grant-in-aid	5,202	50.7
UK overseas aid scheme	353	3.4
UK Colonial Development and Welfare grant transferred to current revenue	1,346	13.1
Total	10,266a	100.0

B. Expenditures

Wages and salaries	5,053	60.3
Other purchases, net	1,607	19.2
Subsidies	207	2.5
Interest payments	133	1.6
Other transfers	1,384	16.5
Total	8,384	100.1a
Current surplus used for capital expenditure	1,882	22.4

Note: in 1965/1966 M1 = US$1.40

a. Rounding error.

Source: Adapted from Michael Ward, "Economic Independence for Lesotho?" Journal of Modern African Studies 5(3):355-368, September 1967, Tables 3 and 4.

For comparison, in that same year the Swaziland equivalent was over $30, and the U.S. federal government spent over $290 per U.S. citizen on national defense alone. Clearly, $11 per resident citizen per year in Lesotho—even at Lesotho's relatively low civil service salaries—could not buy very much in terms of government services for its population.

Education was already widely available at the primary level, but the effectiveness of the education system was questionable. In the early 1960s, although the standardized primary school enrollment ratio was over 90 percent, only about one third of pupils continued beyond the third year of school; the teacher-pupil ratio was about 1:61 (in 1964); schools were denominational, founded by competing missionary groups, and often small and competitive with other local schools of different denominations; for every 1,000 children in primary school, only 17 were in secondary school.[4]

The resource base was extremely limited. The only known minerals of economic value were diamonds, then exploited by individual licensed Basotho diggers using hand methods. Agricultural potential was also very limited. Given the mountainous topography of the country, only about 1 million acres (about 400,000 ha) of arable land are available. Nonarable land totals about 5 million more acres (about 2,000,000 ha), including mountain pasture, steep slopes, rocky hillsides, and deep gorges or ravines. Because of the topography, very little irrigation of the arable land is feasible and even less is practiced. Because most field crops are dependent on rainfall, which is low and extremely variable, the annual yield varies widely with weather conditions. The national slogan "Khotso, Pula, Nala"—"Peace, Rain, Plenty"—is thus partly explained. The major field crops are maize and sorghum, grown largely for consumption by the household growing them, and wheat, peas, beans, and potatoes grown largely for sale. Maize is the staple food, supplemented when necessary with sorghum; however, the preferred use of sorghum is beer-brewing. Maize is more sensitive to both drought and frost than sorghum. Frost can occur throughout the year, and planting cannot take place until after the first spring rains in September or October. Accordingly, to reduce risk, many farmers plant both maize and sorghum, because some sorghum will usually be harvested even when the maize crop is a failure.

In the 1960s, virtually all cultivation involved the use of an ox-drawn plow, and other ox-drawn equipment (planters, cultivators, harrows) was quite often used, although broadcast planting by hand and cultivating with a hoe was still very common. The 1960 agricultural census estimated that less than 10 percent of the acreage planted received any fertilizer or manure in any single year; partly as a result, average yields were low. The first five-year plan put maize yields at two to three bags (of 200 pounds [90 kg] each) per acre although some areas recorded over five bags per acre. This average compares with thirty to thirty-five bags per acre achieved on experimental irrigated plots.

Climatic and topographic conditions inevitably imply that arable agriculture in Lesotho will be relatively low yield and risky. However, agriculture was performing in the 1960s—and continues to perform today—well below its potential because of additional problems largely traceable to socioeconomic structures.

Plowing with oxen. Photo courtesy of L.G.A. Smits.

The land tenure system has been widely viewed as an obstacle to efficient use of the land, although it greatly restrained inequality. The traditional system, in force until the implementation of the 1979 Land Act, vested what Westerners would call ownership in the paramount (king) as representative of the nation. This meant that land could not be alienated and helped to ensure that Lesotho did not face the problem of other African countries (e.g., Swaziland, Kenya) of foreign ownership of much of its land. Use rights only were allocated by the chiefs. Use rights meant the right to plow, cultivate, and harvest crops, but not to fence or harvest straw; after the harvest, any livestock could eat the straw. In theory, each married head of household had a right to an allocation of land, traditionally three (separately located) fields. If fields were not cultivated for several years, they could be reallocated to others. On the death of the landholder, the land would be reallocated. In practice, widows able to cultivate could often keep some land, and the rest would normally be reallocated within the deceased holder's family, if he had sons or junior brothers. However, the landholder could not ensure a transfer to a relative even if he tried to make such a transfer during his lifetime; the final decision remained with the chief.

Inevitably, with increasing population and limited land, in practice land was inequitably distributed, with many (perhaps 10 to 15

Herdboys with sheep and goats. Photo courtesy of Don Gray.

percent) of all households landless, headed either by young males "waiting" for an allocation or by old males or widows unable to cultivate. Sharecropping, in which one household contributed land to which it had rights and another draft power, working capital for seed, or cultivation, was also common, and there were reports of occasional (and illegal) rental contracts on land for cash.

Critics of the pre-1979 land tenure system believed that it discouraged efficient use of land for three reasons. First, fragmentation of holdings and the lack of a market in land rights meant that it was impossible to consolidate holdings into areas large enough to permit profitable use of modern, capital-intensive techniques like mechanization. This observation is somewhat dubious because such techniques may not be profitable in Lesotho conditions anyway. Fragmentation clearly reduced the efficient use of resources in cultivation (because of travel time and access paths), but it also reduced the risk of loss from hail, which is usually very localized. Second, the lack of secure and transferable tenure allegedly decreased the user's incentive to improve the land's productivity by erosion control, irrigation, fertilization, and crop rotation. Again, the criticism is dubious because security of tenure within the family, although not guaranteed, was strong in practice. Perhaps a more valid criticism is the third one, namely that the tradition that fields should be open to grazing (and therefore not fenced) after harvest both increased costs of production (livestock have to be kept out of unharvested fields) and reduced private returns (the straw was a communal product, available to all livestock owners, not a private product appropriable by the landholder). It is interesting to note that as the urban population, and hence urban demand for livestock feed, grew rapidly in the 1970s, more and more farmers within profitable transportation reach of urban centers took to harvesting their straw and selling it, well before the 1979 Land Act implicitly legitimized this departure from traditional mores.

Although the pre-1979 land tenure system may have exacerbated the tendency to low productivity in agriculture, the fundamental problem was almost certainly the impact of the financial incentive for adult males to migrate to South Africa for work. Given the size of landholdings, the high prices of inputs and low prices of marketable outputs, the high transport costs and poor distribution systems, and the effects of rainfall, topography, and soil fertility, for most adult males the return on efforts from farming was inferior to that from migrating, even in the 1960s. By the late 1970s, the gap was enormous. The response of most households to this situation, although perhaps unfortunate from a national point of view, was entirely rational and sensible from the point of view of the individual household. Land and livestock were seen as potentially though not immediately valuable assets, which would allow some diversification of present income sources and some insurance against migrant earnings loss through misfortune, disablement, retirement, or retrenchment by South Africa. But basic microeconomic analysis of the household suggests that the household should, to maximize its welfare, invest its resources in agriculture only up to the point where the return on the marginal input to agriculture equals the return on the marginal input to other uses—in most cases, labor time devoted to migrant work. Given the relatively high wage available in South Africa compared to the average agricultural earnings in Lesotho and given the institutional barriers to amassing sufficient land and capital to permit high marginal return on labor in agriculture at high output/acre levels, it would follow (because the land itself had low or zero opportunity cost) that most households should cultivate, but devote very little labor effort or capital to cultivation. This seems to be entirely consistent with what occurred. Further, it makes sense to cultivate even if the return on the effort involved is very low or negative in the short run, if this increases the probability of retaining the rights to the asset—the land—for the time when the alternative of migration is no longer available.[5] At the national level, this response by households causes a difficulty, because it results in (1) less intensive cultivation than is either feasible or desirable, given the wholly domestic endowments of land and labor, and (2) lowered agricultural output, leading to greater imports of food and a reduction in food security at both the national and the household levels.

Long functional integration into the South African economy and the low level of investment in both social and physical infrastructure also resulted in two other striking features of Lesotho's economy at independence. These are the extremely small and very distorted modern sector and the almost total lack of anything that could be called a "national economy."

The modern sector at independence was heavily dominated by commerce, meaning retail and wholesale trade. In 1964, 90 percent of internal trade was performed by the seventy-two members of the Chamber of Commerce, all but four of them Whites. The other 10 percent was shared by a few Indian traders in the northeast and between 2,500 and 3,000 small Basotho-owned businesses.[6] Manufacturing other than handicrafts was confined to the production of building materials, furniture, one small manufacturing chemist, and one small plant for malting sorghum.[7] Electricity and water supplies were available only in the major towns. The tourism industry in effect did not yet exist. However, the network of trading stores covered the entire country, the economy was essentially wholly monetized, and even in remote areas a wide range of imported manufactured goods were offered for sale.

Entirely consistent with Lesotho's history of being for all practical purposes part of the South African economy for the previous century, at independence there was in no meaningful sense a national economy. Internally, the economy was very heavily fragmented, because transport and communications were so difficult and had been so neglected. Even within the lowlands, the normal route for motor vehicles between places separated by any distance was via the far superior South African road system. In practice, the country was divided into a number of separate rural hinterlands of South African border towns (such as Fouriesburg, Ficksburg, Wepener), and most economic transactions other than the purely local were technically international, either with a rural South African market town just over the border or with the more distant mining and commercial centers in South Africa. As late as the mid-1970s, purchases from firms such as Shell (Lesotho) were routinely invoiced from Bloemfontein, not Maseru.[8]

The implication of this history was that at independence, the new Lesotho government inherited responsibility for a territory that in economic terms was not an "economy." The focus of economic activity was typically in the household, in the immediate local commercial establishments, or in South Africa. In general, the transport and communications infrastructures neither encouraged nor permitted a redirection of links from South Africa to points in Lesotho, and the normal institutions of a national economy did not exist.

MAJOR ECONOMIC TRENDS SINCE INDEPENDENCE

Before discussing government economic policy in detail, it is useful to have a broad picture of what has happened in the economy since independence. Although we stress again that the data are all somewhat suspect and that a spurious degree of precision may be suggested, a sketch of the broad picture is assisted by the numbers contained in Tables 2.3, 2.4, and 2.5.

Table 2.3 gives the most recent available estimates of the percentage distribution of contributions to the gross domestic product (GDP) from various sectors of the economy, for 1967/1968 and 1979/1980. Certain aspects of structural change in Lesotho's economy are suggested by this table. The unreliability of the basic data is clearly shown by consideration of the last column in Table 2.3, which gives estimates of the change in real output by sectors of the economy from 1967/1968 to 1979/1980. This is only indicative of relative changes in real output by sector, because some of the entries must be inaccurate. For example, it is quite unrealistic to suggest that the real value of output in the trade sector and the ownership of dwellings sector fell in this twelve-year period; in both, it must have increased.

Nevertheless, taking the actual numbers with a heavy dose of salt, Table 2.3 does reveal structural change in the economy. In twelve years, overall output grew about 70 percent. This growth was distributed very unevenly between sectors. Agriculture, the largest single sector throughout the period, grew slower than the economy as a whole, by about 50 percent. Sectors involving handicraft production, trade, ownership of dwellings, and other nonprofit services, according to the data, did not grow in real terms at all, although this is very hard to believe. The behavior of the trade sector is particularly noteworthy. According to the data, in 1967/1968 it accounted for over 22 percent of GDP, an astonishingly high percentage, but one consistent with Lesotho as a labor reserve in which cash incomes earned in South Africa were spent on imported goods. The very high value added in wholesale and retail trade for the volume of turnover in 1967/1968 may be partly explained by a high degree of local monopoly. It is also of note that the data suggest that large traders

TABLE 2.3
National Accounts Data

Sector	GDP at Factor Cost,[a] Percent of Total		1979/1980 Output as Percentage of 1967/1968 Output[b]
	1967/1968	1979/1980	
Agriculture	34.5	30.6	150.8
Mining and quarrying	2.3	6.0	446.7
Manufacturing	0.5	3.3	1,019.2
Handicrafts	2.9	1.5	86.6
Electricity and water	0.3	1.0	690.6
Building and construction	4.0	9.2	392.4
Trade, wholesale and retail	22.4	11.1	84.5
Big traders	(11.6)	(6.5)	95.5
Small traders	(10.8)	(4.6)	72.6
Catering (tourism)	0.3	4.0	2,186.8
Transport	0.6	1.9	552.6
Posts and communications	0.7	0.6	155.9
Finance and business services	1.6	4.6	490.1
Ownership of dwellings	13.9	7.8	95.5
Education	4.4	5.7	221.3
Health	1.1	1.2	196.9
Other nonprofit services	0.4	0.3	104.8
Government services	9.1	9.8	181.9
Community and personal services	1.1	1.3	208.9
Total[c]	100.1	99.9	169.9

a. Gross domestic product valued at the cost of the factor inputs (i.e.,
    labor, capital, land); excludes taxes levied on output.
b. Obtained by converting actual output by sector to constant prices by means
    of the price index for GDP, and then expressing 1979/1980 output as a
    percentage of 1967/1968 output.
c. Totals omit items in parentheses and do not add to 100 in first two columns
    of data because of rounding errors. Entry in last column is total 1979/1980
    real GDP as a percentage of 1967/1968 real GDP.

Source: Derived from data in World Bank/United Nations Development Programme
         Team, National Income Accounts of Lesotho, 1967/1968 - 1979/1980,
         (Maseru: World Bank/UNDP Team, 1981).

(mostly foreign) expanded their share of retail and wholesale trade
at the expense of small traders (mostly Basotho).

The posts and communications, government, and health sectors
all expanded roughly in line with the economy as a whole. The
community and personal services and education sectors both more
than doubled their real output, growing about half as fast again as
the economy. The remaining sectors all grew much faster than the
economy; real output increased by multiples of about four and a half
for mining, ten for manufacturing, seven for electricity and water,
four for building and construction, twenty-two for catering, five and
a half for transport, and five for finance and business services. Such

Basotho, at the store and mill. Photo courtesy of Louise B. Cobbe.

rapid growth at first sight seems most impressive, but the impression is, unfortunately, at least partly misleading. In several cases, the growth was from such a small base that at the end of the period the proportional contribution of the sector to GDP was still very small, and thus the effects of the rapid growth in the sectors concerned on the economy as a whole remained commensurately small. The most obvious example is manufacturing; despite the tenfold increase in real output, at the end of the period the sector still accounted for only 3.3 percent of total output (a lower figure than the World Bank reports for any other low-income economy with over one million population), and the relative importance of the sector actually declined between 1975/1976 and 1979/1980.

The growth in mining is also deceptive. The huge increase in real output and percentage contribution to GDP that occurred between 1975/1979 and 1979/1980 is due to the opening of a De Beers subsidiary, a diamond mine at Letseng-la-Terai. However, this mine proved to be unprofitable and was closed in late 1982.

To a very large extent, the increases in real output and relative size in the utilities (electricity and water), transport, and finance and business services sectors reflect the relative absence of such necessary concomitants of a modern economy at the start of the period. Electricity and piped water services were extended to many areas. Many roads

Terminal building, airstrip in the mountains. Photo courtesy of Don Gray.

were constructed or improved, which, together with substantial growth of real disposable incomes in rural areas as mining wages in South Africa increased, permitted rapid expansion of road transport. Banking, financial institutions, and business services greatly expanded as new legal structures and institutions (e.g., Lesotho Bank, Lesotho National Development Corporation, Lesotho National Insurance Company, Lesotho Building Finance Corporation) were established and existing firms expanded (e.g., both foreign commercial banks expanded their operations substantially).

Even the dynamism of construction and catering, where there is very little of this catching-up-with-past-neglect effect, is not necessarily likely to be sustained. The growth in construction reflects three main factors: massive, mostly aid-financed investment in infrastructure, notably roads and government and educational buildings; commercial investment in shops, warehouses, and offices; and residential construction, heavily fueled by the increases in disposable income. It is probable that the last two of these three have largely caught up with the rapid spurt in incomes and spending following the increase in migrant earnings of the mid-1970s, and therefore output in this sector is likely to stabilize if not fall in the 1980s. Catering is a reflection mostly of tourism, which grew very rapidly in the 1970s following the opening of the Maseru Holiday Inn that attracted White South Africans. However, despite continued investment in more hotels and official optimism, tourism began to decline around 1980. This decline is likely to continue, because various bantustans—former "native reserves" within South Africa, now officially there called "homelands" or "national states," some of which are putatively self-governing to some extent—are now able to offer similar if not greater attractions for South Africans closer to their homes.

Hence, the overall implication of Table 2.3 is that the structure of the economy became more "modern," but the basic productive forces changed comparatively little other than an increase in the capacity of the construction sector. Commodity production was still dominated by agriculture, about ten times the size of manufacturing, and the services sector became somewhat restructured to reflect greater "modernization" and purchasing power.

Table 2.4 looks at the national accounts in terms of major standard expenditure aggregates and some per capita indicators. The figures in terms of percent of GDP are more revealing of structural trends in the aggregate than the absolute numbers.

It is noteworthy that private consumption alone has been greater than GDP throughout the period. Investment grew substantially and rapidly until the end of the 1970s, but then started to decline as a proportion of GDP. Exports and imports were probably more severely underreported in the more distant past than recently, but both grew as a proportion of GDP until 1979/1980. In 1982/1983, imports were almost 40 percent greater than GDP, and it is of significance that although exports plus the estimated earnings of migrants were 90 percent of imports in 1971/1972, by 1982/1983 this sum had declined to less than 67 percent of imports. The difference was accounted for by foreign aid inflows and government borrowing.

Table 2.4 shows clearly how the economy became much more dependent on migrant workers' earnings to finance itself, this dependence peaking in the late 1970s. As a result, the gap between GDP and GNP (the latter defined for Lesotho to include the estimated total earnings of migrants, because all migrants are, under South African law, only temporarily absent from Lesotho) also widened. GDP was 81 percent of GNP in 1967/1968; it fell to only 52 percent in 1975/1976 before recovering slightly to 59 percent in 1979/1980 and then declining again to under 57 percent in 1982/1983. The implication is nevertheless marked: Whereas at about the time of independence, Lesotho earned from migrants $1 for every $4 produced at home, by the early 1980s migrant earnings contributed directly over $3 for every $4 produced at home—i.e., by one crude measure, dependence on migration more than tripled. Furthermore, this ten-

60

TABLE 2.4
Major National Accounts Items, Selected Years

A. Aggregates

Aggregates	1971/1972 Million Maloti	1971/1972 Percentage of GDP	1975/1976 Million Maloti	1975/1976 Percentage of GDP	1979/1980 Million Maloti	1979/1980 Percentage of GDP	1982/1983[d] Million Maloti	1982/1983[d] Percentage of GDP
Total consumption	71.9	142.4	207.0	186.5	437.1	167.7	747.0	195.6
Government	8.3	16.4	23.1	20.8	52.3	20.1	90.0	23.6
Private	63.6	125.9	183.9	165.7	384.8	147.7	657.0	172.0
Gross investment	8.1	16.0	27.3	24.6	103.6	39.8	112.0	29.3
Exports	6.8	13.5	16.2	14.6	58.4	22.4	52.0	13.6
Imports	36.3	71.9	139.5	125.7	338.5	129.9	529.0	138.5
GDP at market prices[a]	50.5	100.0	111.0	100.0	260.6	100.0	382.0	100.0
Net factor income from abroad[b]	25.8	51.1	101.0	91.0	181.8	69.8	294.0	77.0
GNP at market prices[c]	76.3	151.1	212.0	191.0	442.4	169.8	676.0	177.0
GDP at constant 1970/1971 prices	47.6		69.6		101.8		122.4	

B. Per capita

	1971/1972 Maloti	1975/1976 Maloti	1979/1980 Maloti	1982/1983 Maloti
GDP/de jure population	46.7	94.0	202.0	271.2
GDP/de facto population	54.6	109.5	229.7	300.8
GNP/de jure population	70.5	179.5	343.0	480.8
GDP/de facto population, constant 1970/71 prices	51.4	68.7	89.7	96.4

Note: Approximate average exchange rates: in 1971/1972, M1 = U.S. $1.30; in 1975/1976 and 1979/1980, M1 = US$1.20; in 1982/1983, M1 = US$0.90. GDP = gross domestic product; GNP = gross national product.

a. GDP = consumption plus gross investment plus exports minus imports.
b. Earnings of migrants less net interest paid abroad.
c. GNP = GDP plus net factor income from abroad.
d. Preliminary estimates.

Source: Derived from data in: Kingdom of Lesotho, Annual Statistical Bulletin 1981 (Maseru: Bureau of Statistics, 1982), World Bank/United Nations Development Programme Team, National Income Accounts of Lesotho, 1967/1968 - 1979/1980 (Maseru: World Bank/UNDP Team, 1981), and Central Bank of Lesotho, Annual Report for 1983 (Maseru: Central Bank of Lesotho, 1984).

dency is probably understated because the national accounts estimates of migrant earnings are consistently lower than estimates inferred from available data on migrants.[9]

Domestic output did grow, however, as suggested by Table 2.3. Table 2.4 shows that, measured in constant 1970/1971 prices, GDP per capita increased from M51 in 1971/1972 to M96 in 1982/1983, or by almost 90 percent. This is equivalent to a real growth rate of about 5.9 percent per annum compounded, although one should remember that the real GDP per capita probably fell during the late 1960s. Table 2.4 shows that most of this growth occurred in the 1970s and that only very slow growth occurred in the early 1980s.[10]

What fueled this growth? As already implied, the two major forces were migrant earnings and foreign aid receipts. Table 2.5 summarizes some data on migration. It is very important to emphasize the ambiguity of migration data. Prior to the early 1960s, Basotho in South Africa were treated officially in the same manner as indigenous South African Blacks. Because substantial permanent migration occurred, especially in the 1930s, 1940s, and 1950s, and Basotho found employment in all parts of South Africa and in all sectors of the South African economy, genuine ambiguities arose concerning the "true" or "correct" citizenship of particular individuals.[11] There are more ethnic Basotho who are permanent residents of South Africa than live in Lesotho—over 1.7 million in South Africa in 1980, compared to about 1.3 million in Lesotho.[12] Since the early 1960s, however, the official restrictions in South Africa on the employment of Blacks, especially foreign Blacks, except as contract migrants have been progressively tightened; therefore, the incentives for migrants from Lesotho to conceal their status are considerable. Furthermore, whether a particular individual is a temporary migrant and intends to return home to Lesotho or a permanent resident of South Africa with no such intention is by definition a subjective question answerable only by the individual. The answer may change with not only the perceived economic, social, political, and legal conditions, opportunities, and constraints in the two locations, but also with the identity of the questioner. Hence, the total number of migrants from Lesotho in South Africa is a quantity that is not objectively measurable, for both conceptual and practical reasons.

Nevertheless, Table 2.5 gives some important and useful numbers. It provides time-series data on three overlapping groups of migrants from Lesotho to South Africa. The first data set includes all migrants employed by mines belonging to the Chamber of Mines (i.e., all gold mines and a few others); these migrants are recruited through TEBA (The Employment Bureau for Africa, formerly Mine Labour Organi-

TABLE 2.5
Lesotho Migrant Workers in South Africa, 1966-1984

		Chamber of Mines Mineworkers		All		
		Average Annual Cash Wage[a]		Mine-	Average Contract	Total Number of
		Current	1970			
Year	Number[b]	Rand	Rand	workers[c]	Length, Months[d]	Legal Workers[e]
1966	64,300	183	208	n.a.	n.a.	n.a.
1967	59,700	187	207	77,414	12	n.a.
1968	65,100	191	207	80,310	12	n.a.
1969	65,000	199	209	83,000	n.a.	n.a.
1970	71,100	208	208	87,384	11	n.a.
1971	68,700	221	209	91,054	12	n.a.
1972	78,500	257	227	98,831	12	n.a.
1973	87,200	350	282	110,453	11	148,856
1974	78,300	552	399	103,288	12	n.a.
1975	85,500	948	602	112,507	10	n.a.
1976	96,400	968	554	121,062	9	152,188
1977	103,200	1,224	628	128,941	11	173,882
1978	104,100	1,476	670	124,491	13	155,623
1979	109,200	1,752	709	124,393	16	152,032
1980	109,000	2,148	808	120,733	16	136,395
1981	109,200	2,495	815	123,538	16	150,422
1982	104,000	3,024	861	117,641	15	147,659
1983	102,800	n.a.	n.a.	115,327	n.a.	140,719
1984	n.a.	n.a.	n.a.	114,071	n.a.	n.a.

Note: n.a. = Not available.

a. For all Black workers in gold-mining; Lesotho-specific figures would probably be higher
   because of Lesotho's above-average skill-mix.
b. On 31 December rounded to nearest 100.
c. Average of monthly data from Lesotho Department of Labour.
d. Average completed contract length, derived by dividing average number in employment by
   average number recruited each month and multiplying by twelve.
e. Except for May 1976, as registered with South African authorities on 30 June.

Source: Derived from data in   Fion de Vletter, "Recent Trends and Prospects of Black
        Migration to South Africa," International Migration for Employment Working Paper
        no. 20 (Geneva: International Labour Office, 1985); Merle Lipton, "Men of Two
        Worlds: Migrant Labour in South Africa," Optima 29(213), November 1980; Kingdom of
        Lesotho, Annual Statistical Bulletin 1982 (Maseru: Bureau of Statistics, 1983);
        Central Bank of Lesotho, Quarterly Review III, No. 4; and South African Institute
        of Race Relations, Survey of Race Relations in South Africa (Johannesburg: SAIRR,
        annual).

zation/Native Recruiting Company). The second set of numbers is
for all migrant mineworkers, including those at non-Chamber mines
(mostly coal and diamond mines), recruited by agencies other than
TEBA. These numbers are usually 15 to 20 percent higher than those
for TEBA migrants only. These two sets of data can be presumed to
be reasonably accurate, because the groups covered are well defined
and recruiting is highly organized and regulated. However, these
statistics are not perfect conceptually or for analytic purposes. For
example, anecdotal evidence confirms that some migrant mineworkers
maintain families in the Republic of South Africa and have only their
travel documents to link them to Lesotho.[13]

The third, and most encompassing, data set includes all Lesotho citizens working in the Republic known to the South African authorities. The numbers here are more uncertain and less useful analytically. It is known that there are illegal migrants. It is also likely that there are many persons who are not regarded officially by South Africa as migrants from Lesotho, yet maintain links with Lesotho and with relatives there (e.g., remittances, sending children to school in Lesotho, intention to retire to Lesotho). On the other hand, some of those officially regarded by South Africa as Lesotho citizens may have no economic links with Lesotho and no intention to return there if they can avoid it.

For all these inadequacies, the data do confirm the broad picture of the evolution of the migrant labor situation, which is not in dispute. Until the early 1970s the Chamber of Mines had for a long time held real wages very low, at a level inadequate for the full support of the migrant and his family, and had as a result relied increasingly on foreign Black labor, the largest contingents coming from Mozambique and Malawi. After Mozambican independence and the temporary withdrawal of Malawian labor, the Chamber of Mines made a policy decision to increase the proportion of its Black labor force from the Republic itself. This required a substantial increase in real wages and was coupled with attempts to decrease the turnover of the labor force to permit greater skill acquisition. The South African government supported the shift to a more South African labor force, but continued to require that at least 97 percent of all Black employees in mining be single, unaccompanied migrants housed in compound hostels. At most, 3 percent of Black mineworkers are allowed to be housed with their families at the mine.[14]

Real cash wages increased very rapidly for mineworkers between 1973 and 1975, with smaller increases continuing until 1981. The number of migrants from Lesotho also increased and the average contract length shortened until 1977. From then on, the mines were in an oversupply situation with respect to Black labor, restrictions were imposed on recruitment, and contract length increased. The number of migrants from Lesotho in Chamber mines increased a little more until 1980; since then the number appears to have roughly stabilized, and it is widely believed (although TEBA usually denies this) that there is a quota for Lesotho of about 100,000 workers on Chamber mines. On non-Chamber mines, the number of Lesotho workers peaked in 1977 and since then has fallen. Correspondingly, recruitment restrictions are tighter for non-Chamber mines. In late 1981, only 5 percent of TEBA's contracts were with novices, i.e., new recruits with no mine experience. A further 25 percent of contracts were with experienced mineworkers without valid reengagement certificates, and 70 percent were with persons with valid reengagement certificates. The other recruitment agencies in Lesotho were not recruiting any novices and rarely took men without valid reengagement certificates.[15] By late 1983, TEBA was taking only a handful of novices, and aspirant but unsuccessful migrant recruits had become a feature of Maseru streets.

The number of known legal workers who do not work in mining has fallen in the period for which data are available, from over 38,000 in 1973 to 21,500 in July 1983. This fact reflects South African government policy, which is to permit "foreign Blacks" to work in South Africa only as migrants at the mines. Thus, Basotho who are not involved in mining in South Africa but who are "legal" consist largely of those who hold so-called Section 10 rights as a result of long and continuous residence or employment.[16] South Africa now no longer permits Lesotho citizens to enter employment in South Africa (except as migrant workers in mining) or to take up permanent residence in South Africa.[17] The penalties for illegal residence and employment, on both employee and employer, have been substantially increased in South Africa since the early 1970s and more stringently enforced. Illegal migration from Lesotho undoubtedly does still occur, but there is no reliable method to gauge its size or composition.

The increases in real mine wages and migrant numbers, together with various institutional factors, were the major stimuli behind Lesotho's apparent economic growth between 1972 and 1982. Mineworkers receive room and board while at the mines, plus their cash wages. At least 60 percent of cash earnings, after the first month, is compulsorily deferred and deposited in savings accounts in Lesotho Bank.[18] Although migrants spend some of their earnings in South Africa on things they do not bring back with them, a high proportion of migrant earnings eventually reaches Lesotho as remittances to relatives, deferred pay, or goods or cash brought back by returning miners. Instead of being saved, the bulk of these earnings is spent, probably mostly sooner rather than later. A high proportion of this spending quickly leaks back into South Africa in payment for imports, but nevertheless two things result from the spending that greatly stimulate the Lesotho economy.

First, the spending is responsible for the level of activity and generates much of the value added in retail and wholesale trade, transport, construction of dwellings, acquisition of livestock, and especially small-scale, informal sector activity at the village level (e.g., beer houses). Particularly at the village level in rural areas, the anthropological evidence suggests that most cash in circulation, and hence most local nonagricultural value added, originates from the earnings of migrants (including migrants in urban areas in Lesotho, whose wages depend indirectly on the earnings of migrants in South Africa to a large extent).

Second, under the Southern African Customs Union Agreement each M1 of imports, from whatever origin, generates about M0.20 of government revenue. Because Customs Union receipts account for the bulk of Lesotho's government revenues, additional migrant earnings—resulting in additional imports and thus government revenue—tend to generate additional government spending and therefore domestic value added.

No published work attempts to quantify these relationships, although it is believed that the Lesotho government has made such attempts. The available macroeconomic data from the national income accounts suggest that at the aggregate level the multiplier for an extra rand of migrant earnings lies in the range 1.25 to 1.85, i.e., each extra rand of income earned by a migrant generates an additional 25 to 85 cents of value added within Lesotho. This implies that 20 to 45 percent of migrant earnings actually buys Lesotho-produced value added, which is not unreasonable given low savings rates, high transport costs, fairly high gross margins in commerce, and a high propensity in recent years to construct or improve dwellings.[19]

The other main stimulus behind Lesotho's growth in the 1970s was foreign aid. Table 2.6 gives available data on foreign aid. Several features are striking. In 1971/1972 , foreign aid was already equivalent to about 25 percent of GDP, and it remained at roughly this level throughout the decade, probably exceeding it in 1981. Net aid receipts were almost as high as gross aid receipts and in most years were comparable to, if not higher than, *gross* investment as recorded in the national accounts (this reflects aid such as technical assistance and food not classified as investment and, probably, underestimation of private investment). Although Lesotho has not received unusually large amounts of aid in per capita terms (in 1982, Lesotho's aid was $64 per person; Somalia, Gambia, Guinea-Bissau, Mauritania, Botswana, and Gabon in Africa alone all had higher receipts per person), this aid inflow is very large and unusual as a proportion of GDP, particularly because it has been sustained at such a high level for so long.

Table 2.6 shows how dependent on specifically British aid Lesotho was prior to 1970. In that year, the UK suspended aid for several months in response to political events, but the United States and various multilateral sources replaced much of what was lost. Since 1970, the UK has declined in importance as an aid donor, although

TABLE 2.6
Lesotho's Foreign Aid Receipts, 1969-1982

	Gross ODA $ million	Net ODA $ million	Percentage of Gross from				
			UK	USA	FRG	EC	Other Multilateral
1969	13.3	13.3	67	15	0	0	15
1970	10.1	10.0	16	40	1	1	38
1971	16.8	16.8	44	24	1	1	28
1972	15.4	14.1	47	19	0	7	22
1973	14.3	14.2	32	14	3	1	41
1974	22.3	22.3	26	13	7	1	42
1975	28.6	28.6	30	7	2	0	49
1976	30.2	30.1	13	13	3	0	40
1977	38.9	38.8	10	10	3	2	46
1978	50.4	50.1	20	10	7	7	35
1979	64.5	64.2	22	14	6	4	28
1980	90.7	90.3	11	18	20	5	29
1981	101.4	101.0	10	25	12	7	35
1982	89.9	89.7	7	28	11	7	33

Notes: ODA is Official Development Assistance, grants and loans,
        disbursements or receipts, in current U.S. dollars; net is gross less
        loan service. EC is European Community; totals of percentages by
        source do not add to 100 since by 1982 some twelve other bilateral
        donors are omitted (the most important are Canada, Denmark, and
        Sweden).

Sources: OECD, Geographical Distribution of Financial Flows to Developing
         Countries, 1969-1975; 1976-1979; and 1979-1982 (Paris: OECD, 1977;
         1980; and 1984).

it remains significant; U.S. aid has fluctuated greatly from year to year, but has become much more important in recent years; West Germany and the European Community have emerged as substantial donors, and multilateral sources (notably the World Bank group, the African Development Bank, the World Food Programme, and UN Development Program) have usually been significant donors. Lesotho greatly diversified bilateral sources of aid as well and benefited in particular from aid relationships with Denmark, Sweden, Holland, and Canada.

Lesotho receives aid of almost all possible types, from all possible sources. Large numbers of expatriate personnel work in the country under technical assistance programs, the absolute number of expatriates probably having grown slowly since independence. Capital projects have been concentrated in road construction, rural development, communications and government buildings, and education, but some funds have also gone to spur industrial development through the

Lesotho National Development Corporation (LNDC) and Basotho Enterprise Development Corporation (BEDCO). Food-aid imports, largely used for food-for-work projects (at very low labor productivities) are also substantial, averaging 33,640 metric tons (37,000 short tons; equivalent to about 55 pounds [25 kg] per person) of grain-equivalent a year in the five-year period 1978–1982. Without food aid, the nutritional status of the rural disadvantaged would be substantially worse than it is.

Aid in Lesotho is a very touchy subject. In the earlier years of independence, limited analytic capability in the government resulted in many projects being designed in London or Washington, not Maseru. Not surprisingly, many aid projects had disappointing results in terms of identifiable benefits. Although analytic capabilities have improved, Lesotho still has little ability to finance its own public capital formation, so that the public sector investment program is still heavily influenced by donor willingness to finance. This results in much frustration for Basotho officials and at least some seemingly rather inappropriate projects, because political pressures make it difficult for the government to turn down offers of aid or to exercise much leverage over project details if donors are adamant. At times, the appropriate adjectives to describe some donor officials include not only adamant but also arrogant and condescending.

The presence of a large community of aid-financed personnel has had some obvious effects on the economy, particularly in Maseru. Housing of a standard considered appropriate for expatriates is in perennially short supply; rents are astonishingly high, and lack of housing often delays the implementation of projects. The tendency of aid projects to provide total employment packages superior to those of government proper puts upward pressure on government salary scales, drains better-quality personnel out of government proper, and leads to frequent job changes for locals with skills in scarce supply. The consumption aspirations and the expenditure patterns of local personnel are also undoubtedly influenced by those of aid workers, who often receive after-tax incomes three to ten times higher than their local counterparts.

Another potentially explosive issue surrounding aid concerns South Africa. Lesotho's dependent position as an enclave surrounded by South Africa has been used by both the government of Lesotho and aid donors as justification for relative generosity by donors toward Lesotho's needs. The UN has on several occasions—e.g., after the Transkei border closure and after the 1982 Maseru raid—used this argument in appeals to the donor community for additional aid for Lesotho. However, the majority of aid donors follow procedures and practices that result in much of their aid disbursements being spent on South African products. Obviously this has to happen indirectly, because a large proportion of consumer spending goes for South African imports, but it is somewhat more surprising and potentially embarrassing that aid disbursements are spent to a substantial extent directly in South Africa, through construction contracts with South African firms, through purchases of materials, equipment, and supplies from South African sources, and from contracts with local firms that are subsidiaries of South African parents. In some cases, it happens despite official "tying" of aid to procurement from the donor's home country: British procedures, for example, permit "tied" funds to be used for purchases from South African companies that are subsidiaries of British parents. In practice, therefore, foreign aid to Lesotho benefits South Africa as well as Lesotho. It is clear and significant that the Lesotho economy is heavily dependent on aid for almost all public sector investment and for a substantial portion of current income.

The facts that agricultural output has grown only a little more slowly than GDP and that manufacturing has grown much faster, although from a tiny base, are grounds for some cautious optimism about the ability of the Lesotho economy to become more self-reliant. Output in all other sectors of the economy is either wholly exogenous (e.g., mining, where output fell back to below 1 percent of GDP after De Beers closed Letseng-la-Terai) or a consequence of the spending of incomes originally earned from aid projects, in agriculture, manufacturing, other "export" industries, or in South Africa. But agriculture, manufacturing, mining, and catering (tourism) combined only amounted to 43.9 percent of GDP in 1979/1980 (a "good" year because harvests were good and De Beers in full operation), or only about 27 percent of consumption alone. It is very clear that the standard of living of the Basotho has been very dependent on foreign aid and migrant earnings from South Africa, probably more so in the late 1970s and early 1980s than in the 1960s.

GOVERNMENT ECONOMIC POLICY AND CONSTRAINTS ON IT

In the conduct of economy policy, all governments are constrained by their resource bases, the external economic environment, the institutional structure, and their perceptions of the political situation and how economic policy affects political advantage. Lesotho is in no sense an exception; rather, it is an extreme case. The resource base is meager. Basically it consists of inadequate agricultural land, too many low-quality livestock, water that can only be exploited with massive investment and cooperation from hostile South Africa, and a relatively well-educated, industrious labor force. The external environment has both positive and negative aspects. On the negative side, Lesotho's location implies high transport costs to or from markets other than South Africa, and inflation and high interest rates have taken their toll. More positively, Lesotho's history, status, and location have implied relatively easy access to foreign aid. Whether such aid has been costless or efficiently used is very debatable, but it has been available. The institutional structure has two major components in Lesotho's case. First, there are the institutions that tie Lesotho to its hostile neighbor—the formal ones of the Southern African Customs Union Agreement, Rand Monetary Area Agreement, and the Labour Agreement in particular—and the more informal ones of commercial and transport links, family ties, migrant movements, broadcasting, the press and magazines, and a largely common culture. Second, there are the more purely domestic institutions, again both formal—parastatals (government-owned but quasi-autonomous bodies), voluntary bodies, and law, education, trade unions—and informal—how people behave, what they expect. At independence, the institutional links with South Africa were either wholly informal or had been established long before by the imperial power, which had a very different perspective on such matters from an independent Lesotho government. Formal domestic institutions were also either rudimentary or nonexistent, with strong South African influence very evident.

Political aspects will be dealt with in more detail in Chapter 4. Here it is important to note that politics have been a strong influence on specific aspects of economic policy throughout the modern period, and it is widely believed that political disunity has acted as a brake on economic progress. The extreme example is sabotage of government development projects by political opponents, but in milder forms the problem has at times been pervasive and serious. In the late 1970s and early 1980s, armed attacks by the Lesotho Liberation Army, the military wing of the opposition in exile, also resulted in substantially expanded government spending on security, which in the 1984/1985 fiscal year accounted for more than 20 percent of current expenditure—the largest single category.

The greatest constraints on the Lesotho government can be summarized as poverty, uncertainty, and South Africa. The three interact: It is because of poverty that the people of Lesotho depend on the income from Basotho migrants' work in South Africa but uncertainty surrounds what South Africa will do and how it will react to events or initiatives in Lesotho. The opinions and interests of aid donors are also very salient, and the government is clearly responsive to them to some extent.

In the circumstances, both the rhetoric and the actual content of government policy are fairly predictable. The rhetoric emphasizes the reduction of dependence on South Africa, especially for employment. In the short run, reducing the dependence is neither feasible nor consistent with other objectives and clearly has not been achieved. However, it is important to stress that no attempt has been made to achieve the reduction in the short run, and, despite the rhetoric, this is in reality very much a long-run objective.[20] Achieving it in the long run implies certain kinds of change in Lesotho. Ultimately, what is required is a vast expansion of opportunities to use labor productively within the country. Comparatively little progress has been made in this respect, largely because of the sparse resource base and the heavy integration with South Africa which, as explained below, makes profitable use of labor within Lesotho difficult. But it can be argued that a necessary prerequisite for this ultimate objective is either the creation of a meaningful national economy or a situation that would permit its appearance if needed. This means the creation and development of the necessary institutions and physical infrastructure (especially transport, storage, commercial infrastructure, and utilities) to allow the focus of economic activity to shift from cross-border transactions to domestic ones.

Consciously or unconsciously—and in explicit statements, apparently mostly the latter—government policy seems to have recognized these necessities. In the period since independence, a very high proportion of government effort has been expended on the creation and development of the elements needed for a national economy to become a reality. Within the public sector, government ministries and departments have been expanded and strengthened; the number of civil service posts doubled to about 12,000. Many parastatals were created, expanded, and strengthened, including Lesotho National Development Corporation (LNDC), responsible for encouraging and holding government equity in industrial and commercial enterprises; Basotho Enterprises Development Corporation (BEDCO), which assists smaller, wholly Basotho firms; Lesotho Bank, a commercial and savings bank; the Central Bank, formally the Lesotho Monetary Authority, which issues the maloti currency and administers monetary policy; Lesotho Housing Corporation, an LNDC subsidiary responsible for much high-cost housing; Lower Income Housing Company (LEHCO-OP), for low-income housing; Lesotho Building Finance Corporation, which finances construction; Lesotho Electricity Corporation (LEC); and Lesotho Telephone.

Further, the government has given considerable encouragement and assistance to the establishment and development of the network of business, professional, and voluntary bodies that represent in practice an important part of the social infrastructure and institutions of modern nations. Prior to independence, there were comparatively very few such organizations. Now, in addition to such obvious bodies as the Chamber of Commerce and Industry and the Red Cross, there are associations or societies for all kinds of groups, from accountants and architects to doctors and nurses. Not all such groups, of course, agree with the government, which rarely provides more than verbal and in-kind support even to those it does favor. The Christian Council, for example, is an outspoken critic that has refused to cooperate with government departments in its work among migrants. Nevertheless, the formation of this social infrastructure is a striking feature of the past two decades and is potentially as important to the development of a national economy as physical infrastructure.

Of course, the government has also stressed construction. Apart from offices to house expanded government services, the most important additions to physical infrastructure are roads, airfields, and telecommunications, although electricity and water supplies and sewage removal have also been substantially increased in urban areas. The expansion and improvement of the road network now allows ordinary road vehicles to reach many areas of the country. On these roads, private transport of persons and goods has greatly increased. The initial impact has probably been simply the deeper penetration of imported goods into rural areas as transport costs have dropped, but the potential for internal specialization and exchange has been greatly enhanced.

The result remains, however, far more the *potential* of a national economy than the actual achievement of one. As the aggregate data presented in Table 2.4 show, import penetration has increased, and exports of goods and services produced in Lesotho—if we take out diamond exports from Letseng-la-Terai, which have now stopped—pay for a smaller fraction of imports than they did at independence. So although domestic production has increased, the economy remains overwhelmingly and desperately dependent on migrant labor to finance consumption, on foreign aid to finance investment, and on the imports that both finance to generate government revenue. One can also wonder, as explored further in Chapter 4, whether government efforts toward building a national economy were not intended mainly to expand the power and wealth of the state itself.

The other main thrust of the government's economic policy has been to attempt to "modernize" the economy and to provide "modern" cash-wage jobs. The government has consistently sought and accepted foreign investment and foreign aid for activities that are in some sense "modern," even if the overall net effect on labor use in the economy may have been negative.

However, it is hard to detect a real strategy behind government's economic policy in the productive sectors. Agricultural policy in particular seems to have been somewhat inconsistent, with initiatives swinging fairly wildly between the preferences of donors (often favoring, in some form, "aid to the poorest," but frequently resulting in economic failures, such as the large area-based projects of the 1970s—for example, the Thaba-Bosiu Rural Development Project) and the government's desires to assist particular groups and further political aims. Even the 1982 annual report of the parastatal Lesotho Agricultural Development Bank bemoans the lack of a central, formally based policy toward agriculture.

Similarly, in industrial development, the policy is to stress generous tax advantages and trade access not only to South Africa but also to Black Africa and the European Community. However, the tax and other investment incentives in Lesotho, although generous, do not match those available in peripheral areas within South Africa, and the trade advantages of Lesotho are identical to those of Swaziland, which can offer a more developed commercial and industrial infrastructure and better transport links to overseas markets. Thus, in practice, most manufacturing investment has been aimed at the domestic market or involves fortuitous circumstances of some kind. Government has appeared willing to accept almost any foreign investment or aid initiative, so long as it provides some modern jobs, regardless of its other qualities.[21]

Integration with South Africa

The 1969 revision of the Southern African Customs Union Agreement, between Botswana, Lesotho, Swaziland, and South Africa, negotiated with considerable outside assistance, was hailed initially as a great advance on previous arrangements, which indeed it was.[22] Important changes included a new revenue-sharing formula; provisions for consultations between governments and annual meetings of a formal Customs Union Commission; provision for Botswana, Lesotho, and Swaziland to give infant industry protection for up to eight years to new domestic activities; and explicit formulation of circumstances under which restrictions on free trade between the partners could be permitted, despite the Customs Union.

The major gain was in revenue. Previously, revenue to Lesotho had been a fixed percentage of collections for the whole area. The new formula determined revenue on the basis of (1) the value of Lesotho's imports from all sources plus excisable production and (2) the average revenue content of taxable commodities in all four countries enhanced by 42 percent to compensate for the negative consequences of membership. The new formula led to very rapid growth of revenue in the early 1970s and permitted the cessation of United Kingdom grants-in-aid to government much earlier than had been expected. However, after the relevant revenue content of taxable commodities declined, the formula was revised to imply that regardless of the actual formula result, Lesotho (and Botswana and Swaziland) would receive as revenue between 17.5 and 22.5 percent of the value of imports. Dissatisfaction still continues with the formula and in particular with the variability of revenue content and the delays in payment (on which no interest is earned; the books on a particular year are not finally closed until a full three years later). Although a technical committee agreed to a new revised formula in 1981, the negotiations to implement the revision were deadlocked throughout 1982, 1983, and 1984. Press reports suggest that South Africa is attempting to couple the revision of the financial formula with issues of wider "closer cooperation," which might involve some form of tacit recognition of bantustans, cooperation with South Africa's Development Bank for Southern Africa, or security concerns.[23]

The Customs Union Agreement gives Lesotho substantially more revenue than it could raise if it was to leave the union but keep domestic final prices at the same level. As seems to be true of many aspects of Lesotho's integration with the South African economy,[24] the Customs Union provides short-term benefits, namely government revenue and wide availability of a full range of manufactures. However, the cost of these benefits is restriction of the long-term development of Lesotho's domestic economy, because the Customs Union ensures South African goods access to the Lesotho market, but does nothing to enhance Lesotho's competitiveness as a production site or, in practical terms, to ensure Lesotho's access to South Africa's markets. Lesotho, as a peripheral country with poor infrastructure close to highly developed industrial and commercial centers in South Africa, is not a low-cost site within the region for most types of production.[25] Access to the South African market is dependent on South African acquiescence, despite the strictures of the Customs Union Agreement, because South Africa has at its disposal many nontariff barriers involving administrative discretion and controls the highly regulated transport system. As a last resort, access to South African markets can be enormously disrupted, deliberately or incidentally, by "go-slows" at border crossings, as occurred during 1983. The long exposure of the Basotho to South African consumer goods, modes of operation, and relative prices may also have induced attitudes that are inimical to appropriate forms of development within Lesotho.

The usage of South African currency within Lesotho was formalized by the Rand Monetary Area Agreement between Lesotho, Swaziland, and South Africa in 1974. This also was an advance over the former, purely informal arrangements. Under the agreement, Lesotho formalized the use of South African currency as legal tender in Lesotho, but in addition acquired (1) the right to receive monetary compensation for such use, based on the application of interest rates on South African government securities to an estimate of the rand currency in circulation in Lesotho, and (2) the right to issue its own currency, the maloti, at par with the rand, backed 100 percent by special rand deposits with the South African Reserve Bank on which interest is also received. Maloti are legal tender in Lesotho but not in South Africa. Further, the agreement formalized Lesotho's access to foreign exchange and specified that the three countries' main reserves of foreign currencies would all be held by the South Africans and that essentially similar foreign exchange controls would be imposed in Lesotho (and Swaziland) as in the Republic of South Africa; however, Lesotho (and Swaziland) were permitted to guarantee access to foreign exchange for purposes of, for example, remittance of profits by foreign investors.

The earliest major formalization of institutional arrangements with South Africa was the Labour Agreement, concluded in 1973. This agreement sets out the conditions under which Lesotho citizens may be employed in South Africa and under which South African employers may recruit in Lesotho. It gives Lesotho very few advantages. The major ones are the provision for a "Labour Representative," an official of the Lesotho government resident in South Africa who, with staff members, is permitted to perform various administrative and welfare functions for Lesotho citizens in South Africa; provisions requiring South African employers of Lesotho citizens to comply with any deferred pay or provident fund wage deduction clauses in contracts of employment (a provident fund system for migrants does not exist, but has been discussed for years and is generally believed to be potentially a very useful innovation); a provision not requiring but pledging cooperation by the South African authorities to ensure that employers deduct any relevant taxes from migrants' wages on behalf of the Lesotho government (however, migrant earnings are exempt from Lesotho income tax); and an exemption from the confinement of Lesotho citizens to employment under contract for not more than two years at a time for those who can prove that they were legally employed in South Africa before July 1, 1963, provided there is no "indigenous" worker to replace them.[26]

The constraints imposed by relationships with South Africa remain immense, and some aspects are still not wholly predictable. One problem surrounds transportation and transit rights. Lesotho's position is that international law gives it, a land-locked state, unrestricted transit rights to the outside world. South Africa, however, has always held that it retains the right to inspect cargoes and passengers in transit to Lesotho and to prevent passage in its national interest—which it does on occasion, recently most notably with respect to defense equipment.

Lesotho also remains dependent on South Africa for supplies of commercial energy, including electricity, coal, and petroleum products. Energy imports have accounted for between 6 and 10 percent of total imports since 1975, with a generally upward trend. Currently, Lesotho has no indigenous sources of energy except a little fuelwood and some experimental wind and solar energy installations, although there is possibly some exploitable peat, and considerable potential for hydropower, both from small (minihydro) installations and from the enormous Highlands Scheme. Some minihydro projects are scheduled for the 1980s with foreign aid. The Highlands Scheme deserves more explicit description.

The Orange River and many of its tributaries have their sources in Lesotho. Water supply is a serious constraint on economic development, and especially industrial development, throughout Southern Africa. This constraint is felt particularly acutely in the most developed core region of the whole continent, the PWV (Pretoria-Witwatersrand-Vereeniging) complex surrounding Johannesburg, which generates more than a third of South Africa's entire GDP. South African planners have long wished to be able to divert water from the headwaters of the Orange system to the Vaal system to supply more water to PWV. Such schemes have been discussed with the Lesotho authorities off and on since the 1960s, but have failed because of an inability to agree on a price to be paid for Lesotho's water and other aspects and guarantees sufficient to make the scheme attractive to both Lesotho and sources of finance.

However, the water crunch in PWV becomes more serious as time passes, and for political and ecological reasons the major alternative outside source of water (by pipeline from the Okavango swamp in northern Botswana) looks less and less likely to materialize. Hence, in its newest incarnation the scheme may finally come to fruition. Current plans call for the expenditure of between one and two billion maloti at 1980 prices, several times Lesotho's annual GDP, to build five dams, 110 km (68 mi) of pipelines, and three hydroelectric stations, which should give Lesotho approximate self-sufficiency in electricity. The feasibility study got underway in 1983, its US$10 million cost being shared equally by South Africa and Lesotho, Lesotho's share being financed by a grant from the European Community. If all goes well, and agreement can be reached on prices, construction could begin in 1987.

If the scheme goes through—which must remain in doubt, South Africa having made negative noises during 1984—it will involve major changes in Lesotho's economy, but in ways that will not reduce dependence on South Africa. The construction activity will give the economy a boost, as will the necessary transport infrastructure for construction in the mountain areas. There may be new tourist development on the lakes behind the dams and along the new roads. The income from water sales will be valuable and a useful diversification of sources of government revenue; nevertheless, the Republic will still be the source of the income, and much of it will no doubt be required to service the loans (which will probably come at least in part from the World Bank) used to finance construction. The availability of cheap hydroelectricity may, however, help to cut manufacturing costs within Lesotho.[27]

Domestic Constraints

Apart from the external constraints imposed by being surrounded by and dependent on South Africa, the government in Lesotho also faces major domestic constraints. Lesotho's current revenue structure is unusual because of the operations of the Customs Union, which provides the bulk of revenue but removes from Lesotho's discretion sales duties on specific goods and all customs and excise duties. Direct taxation has had three major components: basic tax, a flat-rate tax on all adult males that was abolished in 1984; personal income tax, similar to British and South African models; and corporate taxes, subject to many provisions for reduction as investment incentives. One anomaly has already been mentioned: No attempt is being made to collect income tax from migrants, although now all mineworkers earn incomes high enough to be taxed if the income were earned within Lesotho. Presumably the reason is political because given the provisions of the Labour Agreement, the administrative costs of collection could be mainly shifted to the South African mining companies. However, this may change in the future in response to the 1984 South African decision to subject migrants to a unified income tax.

Indeed, income tax rates were effectively lowered for the 1981/ 1982 financial year. The reasons for this are not entirely clear, but because the income tax, despite attempts to strengthen its administration, is to a large extent collected only on salaries and wages and the government is by far the largest employer, it is reasonable to interpret the change as a substitute for an increase in government salary scales. At the levels of professional and technical employment, the government experiences difficulty in attracting and retaining personnel, particularly those of ability, because there are more financially attractive opportunities in the private sector for some and elsewhere in Southern Africa for others. This difficulty is exacerbated by political dissension within Lesotho. It is often alleged that opposition to the government is quite widespread among professional and technical cadres in the civil service and the education establishment. The government is, however, reluctant to raise salary and wage scales to levels that would retain adequate numbers of personnel, including those not well disposed toward it, partly for budgetary reasons and partly because a wage increase would make more pronounced the income inequalities among those employed as well as between the employed and those (the majority) unemployed. A wage increase would also exacerbate the wage restraint problem in the private sector, which is essential to maintain competitiveness with establishments in the Republic. Nevertheless, in 1984 a commission reviewed Civil Service salaries, with instructions to consider "the importance of managerial, professional, and technical skills," and scales were raised in early 1985.

Indirect taxation does offer some scope for raising revenue. Lesotho has managed to use some specific levies on particular industries (e.g., tourism) despite the Customs Union. In other instances, the most notable being alcoholic beverages, the profits of state monopolies have been used as a substitute for indirect taxation. The most interesting case however is the general sales tax (GST). South Africa introduced a GST, initially at 5 percent collected at retail level, at the end of the 1970s. This general sales tax, as opposed to specific sales duties, was not subject to Customs Union provisions. Such a tax was a powerful potential source of revenue for Lesotho, and in late 1982 Lesotho also introduced a GST.

The Lesotho GST was also initially at 5 percent and collected at retail level. Unsurprisingly, early reports suggested considerable collection difficulties and confusion, since in principle all traders, of whatever size, literacy, and accounting ability, were subject to the tax. It appears that by replicating precisely the South African tax, presumably thereby economizing on analytic, decision-making, and planning capabilities in government, Lesotho missed an opportunity to change the tax structure in a way that would have been easier to administer and better suited to the promotion of development. These ends could have been achieved by making Lesotho's GST collectable at the manufacturer or importer level (instead of at retail level), charging a higher rate, but exempting for administrative reasons manufacturers with turnover below a certain volume, and also exempting exports. Such a structure would appear consistent with the Customs Union, but would have given substantial effective protection to small domestic manufacturers. In 1984, the GST rate was raised to 6 percent, and government was considering higher rates on motor vehicles and tobacco.

Table 2.7 contains some information on government budgets, expenditure, and revenue in recent years. These data show how difficult the financial situation of the government was in the early 1980s. The basic causes were the slowdown of the growth of Customs Union receipts in the late 1970s and the decision of the government to attempt to maintain the rate of growth of spending by borrowing. Until 1983/1984, the stagnation of revenue continued, and the inevitable result—in an environment of rapid inflation and high interest rates—was an explosive growth in debt service. Total debt service grew from 1.6 percent of GNP and 7.7 percent of government revenue in 1979/1980 to 5.1 percent of GNP and 29.7 percent of revenue just three years later in 1982/1983. The overall government budget deficit for that year had been planned at 60 percent of revenue, although more conservative views prevailed, and the actual deficit was only half that level. However, this was achieved by severe restraints on spending, followed by the introduction of new taxes. Maintained financial stringency had reduced the deficit to manageable levels by 1984/1985, although debt service remains at worrying levels compared to total revenue. Two other points evident from Table 2.7 are the government's recurring optimism about how much foreign aid will be available for spending through government and where the axe falls when cuts in spending are made. In recent years, the government has budgeted for between four and eight times the amount of grant aid it actually received, and actual capital expenditure was only 42 percent in 1983/1984 and 59 percent in 1984/1985 of that planned at budget time.

A second example of domestic constraints and policy actions designed to induce substantial institutional change is the issue of land tenure. The necessary legislation to change land-use practices was embodied in a series of acts, from the Land Husbandry Act of 1969 through the 1979 Land Act to the Town and Country Planning

TABLE 2.7
Government Budgetary Operations, 1982/1983–1984/1985 (millions of Maloti)

	1982/1983		1983/1984		1984/1985	
	Budget Estimates	Outcome	Budget Estimates	Provisional Outcome	Budget Estimates	Forecast Outcome
Total recurrent revenue	138.5	134.8	166.4	169.9	229.7	215.0
Income taxes	15.3	11.5	17.1	10.5	11.3	11.1
Sales tax	5.0	2.7	12.0	14.7	15.0	18.0
Customs Union	76.7	76.7	109.8	109.9	151.5	151.5
Other	41.5	38.6	27.5	29.1	46.4	28.1
Customs Union as percent of total	55.4%	56.9%	66.0%	64.7%	66.0%	70.5%
Grant aid[a]	47.7	9.4	59.2	7.4	46.8	10.0
Overall deficit (-) or surplus (+)	-83.0	-41.0	-79.1	-21.9	+5.7	-8.0
As percent of revenue	-60.0%	-30.4%	-47.5%	-12.9%	+2.5%	-3.7%
As percent of GNP	-10.3%	-5.2%	-8.8%	-2.4%	+0.5%	-0.8%
Total expenditure	269.2	185.2	304.7	199.3	270.8	233
Debt service	36.0	40.1	41.9	44.0	65.7	58.1
As percent of revenue	26.0%	29.7%	25.2%	25.9%	28.6%	27.0%
Wages and salaries	66.0	63.5	65.5	65.7	71.9	80.0
Capital expenditures[a]	63.0	63.5	137.1	57.8	119.2	70.0

a. Excludes grant aid received in kind and direct expenditures by donors (estimated at M36.5 million in 1984/1985); on expenditure side, includes net lending in 1982/1983.

Source: Derived from data in various issues of Central Bank of Lesotho, Quarterly Review and annual budget speeches.

Act of 1980. Effective implementation of the powers granted by these laws only really began in 1980. Taken together, when fully implemented the laws will transform the institutions of land use for arable farming, for livestock raising, and in urban areas from the relics of the precapitalist era to fully commercialized, capitalist relations.

The clear intentions in rural areas are to encourage "progressive" farmers, to improve productivity of both arable and livestock farming, and to facilitate a transformation from largely subsistence to more commercial farming. Inevitable consequences will be more landless people and greater inequality of income and wealth in rural areas. The recent land-use legislation also will complete a process that has been underway since independence—removing the main source of the chiefs' influence in rural areas by progressively decreasing their powers over land allocation, initially eroded by the 1967 Land Act that set up elected land committees.

Given that the land tenure system has been criticized for so long, the delay in reforming it is evidence of the constraints felt by the government. Even if implementation is evenhanded, those who will benefit are largely the economically better off, who will be better able both to negotiate titles and to benefit from their possession.[28] In addition to the chiefs, those who may lose are the rural and urban poor and uneducated who may neither be able to obtain titles nor, if they do, have access to sufficient capital to make productive use of the land so obtained. The timing of the change is not easy to explain, but it may have been influenced by a feeling that high mine wages for several years had greatly increased superficial prosperity in rural areas and, therefore, that the poor might not oppose it too vociferously. Certainly, the government was increasingly desperate about the stagnant state of agriculture.

THE ECONOMICS OF THE LABOR RESERVE

In the 1980s Lesotho is becoming more and more a pure labor reserve for a single South African industry, mining. For the medium-term future, this situation represents a very insecure and dependent position but also an opportunity to transform the economy. Insecurity arises from the heavy concentration of national income, especially foreign exchange earnings, on the single source, the South African mining industry's demand for Basotho labor. The labor market situation within South Africa, with male Black unemployment estimated at various levels from half a million up, makes clear that if either the mines, or the South African government, decided to eliminate Lesotho's migrants it could be done quickly. Fortunately for Lesotho, all indications are that the mining industry sees substantial advantages in a stable and sizable contingent of Basotho workers. The South African government may not agree, but must appreciate that expelling Lesotho's migrants rapidly would wreak havoc in Lesotho and therefore bring upon South Africa heavy disapproval from Lesotho's donors, who include the U.S., West Germany, the UK, and the European Community. Such an action would, therefore, probably be a last resort in conflict between the Republic and Lesotho, but the possibility remains and the threat of it was used in 1983.

It is obvious how dependence arises from this situation. The opportunity needs to be made explicit. Lesotho's migrants earn, on average, around U.S. $2,000 a year now, for a total of well over U.S.$200 million. These earnings, some three times in real terms the level of the early 1970s, have permitted Lesotho's population, on average, to greatly improve living standards. The opportunity is to divert enough of this flow of earnings into productive investment in physical and human capital and institutions to transform the economy into one that could sustain itself without such massive export of labor.

As yet, little advantage has been taken of this opportunity. Lesotho has continued to develop as a consumer society without the requisite productive base. Inequalities are increasing and the situation is likely to worsen. The reality of labor use within the country is frighteningly inappropriate. Education has expanded enormously, but there is little evidence of social return on the investment involved. The expected private return to education for males has been zero except at university level.[29] To a very large extent, Lesotho remains stuck in the classic dilemma of the labor reserve in a peripheral region close to a much more developed one: Current income is maximized by promoting integration with and labor flow to the developed core, but long-term development of a self-sustaining nature probably requires some disengagement and the imposition of barriers to the free flow of goods, services, labor, and finance.

For Lesotho, this dilemma is exacerbated by four considerations. First, permanent migration, producing a lower home population and the possibility of higher GDP per capita—the classic adjustment mechanism for peripheral regions within single national economies— is not permitted by South Africa, is inconsistent with national aspirations, and is not even desired by the majority of current migrants.[30] Second, the formalization of integration with South Africa into agreements such as those covering the Customs Union and the Rand Monetary Area greatly constrains the policy possibilities for disengagement. Third, Lesotho's weak resource and infrastructure base and the very wide exposure of its population to South African income levels and methods make it very hard to find activities that both are profitable in Lesotho and meet the population's expectations of what is "modern" and represents "progress." Fourth, it seems plausible that the short- to medium-term interests of almost all influential groups within the country are better served by continuation of the status quo or something close to it, rather than by radical change that in the long run may be necessary for the national interest as a whole.

This last point deserves more detailed treatment. The most concentrated, vocal, and articulate group in Lesotho are the wage- and salary-earning employees who depend on the government for their incomes—civil servants, teachers, and the police and military. These groups benefit from having unrestricted access to a full range of goods and services from South Africa at South African prices, and they would tend to lose in the short run from any policy that slowed the growth of government revenue or diverted government expenditure from personnel costs to other items (such as production subsidies). Hence, from a relatively short-run, personal point of view, these groups tend to benefit from the unrestricted operation of the Customs Union and maximum migrant labor. High levels of migration benefit this group because they both boost government revenue via the workings of the Customs Union and reduce pressure for alternative sources of income in rural areas.

In practice, there is no group that can match the government employees in numbers, cohesiveness, or influence. Commercial farmers and manufacturing entrepreneurs might prefer a delinking, disengagement type of policy to encourage profitable productive activities at home, but they are outnumbered by trading and transport interests, which are better served by migration and high cash incomes of migrants. Migrants and potential migrants would rather stay home, of course, but there is no feasible way to devise uses of unskilled labor (or labor with mining skills) that will allow profitable operations and wage levels comparable to those in the gold mines. Those who are unable to migrate and who lack substantial agricultural, educational, or other assets—women, the old, the unlucky young—are the groups who in the short run would benefit most from a reorientation of policy. But these are also the groups with the least "voice"—at least until they become concentrated in large, jobless, and destitute groups in towns.

The economic challenge facing Lesotho is to find policies that will permit and encourage a growing portion of migrant earnings to be invested in the country in ways that will permit more productive use of labor time internally and that are viable and profitable in the long run. As of now, migrants appear to have judged, probably very sensibly, that from their individual, private points of view, the best uses of their increased earnings are higher current consumption; investment in better housing and consumer durables; education for their children; livestock; and transport, retail trade, and small-scale service activities. These choices do little to enhance the productive base of the society.

But those who influence policy are not likely to do anything to change the situation, despite the fact that they as a group are the obvious source of the entrepreneurs and managers who would benefit most from a redirection of the economy. Such a redirection would be risky, would involve losses for some, and might be hard to explain. Those at the top are doing very well under present policies and will face little pressure to change until the numbers, conditions, and protests of those who have no stake in the system—those without access to migrant earnings, without jobs, without substantial assets—worsen considerably.

However, one can predict with confidence that conditions will worsen, perhaps sooner than expected. Close to 30,000 young people enter the labor market annually; only 2,000 to 3,000 at most can hope to become legal migrants, and a comparable number might get formal sector wage jobs according to recent trends. Over 20,000 young people a year cannot be absorbed indefinitely in the informal sector and rural areas, with incomes grossly inferior to migrants or junior civil servants, without some form of social disruption. South Africa's policies represent a useful, and real, scapegoat for the economic difficulties in Lesotho, but the true danger is an ever-worsening youth employment crisis and deepening internal inequality. As yet, the government has no answer to this problem.

NOTES

1. On this, see Colin Murray, *Families Divided: The Impact of Migrant Labour in Lesotho* (Cambridge: Cambridge University Press, 1981); Andrew Spiegel, "Migrant Labour Remittances, Rural Differentiation, and the Developmental Cycle in a Lesotho Community," (M.A. thesis, University of Cape Town, 1979); and Chapter 3 of this book.

2. E. H. Ashton, "A Sociological Sketch of Sotho Diet," *Transactions of the Royal Society of South Africa* 27, Part II (1939), p. 147–214, is one of the earlier explicit observations of this phenomenon.

3. G.M.E. Leistner, *Lesotho: Economic Structure and Growth* (Pretoria: Africa Institute, 1966), p. 19.

4. Ibid., p. 5.

5. This aspect is stressed by Murray, *Families Divided*, and Spiegel, "Migrant Labour Remittances."

6. Leistner, *Lesotho: Economic Structure*, p. 18.

7. Ibid., p. 22.

8. James Cobbe, "Wage Policy Problems in the Small Peripheral Countries of Southern Africa, 1967–76," *Journal of Southern African Affairs* no. 2, 4 (October 1977): note 13, p. 464.

9. For example, the most conservative assumptions applied to the data in Table 2.5 suggest migrant earnings in 1979/1980 in excess of M200 million, whereas the national accounts data report only M183 million.

10. K.T.J. Rakhetla, "Budget Speech Presenting the 1983/84 Estimates of Revenue and Expenditure" (Maseru: Ministry of Finance and the National Assembly, April 1983, Mimeographed), p. 2.

11. Consider as an example a child born in South Africa in the 1950s. In the South African government view, the child's citizenship would depend on the place of birth and citizenship of the father. Lesotho would normally grant citizenship only if the child could prove the father was from Basutoland. The adult in the late 1970s might find himself or herself able to obtain one, all, or none of Lesotho, South African, and one or more bantustan-issued documentation. It is easy to find anecdotal evidence in Lesotho of persons with two sets of travel documents (e.g., from both Lesotho and a bantustan) and of others unable to obtain any travel documents.

12. South African data are from the 1980 census. On Basotho in the Republic of South Africa, see, for example, William F. Lye and Colin Murray, *Transformations on the High Veld: The Tswana and the Southern Sotho* (Totowa, N.J.: Barnes and Noble, 1979).

13. TEBA annual reports even confirm that at least until 1981, small numbers of migrant workers were still engaged on new contracts at the mines, although this practice had officially not been allowed for many years.

14. Few mines achieve even close to the 3 percent figure. In 1975, when only 22 percent of Black mine employment was South African, the Chamber of Mines adopted a target of 50 percent South African and 50 percent foreign. By 1982, 60 percent South African had been achieved. "Mining Survey," Supplement to *Financial Mail* (Johannesburg) (22 October 1982), pp. 23–24.

15. Reengagement certificates are the main instrument of employment stabilization; they are documents issued to mineworkers at the end of contracts, guaranteeing various privileges (cash bonuses, reemployment in the same pay grade on the same mine) if a new contract is signed within a given period of time (the privileges are graduated and decrease with the time spent between contracts; eventually, the certificate ceases to be "valid," but is still of value as proof of mine experience).

16. Section 10 refers to the section of the relevant South African legislation that set out the requirements to be met by Blacks to qualify for permanent residence (as opposed to migrant worker status) in the common areas of South Africa. Basically, the requirements are ten years of continuous

employment with one employer or fifteen years of continuous employment with more than one employer. Blacks who entered the Republic from the former High Commission Territories before South African law differentiated them from South African Blacks could qualify for such rights.

17. There are two potentially important categories of exception. First, if no suitable workers can be found within South Africa, employers may seek permission to contract with foreign Blacks. On this basis, Lesotho citizens may be temporarily legally employed in agriculture in the Orange Free State, and those with skills may be legally employed when economic conditions produce shortages of South African Blacks with required skills, for example, in the construction trades during boom periods. In the past, however, probably most such employment has been illegal but tacitly ignored by the authorities. Second, South African labor legislation does not necessarily apply in the supposedly "independent" bantustans (Transkei, Venda, Bophuthatswana, Lebowa). No information is available on numbers of Basotho working in such bantustans, but highly publicized individual cases (as of National University of Lesotho academic staff hired by bantustan universities) make clear that there are some. Probably most are highly skilled, since the bantustans have considerable surpluses of unskilled labor.

18. This Compulsory Deferred Pay Scheme has been in force since 1975. Mineworkers receive 5 percent interest on their deposits. The total amount in the deferred pay fund is much lower than one would expect from the rules of the scheme, largely because mineworkers can withdraw their balances whenever physically in Lesotho. Since the introduction of the "eleven shift fortnight" in gold mining in 1977, mineworkers only work on alternate Saturdays, and many are close enough to make occasional weekend visits to Lesotho—and to Lesotho Bank on Saturday morning to withdraw deferred pay. There are also various other strategies individual migrants can adopt to minimize the balances of deferred pay held on their behalf—something many of them, apparently, wish to do.

19. These estimates are very crude and have a distressingly wide range, but are the best the data can support. They are derived in J. Cobbe, "Modeling a Labor-Reserve Economy: Lesotho," paper presented to the African Studies Association Meetings, Los Angeles, October 1984.

20. An example would be the second plan document, which after stating the reduction of migrant employment as a goal, nevertheless projected that over the plan period, 50 percent of the *increment* to the labor force would migrate. Kingdom of Lesotho, *Second Five-Year Development Plan,* 1975/76–1979/80 (Maseru: Government Printer, [1976]), p. 22. For a more extended discussion of rhetoric and reality in government policy, see James Cobbe, "The Changing Nature of Dependence: Economic Problems in Lesotho," *Journal of Modern African Studies* 21, no. 2 (June 1983), pp. 293–310.

21. There are manufacturing plants whose output is aimed at export markets in South Africa (e.g., ice cream) and Europe (e.g., umbrellas). Lesotho is quite well-placed to serve the inland South African market, if either cost conditions are not too out of line or the investor has a political preference

for not having his or her plant inside South Africa. Some of the more dubious ventures have included a lab that paid Basotho donors for blood and exported plasma and other blood products; a factory manufacturing both sports and military parachutes, with some uncertainty surrounding the identity of its customers; and a vegetable canning plant, originally intended to can asparagus (only available for a few weeks a year), that was kept running all year producing canned beans at a manufacturing cost greater than the retail price of imported off-brand baked beans in Maseru supermarkets. Job creation in manufacturing averages under 2,000 a year.

22. There is a large literature on the Customs Union. The best description of the 1969 revision is P. M. Landell-Mills, "The 1969 Southern African Customs Union Agreement," *Journal of Modern African Studies* 9, no. 2 (August 1971), pp. 263–281; a very useful discussion of the details and technicalities of the functioning of the Customs Union is found in Derek J. Hudson, "Botswana's Membership of the Southern African Customs Union," Chapter 9 in *Papers on the Economy of Botswana*, ed. Charles Harvey (London: Heinemann, 1981); a broad assessment of the union's effects, which includes references to many assessments of it, is James H. Cobbe, "Integration Among Unequals: The Southern African Customs Union and Development," *World Development* 8, no. 4 (April 1980), pp. 329–336.

23. See "Customs Union: Revenue Impasse," *Financial Mail* (Johannesburg) (11 March 1983), p. 1060; and K.T.J. Rakhetla, *Budget Speech*, Maseru (27 February 1984), para. 24. Internally, South Africa treats its "independent bantustans" as though they were members of the Customs Union, although formally Botswana, Lesotho, and Swaziland (BLS) all steadfastly refuse to recognize them as independent entities. The Development Bank for Southern Africa is part of South Africa's scheme for a "constellation of states" and began operation in late 1983. South Africa has used economic leverage on the BLS states to achieve political or security ends in the past; see discussion in Chapter 5 in this book.

24. For example, for the effects of migrant labor, see James Cobbe, "Emigration and Development in Southern Africa, with Special Reference to Lesotho," *International Migration Review* 16, no. 4 (Winter 1982), pp. 837–868; and for the effects of erosion, see Stephen D. Turner, "Soil Conservation: Administrative and Extension Approaches in Lesotho," *Agricultural Administration* 9, no. 2 (1982), pp. 147–162.

25. This argument is explored at length, with empirical evidence, in Percy Selwyn, *Industries in the Southern African Periphery* (London: Croom-Helm, 1975). The situation has changed little since Selwyn did his research.

26. "Indigenous" is ironical here because in South African official eyes there are no Black South African citizens; however, the clause implies that those Lesotho citizens who do possess Section 10 rights from before 1963 have little security. The full text of the agreement is reprinted in W. J. Breytenbach, *Migratory Labour Arrangements in Southern Africa* (Pretoria: Africa Institute, 1979).

27. Electricity in South Africa is inexpensive, since it is generated largely from very low-cost coal. Currently, LEC purchases electricity from ESCOM,

the South African Electricity Supply Commission, and resells it. Commercial and industrial users in Lesotho generally face higher electricity charges than they would in major urban centers in South Africa.

28. Anecdotal evidence suggests that the process of obtaining titles can, as might be expected, be influenced in discretionary ways by the bureaucracy and chiefs as a result of both individual favoritism (e.g., political affiliation) and corrupt practices.

29. See James Cobbe, "The Education System, Wage and Salary Structures, and Income Distribution: Lesotho as a Case Study, Circa 1975," *Journal of Developing Areas* 17, no. 2 (January 1983), and Chapter 3 in this book.

30. See Cobbe, "Emigration and Development."

3

The Social Dynamics
of the Labor Reserve

Lesotho's extreme dependence on the export of labor has had a massive effect on not only its economy but also its social structure. Much of this impact has been negative. Even if the South African government refrains from implementing the threats it has made to repatriate Basotho migrants, the opportunities for new migration are very few, and it is very likely that eventually the number of migrants will decline.[1] This implies that as population grows, social and economic problems arising from poverty and unemployment will also grow.

This chapter focuses on the social consequences of the labor reserve status of Lesotho and on the strategies adopted by the Basotho in their efforts to survive. Most attention will be paid to the rural areas, because 90 percent of the population lives there, but urban issues will also be addressed. The discussion will include attempts to assess the income and wealth distribution in the country and to measure the extent of poverty. The chapter concludes with a tentative analysis of the country's contemporary class structure.

THE RURAL MILIEU

For the roughly 150,000 men and 20,000 women who migrate regularly to South Africa for work, the rural areas provide a home base rather than a continuous place of residence. Furthermore, migrant earnings are essential to the survival of rural life. For most farmers the returns from agriculture are extremely low and in bad years frequently fail to cover costs.[2] In a survey of both lowland and mountain areas conducted by Arie van der Wiel in 1975 and 1976, it was found that agriculture contributed only 17 percent of total rural income. Domestic off-farm activities provided another 12 percent, but by far the largest contribution came from migrant remittances, which provided 71 percent—a dramatic increase from the 40 percent that they contributed in 1969.[3] Under such circumstances, it is easy to agree with the observation of the influential report of the Jobs and Skills Programme for Africa (JASPA) that "the result is the attitude of an industrial proletariat to its dormitory; rural Lesotho is a place to live, a place to preserve traditional ties and norms, . . . and a place to retire, but not a place on which to depend for sustenance and income."[4]

The contribution of migrant remittances was enhanced in the mid-1970s by the dramatic increase in mine wages. This had an obvious impact on the incomes of rural households in Lesotho, which in 1977–1978 prices rose on the average from R500 a year in the late 1960s to R1,000 a year in 1976.[5] Despite such increases, however, a high proportion of households continued to experience great difficulty in satisfying their basic needs for food, shelter, health, and education. The National Food and Nutrition Planning Conference of 1978–1979, for example, estimated that one third of rural households suffered from malnutrition and from deficiency-related diseases such as kwashiorkor.[6] With Lesotho's population rising rapidly, with mine wages barely keeping pace with inflation since 1977, and with the likely reduction in migration to South Africa, the prospects for the future look very bleak.

Although mitigating the extent of rural poverty in recent years, the migrant labor system has clearly not eradicated it. Moreover, the system has had many damaging social effects, both to the migrants who are exposed to the daily rigors and humiliations of apartheid and to the families left behind to face long periods of separation and the anxieties and uncertainties inevitably involved. These and other problems of the migrant labor system have been well-documented in recent years at both the macro and micro level.[7] What follows is a sketch of the major features of rural life as revealed by these studies.

Rural Differentiation and the Developmental Cycle

From its examination of income distribution in 1973–1974, the World Bank mission concluded that Lesotho's rural areas, though poor in general, manifested "a degree of equality which is not matched in any country known to the mission."[8] The Lesotho government went even further in its Second Five-Year Development Plan to declare that Lesotho's rural equality was "unlikely to be matched by any other country."[9] It was argued that this unusually equitable division of rural resources resulted from (1) the relatively even distribution of productive assets, such as land and livestock, and (2) the equalizing

Thabana-li-Mele, a village in the foothills. Photo courtesy of Joe Alfers.

Transport by ox-sled. Photo courtesy of Don Gray.

Building with empty beer cans. Photo courtesy of Louise B. Cobbe.

effect of migrant remittances, which enabled those households with fewer assets to compensate by a more active engagement in migrant labor.

Unfortunately, these claims seriously misrepresented the true situation. For example, recent evidence on livestock ownership reveals much wider disparities than those suggested by the World Bank. In his survey of 1,286 households, van der Wiel demonstrated that whereas 20 percent of households owned 80 percent of livestock, 48 percent owned no stock at all. The claims concerning the equitable distribution of land have more justification, admittedly, because of the pre-1979 land tenure system. Nevertheless, there are signs of growing inequality. The JASPA report showed that the bottom 21 percent of farmers held only 5 percent of the land, whereas the top 9 percent held 26 percent. Equally important is the increasing evidence of landlessness in the countryside. The proportion of landless house-holds rose from 7 percent in 1950 to 13 percent in 1970, and the small national sample surveyed in 1975 revealed a figure of 23 percent.[10]

When we incorporate migrant remittances into the picture and consider the distribution of total rural incomes, rural inequality becomes even greater. The data in Table 3.1, which summarize the evidence from van der Wiel's survey, conflict markedly with the World

TABLE 3.1

Distribution and Source of Average Annual Income: Thaba-T'seka and Phutiatsana
Project Survey, 1975-1976

	Income Strata (Maloti)				
	0-199	200-599	600-999	1000+	All Strata
Households (percent)	27	20	27	26	100
Individuals (percent)	16.1	18.9	26.5	38.5	100
Income (percent)	2.3	10.5	28.9	58.3	100
Average household size	3.1	4.9	5.1	7.1	5.2
Average annual income					
Households (Maloti)	66	408	859	1,739	783
Individuals (Maloti)	21	83	168	226	151
Source of average annual income					
Agriculture (Maloti)	46	151	81	279	137
Off-farm (Maloti)	15	42	80	222	92
Remittances (Maloti)	5	215	698	1,238	554
Agriculture (percent)	70	37	9	16	17
Off-farm (percent)	22	10	10	13	12
Remittances (percent)	8	53	81	71	71

Source: Derived from data in A.C.A. van der Wiel, <u>Migratory Wage Labour:
Its Role in the Economy of Lesotho</u> (Mazenod: Mazenod Book Centre,
1977), pp. 84 and 88.

Bank's estimates. Table 3.1 suggests substantial inequality: the lowest
35 percent of the population receive only 13 percent of the total
rural income, and the highest 38 percent of the population receive
58 percent of the total rural income. Moreover, it is only this highest
38 percent that lies above the poverty datum line (PDL), calculated
by van der Wiel at M1,152 per annum for an average rural household
of 5.2 persons in 1976. The JASPA report, using a more conservative
estimate of basic needs, estimated that fewer households, between
30 and 40 percent of all households, were below the PDL, but
acknowledged that almost all of these households were living in
conditions of abject poverty. Rapid inflation in the late 1970s and
early 1980s resulted in a recalculation of the PDL for the average
rural household by the Lesotho Bureau of Statistics, producing a figure
of over M3,100 per annum for April 1984.

The data in Table 3.1 also refute one of the principal assumptions underlying Lesotho's alleged egalitarianism, namely that the poorest households can compensate for their lower incomes from crop production and livestock by devoting more energy to migrant labor. In fact, the reverse is quite clearly the case. It is the poorest households that are the least dependent on migrant labor, as well as being the least prosperous in terms of agricultural and off-farm incomes. This lack of dependence is not the result of conscious choice, of course, but because such households do not contain adult males able to engage in migrant work. Denied access to migrant earnings, these small and frequently female-headed households not only experience considerable difficulty in satisfying their consumption requirements but also in obtaining the necessary cash inputs for more successful agricultural and off-farm activities. In 1976 it was estimated that 40 percent of rural households were in this position and were living in conditions of extreme deprivation.[11]

The picture of rural inequality painted by van der Wiel has been substantiated in several other studies and belatedly acknowledged in the Lesotho government's third and latest development plan. The situation is likely to deteriorate in the future as a result of two developments in particular. The first is the inability, for reasons already mentioned, of South Africa to absorb the increase in Lesotho's male labor force. If recent trends continue, the government estimates that at any given time, the proportion of households without a migrant will rise to 67 percent by 1985.[12]

The second development results from changes introduced in Lesotho's land tenure system by the 1979 Land Act discussed in Chapter 2 of this book. One aim of the land tenure changes is to halt the fragmentation of land holdings and to provide for their consolidation under "progressive" farmers who possess the necessary capital and technology to raise agricultural productivity. Undoubtedly, a side effect of this process will be a rise in landlessness and a widening of the gap between the rural "haves" and "have nots."[13]

This account of rural inequality, although by no means inaccurate in aggregate terms, does obscure some complexities at the village and household level. First, there are various networks through which a portion of the incomes of the more affluent households is diffused and redistributed to the less prosperous ones. Second, in focusing on the differences between households, the analysis has neglected the fact that households change as they develop over time. Spiegel has usefully employed the concept of a "developmental cycle" in his examination of this phenomenon in Lesotho.

In his anthropological study of two villages in Qacha's Nek district in the southeastern part of Lesotho, Spiegel relates differential access to wage earnings, land, and livestock to a number of different stages in the developmental cycle of a typical or model household. The earliest stage is typified by a young married couple, living initially with the husband's family but seeking to establish an independent household. The husband's remittances from migrant employment will be used for bridewealth payments, for gifts or bribes to the land-allocating authorities for the grant of a homestead site, and for payments for materials and labor to build a house. In the second stage, remittances will form the basis for further house building to accommodate the expanding family, for acquisition of land, livestock, and agricultural implements, and for hiring laborers to work in the household's fields. The third stage, which represents the zenith of household development in terms of size and income, will be reached when the household's sons are old enough to migrate and when the household head, now retired from his own migrant career, turns his attention to managing his land and livestock. The earnings of adult sons will be supplemented by agricultural production and by the hiring out of labor and implements to neighboring families. The final stage is one of decline, as wage-earning sons leave to establish households of their own. Denied direct access to migrant earnings, the household, now frequently headed by a widow, must rely on its own resources to gain access to the remittances of others. Such resources are likely to be depleted over time. Agricultural implements will tend to fall into disrepair without the cash income to ensure their maintenance and replacement. Livestock may well have to be sold. Finally, land may have to be sublet on a sharecropping basis or transferred to married sons in return for the promise of their future support.

Documented as it is with detailed and vivid case studies, Spiegel's analysis shows how incomes are diffused within the rural community at different points in the developmental cycle and the variety of interhousehold linkages that result. Clearly, certain indicators of rural inequality owe their existence to the cyclical rise and decline of households as much as to the underdevelopment of the labor reserve. Landlessness, for example, can be a product of a particular stage in the cycle as well as a result of rural stratification and population pressure. The variation in the size of households and the positive correlation between household size and wealth can also be attributed in part to the developmental cycle.

Nevertheless, as Spiegel observes, there are many variations on and deviations from the typical cycle. Variations result from differences in the level of migrant earnings and the regularity with which they are remitted, the number and gender of the household's children, the proportion of remittances spent for household consumption versus investment, and the proximity of the household, in terms of kinship and political affiliations, to the power structure of the local community.

Of perhaps greater importance are the deviations from the typical cycle. These are of two broad types. First, there are a few rural households, often among the most prosperous, that rely on incomes from within Lesotho rather than on migrant remittances. These are largely progressive farmers, traders, and salaried officials who form "a nascent petty bourgeoisie in the Lesotho countryside."[14] Second, there are households that deviate from the typical cycle in ways that preclude them from ever achieving the zenith of household development. A common example is a household whose male head is forced to curtail his migrant career because of ill health, injury, or redundancy. Another example is the household that is deprived of the male head's earnings through death, divorce, or desertion.

We should not expect too much from the developmental cycle, therefore, and both Spiegel and Murray caution that the temptation to use it as the major determinant of inequality in the countryside, as A. V. Chayanov did in his analysis of the Russian peasantry, must be resisted in the Lesotho case. The degree of access to migrant earnings is largely responsible for the inequalities that exist and how they are modified during the cycle. Therefore, the inequalities can be understood effectively only in the wider context of Lesotho's position as a structurally underdeveloped labor reserve.

The Role of Custom

It almost goes without saying that Lesotho's social and cultural landscape has been inevitably transformed by the dramatic changes that have affected the country during the past century: from the commoditization of its economy and the proletarianization of its work force to the assault on its values by Western religion and education. Many of the traditional practices, outlined so vividly in Ashton's authoritative work on Basotho law and custom,[15] have been modified accordingly. Polygyny and male initiation, for example, have both declined in importance, and female initiation has declined even more markedly.[16]

Nevertheless, it is equally obvious to even a casual visitor to Lesotho that respect for traditional norms and behavior is still very much a part of everyday life in the rural areas. In explaining this apparent paradox, two principal schools of thought have emerged. The first sees the persistence of customary practices and values as

Pitso at Thaba-Bosiu. Photo courtesy of L.G.A. Smits.

occurring in spite of rapid social transformation; the second sees their survival as a direct consequence of such transformation. The first school is represented in the works of liberal dualist scholars. (The word *dualist* is used here to imply the belief that modern and traditional society and economy are sharply differentiated and separable.) Such scholars see the inherent traditionalism of societies such as Lesotho as a stubborn and irrational impediment to the modernizing forces of capitalist economic growth and Western education and values. The oversimplified and distorted reductionism of this approach has been exposed by the second school of thought, rooted in a more radical approach to Southern African historiography. These neo-Marxist scholars have shown convincingly that the survival of traditional or precapitalist social relations, far from providing an irrational obstacle, has in fact served the interests of rapid capitalist development in South Africa's mining and industrial centers.[17] Concerning the regions that send migrants to the South African core, such as Lesotho, the bantustans within South Africa, Botswana, Swaziland, Mozambique, and Malawi, which collectively can be termed labor reserves for South Africa, this approach interprets the role of custom as anything but an impediment to capitalism. The preservation of customary forms of land tenure in the labor reserves, for example, enabled South African employers to rationalize the inordinately low wages historically paid to migrant workers and to derive in consequence extremely high rates of profit. Instead of paying a wage sufficient to meet the costs of reproduction of the worker and his family, they provided merely for the worker's own subsistence and left his dependents to fend for themselves in Lesotho.

Although providing a useful antidote to earlier dualist interpretations, the neo-Marxist approach is by no means devoid of limitations. Perhaps the most important, in the present context, is the tendency to confuse cause and effect. Undoubtedly the persistence of traditional social relations had the effect of facilitating capitalist accumulation. But to argue, as many advocates of this approach do, that the latter was the principal cause of the former is much more doubtful, unless we are prepared to accept the clearly unwarranted assumption that traditional societies were a tabula rasa, awaiting the arrival of capitalism to write its grand design upon them.[18]

Instead of seeing the survival of custom as functional or dysfunctional to capitalist development, therefore, a new perspective would seem to be needed. The dimensions of such a perspective have been suggested recently by scholars such as Colin Murray, who have argued that the persistence of traditional norms and social relations should be viewed as a result of subtle and complex processes of adaptation to ensure survival in the rural malaise created by Lesotho's labor reserve position.[19] Such adaptation has been rendered all the more necessary by the failure of South African employers and the Lesotho government to ensure adequate alternative provision for social security and welfare. A few illustrations follow to show the utility of this perspective.

Customary Land Tenure

According to customary law, as codified in the Laws of Lerotholi, every married male Mosotho who resides within the jurisdiction of a chief is entitled in principle to the use of three fields of approximately two to three acres each. In practice, the actual distribution of land is far more uneven than this. Landlessness is increasing, and for most landholders the average size of holdings is decreasing.[20] More and more fields (mostly the less fertile) are being allowed to lie fallow, and in years of poor harvests, many farmers fail to recover their original investment. Sandra Wallman has argued that this situation has been exacerbated by the development of an ideology of despair concerning the continuing relevance of farming as a way of life.[21] If this interpretation is correct, it seems strangely paradoxical that so many people in the rural areas continue to value access to land. That they do so, however, is clearly evident, despite Wallman's reductionist disclaimer to the contrary, not least from the extensive amount of energy devoted to the complex and frequently acrimonious litigation that accompanies the question of land allocation.

We have already argued that this behavior is not irrational even from a narrow economic viewpoint, once we recognize the existence of the household developmental cycle and the risks (and eventual certainty) of the household losing access to migrant earnings. It becomes even less paradoxical still if we take a wider social view of land and view it not simply as a directly productive asset but as a fundamental part of the ties that bind together rural communities. The customary land tenure system, as adapted over time, provides such bonds and forms a basis for the creation of complex and diverse networks of cooperation between households, for the provision of security in old age, and for the diffusion and transfer of incomes at different stages in the developmental cycle.

We do not suggest that rural life in Lesotho is a model of harmony and cooperation. Given the poverty and uncertainty that prevail, disputes are frequent, and violence is by no means uncommon. What we do suggest, however, is that the long-standing appeals for a more rational land tenure system, contained in reports from those of Pim to those of JASPA, should be assessed in the wider context of their possible implications not merely for productivity and efficiency but also for the complex networks of rural interdependence outlined above. The 1979 Land Act, we argue, may well lead to increases in landlessness and rural poverty that more than negate any gains in agricultural productivity. If this legislation leads to the destruction of the more subtle networks of rural interdependence, as seems likely, its effects could be far more serious, particularly with respect to social cohesion in rural areas.

Bohali (Bridewealth)

Despite the fierce moralistic onslaught waged by the missionaries, marriage by cattle has demonstrated a remarkable though by no means unmodified persistence.[22] In virtually all customary marriages, which account for approximately half the marriages in Lesotho,[23] bohali transactions form a fundamental part of the marriage agreement. They also take place in the vast majority of Christian or civil marriages.[24]

The number of cattle involved in the bohali agreement varies according to the social status of the families involved and, nowadays, the education of the wife. But from the turn of the century, the number for an average rural family has remained fairly constant at about twenty to twenty-two head of cattle or their equivalent in cash or small stock. The real value of the actual outlay has probably increased, although it is difficult to be sure. With Lesotho's transformation from granary to labor reserve, the proportion of *bohali* transfers paid in cash has risen dramatically. Whereas the real value of migrant earnings remained static for much of this century, the market price of cattle doubled in real terms from 1936 to 1974 alone. The wage increases of the mid-1970s reversed this trend, but since 1978 incomes have barely kept pace with rising cattle prices.

Historically, therefore, it has proved increasingly difficult for a husband to meet his *bohali* commitments for even one wife, and this problem is partly responsible for the progressive decline in polygyny. Despite the fact that the nominal cash equivalent of cattle is normally set below the prevailing market price and the fact that *bohali* payments are usually staggered over many years, such payments clearly represent a major strain on economic resources. Hence, many *bohali* agreements remain unfulfilled; the bridewealth debts created frequently span several generations and result in vast amounts of litigation.

The high bridewealth rates have also prompted scholars such as Sebastian Poulter to question the contemporary rationality of the *bohali* system.[25] Given the conditions of poverty that prevail in Lesotho, it seems incredible to Poulter that such large amounts should be squandered on marriage when it appears they could be put to more effective alternative use. Although understandable at one level, this type of argument overlooks important functions performed by *bohali*. In the first place, it is through *bohali* that a husband establishes rights to his children. This occurs when a proportion of the *bohali*—normally ten head of cattle or their equivalent—has been transferred. Until such time, children legally belong to the mother's family. In light of this custom, it is by no means clear that the husband's investment in *bohali* is irrational, for it is an investment that entitles him to the labor and earnings of his children and to their support in old age. In the second place, although representing an immediate net loss to the husband and his family, the *bohali* transfer represents an obvious net gain to the wife's family. Far from squandering resources, therefore, *bohali* payments form part of the complex mechanism through which incomes and wealth are diffused and redistributed within the rural community.

Family Life and the Role of Women

The various redistributive networks that we have considered so far have undoubtedly mitigated the extent of rural squalor and the pressures on social cohesion created by Lesotho's labor reserve position. Problems have not been eradicated, however, and are particularly evident in families. Although forming the economic basis for the

Mosotho woman. Photo courtesy of Joe Alfers.

establishment and survival of most rural families, the migrant labor system places considerable stress on marital stability. Surrounding this issue are other complex issues relating to the nature and changing role of marriage, the extended family, the legal position of women, the division of labor according to gender, and the value of women's unpaid domestic labor. The effects of gross social injustice on the migrants have been researched extensively, but little attention has been devoted to these related family issues. Recently, however, such issues have been penetratingly studied by such scholars as Gay, Gordon, Murray, and Spiegel.[26] We cannot unravel all the complexities involved, but merely address some of the themes revealed in such works through a brief analysis of the problems faced by three groups of women: wives, widows, and those who have separated or divorced. We omit the "never married," because there are very few never married adult females in rural areas, although there are growing numbers in towns. It should also be noted that there is often considerable difficulty in accurately characterizing the marital status of individual women, particularly if the husband is absent and his future intentions are uncertain.

Wives. Most rural wives are married to migrants, a fact that should cause little surprise given the lack of alternative domestic employment for men. Further, wives and children are legally barred from entering South Africa to live with their husbands. Periods of separation are longer now than in the past because the pressure to obtain and retain jobs in South Africa has forced migrants to extend their average length of contract and to curtail their periods of leave.[27] This situation places considerable responsibility and stress on the wives left behind.

Customary law continues to regard women as jural minors who must defer to the authority of their husbands and other male relatives. Nevertheless, although guided by their husbands, wives have been forced in practice to assume the day-to-day management of the household while their husbands are away. This involves an awesome range of duties: supervising the fields and livestock, maintaining and extending the household's buildings, fetching water and fuel, attending to domestic chores, ensuring the children's education and health, and much more. Although assisted by older children and by husbands when home on leave, women devote an estimated eleven or more hours a day to such tasks.[28] Nor is this all. With the cost of living rising rapidly, incomes from remittances and agriculture are rarely sufficient for the needs of the household. To supplement them, most wives must engage in additional activities. A few might be able to obtain employment in the village or a nearby town. The rest must turn to the informal sector, where the most common activity is the brewing of beer for sale. Many wives, in addition, take a lover from whom gifts are expected.

The separation of families and the onus thus placed on wives cause enormous strain. In her survey of 525 wives, Gordon shows convincingly that the large majority of wives experience considerable anxiety about the welfare of their families. She also demonstrates that the degree of strain increases with the wives' age, the length of marriage, and the number of children. In the process she casts severe doubt on the view that sees the migrant labor system as having few disruptive effects on family life, a view that is based on the clearly dubious assumptions that (1) women over many years have become accustomed to their role and (2) in any case, their reliance on extended kinship relations adequately compensates for the absence of their husbands.[29]

Tension within the family is often accentuated rather than relieved by the return of the husband on leave, because then the essential irony of the wife's position is brought into focus. Although she assumes the responsibility for the household, it is the husband, through his wage-earning capacity, who controls the major resources for its effective management. Wives often chastise their husbands for failing to remit their earnings regularly and for returning home with luxury items such as radios and record players when food and clothing are desperately needed. Husbands frequently berate their wives for ignoring their directives concerning the disposition of remittances, directives that are often based on different priorities from those of their wives. Quarrels frequently ensue, especially if the husband discovers that his wife has been having affairs with other men, and wife beating is by no means uncommon.[30]

Not all husbands beat their wives, of course, nor are all households the scene of constant friction. The state of family relations obviously depends on many factors, especially on the amount and regularity of the wages remitted. Some husbands are conscientious in this respect and show considerable concern for the welfare of their families. Many are more remiss, however, and in their households much tension occurs.

So far we have examined the experiences of the largest category of wives: those married to migrants and living in independent households in the second stage of the developmental cycle.[31] The experiences of those in the first and third stages are different in a number of respects, but by no means devoid of stress. In the first stage, residence with the husband's family frequently leads to additional friction between the wife and her in-laws, especially over the disposition of her husband's remittances to which both have a claim. In the third stage, the return of the migrant husband may lead to an improvement in marital harmony. Tensions are not ruled out, however, and the return to coresident married life after many years of separation quite commonly poses serious problems of adjustment for both partners.

Widows. Lesotho has one of the highest proportions of female-headed households in the developing world, and approximately 90 percent of such households in Lesotho are headed by widows. The large number of widows compared to widowers in the country can be attributed in part to the general tendency of women to outlive men and to the fact that Basotho men tend to marry later in life than women. But two additional factors are peculiar to Lesotho. The first is the high rate of early mortality for miners, either due to accidents at work or to prevalent work-related illnesses such as silicosis and tuberculosis. The second factor is the difficulty experienced by widows in remarrying, a difficulty not encountered to the same extent by widowers. The most important obstacle is the fact that if a widow remarries she loses all rights to her ex-husband's fields, to the house and property of the household, and to her children if bridewealth has been paid. Very few widows are prepared to sacrifice the security, however limited, that such rights represent for a remarriage that may well result in tension and frustration.

In rural areas when a woman becomes a widow, the pressure on her intensifies. Although some older widows may receive remittances from adult sons, such gains are offset by advancing age, which makes it harder to earn income from work in agriculture or in the formal and informal sectors. For women with young children, widowhood poses different problems. Denied access to migrant remittances and often unable to leave her children to look for work farther afield, a young widow has to rely almost entirely on agriculture; on local employment, which is in short supply; on the informal sector; and on the limited support that her kin might provide. It is hardly surprising, therefore, that households headed by widows constitute the vast majority of the 27 percent of extremely disadvantaged households listed in Table 3.1.

Separated and Divorced Women. The disharmony typical of rural family life often leads to marital breakdown. Divorce is rare[32] although recognized under both civil and customary law. Divorce proceedings are frequently complex, especially when bridewealth has been paid and the custody of children is at stake. Therefore, married couples are reluctant to initiate divorce proceedings, and separation is much more common. By separation in this context we are not referring to the temporary separation that inevitably accompanies family life in the labor reserve, nor to the extended separation experienced by women whose husbands have deserted them, tragic as this often is for the women concerned. For in both cases, the women continue to reside in their marital homes with rights to house, land, and property. In contrast, the separation associated with marital breakdown is characterized by the permanent return of the woman and her children to her natal home, thereby sacrificing her rights to the husband's land and property. Such a step is not taken lightly, and the fact that it occurs as frequently as it does attests to the serious nature of the strains on married life in Lesotho's rural households.

Once reestablished with her natal kin, the separated woman is unable in most cases to rely fully on the hospitality of her family, whose own meager resources can rarely stretch to accommodate the additional burden. Remarriage is possible, but unusual. More commonly she has to seek employment to support herself and her children. With local opportunities limited, this often involves leaving the children with grandparents or relatives and searching for work in Lesotho's urban areas or in South Africa.

Given the hazards of work in the Republic, most women would prefer employment in Lesotho's towns. But despite the recent acceleration in urban growth, which has created more jobs for women, the demand for jobs far exceeds the supply.[33] Many separated women must resort to migrant work in South Africa; however, for nearly all women, such work is illegal. Nevertheless, there are an estimated 20,000 female Basotho migrants in South Africa, of whom a large proportion are separated.[34] The vast majority must enter South Africa illegally by avoiding the border control posts, and once in the Republic they must face the daily threat of arrest and imprisonment. Moreover, the illegal nature of their situation forces them to opt for extremely low-paying jobs with employers who are prepared to ask few questions. The majority obtain work as domestic servants, with appalling wages and working conditions that have been graphically documented by Jacklyn Cock.[35] Because of the low wages they can remit only small amounts to their families in Lesotho. In addition, the risks inherent in travel prevent them from visiting home often, with obvious implications for their children.

Positive Effects on Women. It is also worth noting that structural conditions in Lesotho result in some unusual outcomes with respect to women's roles. For example, because livestock care is a male task and so many adult males are absent as migrants, younger males are absent from enrollment in education, working instead as herdboys. Consequently, female students outnumber males at all educational levels except the university. Even at the university, there are almost as many females as males, a very unusual situation in Africa.

Both because more females than males have any given educational qualification below a university degree and because females cannot migrate to South Africa as easily as males can, females are unusually well represented in formal employment in both the private and public sectors. A number of government departments have professional staffs that are predominantly female. Female workers account for much of the increase in wage employment in urban areas since the mid-1970s. The asymmetric supply and demand situation for employment of men and women implies that the wage differential between Lesotho and South Africa is much greater (Lesotho wages being lower, of course) for women (who cannot migrate) than for men (who can). Thus, employers have a greater incentive to employ women rather than men in Lesotho than in most countries. However, few women manage to achieve positions of real power and authority, such as permanent secretary in government. Perhaps, as has been argued, this situation exists because males still expect deference from females and females experience difficulty in supervising males.

The pressure of circumstances forces many women into entrepreneurial activity, often initially in the informal sector. A few such women have been spectacularly successful, and it is clear that in the private sector there are no insuperable barriers to female success. Prominent businesswomen are found in the retail sector, catering and entertainment (shebeen-queens, cafes), transportation (taxi-owners), housing rentals, farming (especially poultry, pigs, and vegetables), and small-scale manufacturing (knitting by machine and dressmaking).

Children. Some of the most disturbing social consequences of migrant labor affect children. It is common that a migrant father sees his children only for widely separated short periods, a matter of weeks once each year to year and a half. Often, children of migrants suffer from the uncertainty and deprivations that result from irregular remittances and the strategies adopted by their mothers to overcome such problems. Family life is often unstable, and the children may spend long periods with grandparents or other relatives who in some cases treat them as unpaid domestic servants. Many males become herdboys at surprisingly early ages. Boys as young as four years old may care for herds near villages, and boys of six or seven may spend perhaps months at a time at mountain cattle posts fending for themselves in the company of only other boys and male adolescents. Even if children otherwise manage to remain at school, there is frequently great uncertainty as to whether fees and other expenses can be paid. Secondary schooling for the vast majority is not consistent with remaining at home, since most secondary schools are in towns. This situation implies either boarding and hence greater financial strain on families—or staying with relatives, strangers, or even alone. In urban areas, the temptations and stresses that affect the young are substantial: Instances of prostitution by teenage secondary school students have occurred, tensions between rich and poor among the young are clearly present, and juvenile crime and abuse of alcohol and cannabis are increasing.

At the risk of facile generalization, it is worthwhile saying that most outside observers would agree that the Basotho are very fond of children, and many families make substantial sacrifices on behalf of their children. But structurally for the bulk of the rural population, Lesotho is a very harsh and uncertain environment. The immediate effects on children—particularly those living in poverty—are self-evident and serious. Less easy to establish firmly, but potentially more serious, is what growing up in these circumstances does to children psychologically and what the implications of this are for Basotho society in the future.

THE URBAN MILIEU

At independence less than 5 percent of Basotho lived in the urban areas, about half of them (27,000) in the capital, Maseru. With the possible exception of Maseru, the towns that developed during the colonial period were small enclaves, usually explicitly referred to as "camps." These lacked the most elementary amenities of modern urban development and served essentially as administrative headquarters for the country's districts and as economic service centers for the surrounding rural communities. In comparison with other parts of Africa, the low level of migration from rural to urban settings in Lesotho during this period reflected the migration to South Africa's mining and industrial centers, not economic viability in Lesotho's countryside.

However, urbanization has risen rapidly since independence because of the increasing inability of both South Africa and domestic agriculture to absorb the growth in Lesotho's labor force. By 1980 about 125,000 people (10 percent of the population) were living in the urban areas. Close to 60,000 were based in Maseru. The remainder were spread between fifteen urban or peri-urban centers, none of which had a population greater than 10,000. Maseru's growth rate since independence has been an alarming 6 percent a year, and if this trend continues its population should reach 100,000 well before

Stonecutting. Photo courtesy of Louise B. Cobbe.

the end of the century. It is to Maseru, therefore, that our attention will largely be directed.

The recent rapid growth of urbanization in Lesotho has led, as in most developing countries, to the emergence of extremes of affluence and poverty. For the minority of Basotho and their expatriate counterparts in well-paid employment in the public and private sectors, Maseru offers an increasingly wide range of amenities: from spacious and well-equipped housing to fashionable shopping centers; from elegant restaurants to hotels such as the Holiday Inn and the Lesotho Sun Hotel whose casinos prove a major attraction. For the majority of Maseru's population, however, confined to overcrowded locations on the outskirts of town, such amenities are a distant pipe dream. In contrast, their lives consist of low and uncertain income, of inadequate and unsanitary housing, of frustration and despair, and not uncommonly of violence.

The extent of urban inequality was acknowledged in the 1975 World Bank report and in the government's Second Five-Year Development Plan. According to their estimates, the lowest and highest 40 percent of urban dwellers received 14 and 72 percent, respectively, of total urban incomes and the lowest and highest 5 percent received shares of 1 and 26 percent, respectively.[36] Furthermore, the urban areas, although small in size, account for a disproportionately large share of the country's national income, a share that increased from 27 percent in 1972/1973 to 33 percent in 1977/1978.[37]

The existence of inequality does not, of course, imply the prevalence of poverty. Poverty can only be ascertained by establishing the proportion of urban households that fall below the PDL. The most comprehensive study of this question to date was the one undertaken for Maseru households by Pieter Marres and Arie van der Wiel in 1974.[38] From a set of very detailed calculations concerning the minimum income required to cover essentials such as food, clothing, soap, fuel, accommodation, medical and school fees, and tax, they estimated that the PDL for an average Maseru household of 4.3 persons was M55.24 per month in April 1974. Comparing this figure with the most comprehensive evidence available for total household income, including an imputed value for agricultural production undertaken on urban homestead sites, they calculated that 60 percent of Maseru households fell below the PDL in 1974. An update of this calculation, using the same consumption basket but 1984 prices, showed a 376 percent increase in the urban PDL to M207.63 per month in April 1984.

The other major investigation of the urban PDL, contained in the JASPA report, estimated that the proportion of urban households below the PDL was closer to one third than two thirds—still a high proportion in the view of the investigators. By its own admission, however, the JASPA report conservatively estimated the minimum requirements for the PDL. But JASPA felt it was thus able to identify more clearly the real "hard core poverty groups" in the urban areas. There are grounds for suspecting that the report was too conservative. Its estimate of the PDL for an average urban household in 1978 was M54.72, slightly less than Marres and van der Wiel's figure of four years earlier and also much less than the figure of M98.06 per month determined by Thabo Khaketla as the PDL for an average Maseru household in October 1978.[39] Such disparities in estimates of the PDL reveal an obvious limitation of this approach to the study of poverty: One person's estimate of basic needs is not necessarily the same as another's. Nevertheless, poverty is clearly widespread in Lesotho's urban areas.

There is little reason to suppose that the trends revealed in these studies have been reversed in recent years. The major increase in migrant remittances in the mid-1970s, which undoubtedly benefited the lower-income groups, had already been felt by the time the JASPA report was written. And in any case, remittances are a much smaller proportion of urban incomes (15 percent) than of rural incomes (70 percent).[40] With respect to wage-earners, it is true that money wages have risen. In 1981 the minimum wage for unskilled labor was raised to M732 per year for light physical work and to M840 per year for heavy physical work. This compares with an average wage for unskilled work of M480 a year in 1977–1978. Nevertheless, any impact that this might have had on narrowing wage and salary differentials was offset by the substantial salary increases awarded to middle- and high-level personnel in government service in 1980, increases that were soon reflected in the private sector. A minimum wage of M840 per year begins to look less impressive when compared, for example, with the starting salary of M5,460 per year for a university graduate with a general B.A. degree and little or no experience, especially as the generous tax reductions of 1981 enabled salaried employees to retain a higher proportion of their salaries than previously. The gains from recent wage increases have also been offset by inflation. In October 1984, the retail price indices (based on October 1975 = 100) reached 316.4 for all urban households and 326.2 for low-income households. It is also probable that minimum wages are neither observed by nor enforced on small, wholly locally owned businesses, which largely escape the government's data collection but may be accounting for a growing proportion of employment in towns. New government salary scales were introduced in early 1985, but they are not likely to have narrowed income differentials much if at all.

The extent of urban inequality and poverty is also being compounded by the rising rate of unemployment. Although there are no reliable statistics on urban employment, certain conclusions can be extrapolated from the data that exist for the country as a whole. According to recent figures from the government's Central Planning and Development Office (CPDO), the proportion of the total labor force not gainfully employed in South Africa or in the agricultural, wage, or informal sectors in Lesotho rose from 35 percent in 1975 to 43 percent in 1980. With the labor force increasing much faster than its likely rate of absorption into employment in Lesotho or South Africa, this proportion would rise to at least 60 percent by the end of the century if present trends continued unchanged.[41]

There is little doubt that the deteriorating employment situation in the country as a whole has been a major factor in the recent growth in urbanization. Most people who move to the towns do so to obtain work. But their hopes are frequently frustrated, and one of the most plaintive cries heard these days in the urban as well as rural areas is that of *mosebetsi ha o eo*, "there's no work (here)." Nevertheless, while the prospect, however remote, of a small and unreliable cash income in the towns continues to have more appeal than the certainty of poverty and hunger in the rural areas, the trend toward urbanization will continue. So too will the inevitable growth of urban unemployment.

Unemployment and poverty are accompanied by other problems common in developing countries with rapid urban growth.[42] Accommodations for low-income groups are in short supply. Rents are often exorbitant, and living conditions are frequently squalid. Few urban locations have adequate provision for sanitation or water supply, let alone electricity, and diseases such as gastroenteritis are prevalent. In addition, the generally unplanned nature of urban expansion has led to serious incursions onto valuable agricultural land. Another common problem is the sense of alienation experienced by many urban dwellers. A high proportion of them are relative newcomers to the towns, and many find the process of adjustment a difficult and traumatic one. Gone are the networks, long-established in the rural areas, through which families in difficulty can obtain material support and comfort and through which incomes can be diffused and redistributed. Instead, such families are often confronted with loneliness and frustration, not to mention the more sordid realities of urban life such as crime, alcoholism, violence, and prostitution. Although present in the rural areas, such problems occur on a much more widespread scale in the towns. Finally, the urban malaise stresses family stability at least as much as the pressures experienced in the countryside. Not surprisingly, there are repercussions on the children involved. In her survey of juvenile delinquents at the Juvenile Training Centre in Maseru, Bereng discovered that 70 percent were the children of separated or divorced parents, a higher percentage than would be expected from the proportion of marriages that end in separation or divorce.

These and many other problems await the urgent attention of sociologists, who have tended so far to concentrate almost exclusively on rural Lesotho. Solutions also await the attention of the government, which although acknowledging that the problems exist,[43] has done little as yet to confront them effectively.

RELIGION AND CULTURE

Religion plays an important part in Basotho social life. Recent data on denominational affiliations are not available, but the 1966 census recorded 39 percent of the population as Roman Catholic, 24 percent members of the Lesotho Evangelical Church (LEC), 11 percent Anglican, and 8 percent belonging to other Christian churches (including the African Methodist Episcopal Church [AME], Assemblies of God, Dutch Reformed, Seventh Day Adventist, Methodist, and several independent Zionist sects). Only 18 percent were non-Christian.

The churches run almost all schools and about half the hospitals and have an important role in social work and politics. Although relations among the hierarchies and clergy have improved, substantial hostility between individual lay members of different denominations still exists. It is not unusual for a sick person to undertake a long journey to a hospital of the "right" denomination, never considering going to a much closer hospital of a different denomination. Most clergy are now Basotho, but many missionaries are still present. Many Catholic missionaries are French Canadian; the Catholic missionaries tend to be conservative. Each denomination maintains close links with churches of the same denomination in South Africa and personnel move back and forth. Desmond Tutu, current Anglican Bishop of Johannesburg, for example, was earlier Bishop of Maseru and, earlier still, was a chaplain at the university at Roma.

The earlier close alliance between the Catholic Church and the BNP has weakened considerably in recent years, and leaders of the Catholic Church have joined with other religious leaders to call for reconciliation and peace in the kingdom. Nevertheless, in popular eyes the Catholic Church still tends to be associated with the BNP; the LEC and, to a lesser extent, other protestant denominations are associated with the opposition. This alignment partly reflects the religious adherence of the political elite, but perhaps more the fact that the only independent press in Lesotho is the religious, vernacular press, consisting of weekly and less frequently published newspapers of very long standing (for example, *Leselinyana La Lesotho* has been published for more than 110 years). The LEC paper has been highly critical of government, the Catholic paper much less so.

The comparatively well-established vernacular press reflects the long tradition of literacy in the country and the early establishment of printing presses by missions. The extensive literature in Sesotho reflects the same; Thomas Mofolo's novels, for example, have been translated into English, French, German, and Italian as well as other African languages. The two modern church-controlled printing works publish not only religious and educational works for both local use and for other countries throughout Southern and Central Africa, but also a substantial stream of fiction, verse, and nonfiction in both English and Sesotho.

To a large extent, cultural life in Lesotho has become part of the hybrid Black culture of modern Southern Africa. However, certain distinctive features exist, some remnants of past tradition, others partly new inventions. In the field of craftwork, for example, distinctive grasswork, such as the famous Basotho hat, is still widely made; traditional pottery coexists with modern, but distinctive, techniques and designs; modern handweaving and handloom techniques are combined with local designs to produce unusual textiles, notably mohair tapestries. Various traditional dances still play an important role in various ceremonies, although perhaps the most well-known Basotho dance is the "gumboot dance," a hybrid of dubious origins associated with mine hostel compounds. Singing is an important part of initiation schools (in which traditional preparation for initiation into adulthood takes place), of religious and school life, and accompaniment to dances and communal work. Basotho choirs, whether from a primary school or a church, are typically impressive. Songs may be traditional, foreign, or modern but local and usually are not accompanied by musical instruments. Several traditional instruments exist and are used mainly for solos. Herdboys frequently possess such instruments, whose music is believed to be beneficial to cattle. However, popular culture is dominated by urban Black South African models, and the guitar, accordion, "gram" (battery-operated radiogramophone), transistor radio, cassette player, and discotheque are more common in urban areas than their traditional counterparts; they have also penetrated village life to a considerable degree.

CLASS FORMATION AND CONSOLIDATION

The inequalities prevalent in Lesotho's rural and urban areas reflect a long-standing process of class formation, the origins of which were visible by the time of the first contacts between Moshoeshoe's kingdom and the Cape in the mid-nineteenth century. Based on the emergence of different and opposed interests in the production and appropriation of social wealth, such class divisions were intensified by contact with the mercantilist nexus in the Cape and enhanced and modified by Lesotho's subsequent incorporation into South Africa's expanding industrial economy. It is to the changing nature and reproduction of these divisions that we now turn briefly.

By the second half of the nineteenth century, communal cultivation in Lesotho was beginning to give way to peasant production both for subsistence and for the expanding external market. The rise of the Lesotho peasantry was short-lived, however. With the transition from granary to labor reserve, agriculture ceased to provide an adequate livelihood for all but a tiny minority of rural dwellers. The vast majority came to rely either directly or indirectly on the earnings of migrant workers. For this reason, scholars such as Murray and Spiegel have argued convincingly that the Basotho peasantry should be seen

Roadworks. Photo courtesy of Joe Alfers.

not as a self-sufficient peasantry but as a rural-based proletariat, part of South Africa's regional working class.[44] This class must not be seen as a homogeneous mass because, as we have seen, considerable differences exist between rural households and also within them as they develop over time.

Alongside the rural proletariat is a small urban working class, also divided according to skill and income. With the possible exception of the relatively highly paid skilled workers, who constitute about a fifth of this class, the urban workers earn about the same amount as their rural-based brethren. In general, the earnings of both unskilled urban and rural workers are lower than those of migrants. However, the urban workers—simply because their urban location within Lesotho provides for the emergence of working-class consciousness—have a more effective base for organization and protest. To their voices of dissatisfaction will be added the protests of the growing structurally unemployed or underemployed class. Clearly, the difficulties of the proletariat pose a serious challenge to the government.

Above the proletariat in the class hierarchy stands the petty bourgeoisie, a heterogeneous class that is divided both vertically and horizontally. The petty bourgeoisie can be separated by vertical boundaries into a number of segments or fractions, the most important of which are a commercial segment of traders, shopkeepers, and businessmen; a rural segment of relatively prosperous farmers and rural contractors of the kulak variety;[45] and a bureaucratic segment, which in Lesotho is the largest, of civil servants, teachers, and professionals. Although frequently forming the basis for political conflict in other parts of Africa, these divisions are not as troublesome in Lesotho, where bureaucratic salaries are commonly invested in private commercial ventures and where both bureaucratic and commercial incomes are often invested in agriculture. Of perhaps greater importance, therefore, are the horizontal divisions that characterize the petty bourgeoisie. Wide disparities in income and wealth exist between the lower and higher echelons of this class: between the primary school teacher and the university professor, between the small shopkeeper and the prosperous wholesaler who supplies the small shopkeeper's wares, and between the civil service clerk and the high-ranking official for whom the clerk works. Such differentials reflect variations in the level of educational attainment and in the degree of access to the agencies of central and local government patronage. Accordingly, the distinctions that can be drawn between the lower levels of the petty bourgeoisie and the proletariat on the one hand, and between the higher levels of the petty bourgeoisie and of the national bourgeoisie on the other, are far from clear-cut. As a result, the political outlook of the petty bourgeoisie class will normally be ambivalent, some sections tending to side with the dominant class (which controls the state) and other with the dominated. The distinction between the lower levels of the bourgeoisie and the working class became more blurred in Lesotho following South African mine wage increases when some of the petty bourgeoisie, particularly primary school teachers, left Lesotho to join the ranks of the migrant labor force.

It has always been difficult in the Third World context to determine precisely where the petty bourgeoisie ends and the national bourgeoisie begins. Scholars associated with the dependency school (which emphasizes the dependence of society, economy, and polity in the Third World on external forces) have argued that it makes little sense to talk of a national bourgeoisie at all, or even of a national economy, in situations where the ownership and control of the major capitalist means of production are vested largely in the hands of foreign enterprises. At most, such a bourgeoisie can play a merely auxiliary role in the service of foreign capital. Recently, however, conflicting evidence drawn from countries such as Nigeria and Kenya has been put forward to challenge this view as seriously underestimating the prospects for indigenous capital accumulation in African and other Third World countries. So far this has failed to impress the dependency theorists, and the debate continues.[46] So too does the controversy surrounding the question of the bureaucratic bourgeoisie. Although most scholars seem agreed that senior state officials play a crucial role in developing countries, there is serious academic contention over whether they constitute a dominant bureaucratic class in their own right or a petty bourgeois stratum serving the interests of dominant internal and external classes.[47]

Evidence from the Lesotho case is unlikely to resolve these issues, for in some ways it is ambivalent. On the one hand, it is evident that the economic survival of the country is heavily dependent on foreign capital in general and South African capital in particular. Hardly any major industrial infrastructure exists and the little that does is largely in the hands of foreigners. So too are large parts of the commercial and distributive sectors. On the other hand, it is equally evident that a growing number of Basotho are involved in capitalist production and accumulation, especially in construction, transport, wholesale and retail trade, the service sector, and to a more limited extent in small-scale industrial ventures. It is also clear that much of the local capital accumulation since independence has been under the auspices of the state, either directly through the establishment of parastatals such as LNDC or indirectly through private accumulation by senior state officials, whose salaries and political influence have been used to good effect in this direction.

What seems to be required, therefore, are several analyses: (1) of the contradictions that exist between local and foreign accumulators, between them and the state, and between all these groups and the other classes and strata that exist in Lesotho; (2) of the ways in which such class contradictions are affected by other types of cleavage in society; and (3) of the impact of all these factors on the social, economic, and political life of the country. In the search for such analyses, the quest for conclusive proof of the existence or nonexistence of a national or bureaucratic bourgeoisie may well prove an illusory distraction rather than a helpful focus.

One final group, which has been neglected so far, is the chiefs. Although providing the basis for the earliest forms of stratification within Basotho society, the chiefs have never been a homogeneous class; the divisions within the chieftainship have played and continue to play an important role in Basotho politics. Since the 1940s, however, it is doubtful whether the chiefs have constituted a separate class at all, a fact attributable in part to the effects of social change and in part to the effects of the British administrative reforms that deprived them of most of their traditional sources of wealth. With the gradual erosion of their control over land allocation since independence, whatever economic and political power they possess has come increasingly to rest on their position as officially recognized and paid functionaries of the state—a position from which they can be dismissed, their hereditary status notwithstanding. Many have been able to supplement their official incomes by engaging in farming and commerce. Some have combined their roles in local government and important positions in the central political and bureaucratic hierarchy. Others have been less successful and have sunk into the ranks of the rural proletariat. As such, the chiefs need not be considered as a distinct class.

The contemporary class structure of Lesotho and the wide disparities in income and power that it reflects are reinforced by several factors, especially the educational system.[48] The important role of education in this respect is recognized by the government's Education Task Force, which observed, "In government as well as in private sectors income is associated with the level of educational qualification. Higher educational qualifications lead to higher income remuneration."[49] What is of special interest in the Lesotho case is the fact that the handsome returns from education are realized almost solely at the tertiary level. Economic returns from primary and secondary education are virtually zero, at least for men. In the early 1980s, a person with a primary school education on entering the public service received M900 per year, a person with a secondary school education—that is, with five additional years of education and the Cambridge Overseas School Certificate (COSC)—started at M1,260, a difference of only M360 per year. In contrast, a B.A. graduate with four additional years of university education after COSC began at

M5,460, a salary that the COSC entrant to the civil service could attain only after twenty-four years of service.[50] Furthermore, an uneducated novice mineworker could earn in ten months in South Africa what a COSC new civil servant earned in a year in Lesotho. The minimal returns from secondary as well as primary education are brought sharply into focus by this fact. Changes in scales in early 1985 increased the lowest rate in government service by 50 percent, from M900 per year to M1,344, but made no significant change to these relationships.

An obvious implication of the connection between education and salary structure is the important premium placed on tertiary and especially university education, a premium for which the country has to pay dearly. In academic year 1981/1982, the country's only university—the National University of Lesotho—accounted for 20 percent of the government's recurrent expenditure on education, only slightly less than the 24 percent spent on the whole secondary school system. The unit cost of primary education was M35 per student in 1981/ 1982, compared to M5,110 per university student.[51] This obviously raises the question of which sections of society benefit from such expensive and clearly rewarding university education. From a study of the socioeconomic backgrounds of first-year undergraduates undertaken by Cobbe in 1976 it became clear that "rich families, better-educated families, families where the father had cash employment within Lesotho, and families with homes in the more educationally-favored districts are all over-represented at the University."[52]

Such a conclusion is hardly surprising, given the obstacles that exclude almost all but the privileged classes from obtaining adequate secondary schooling for their children, itself an essential precondition for university admission. Two obstacles are of particular importance. The first is the high cost involved. Although primary education is quite cheap and although those fortunate enough to gain entry to the university are normally provided by the government with loan-bursaries (that is, loans much of which may be forgiven if the student graduates and works in specified employment for a certain number of years), secondary education is prohibitively expensive for most Basotho families. Fees alone stood on average at M163 a student, or 35 percent of per capita income, in fiscal year 1980/1981. The second is the high risk involved. With the well-documented decline in the facilities and teaching standards in many schools in recent years,[53] the failure rate, especially at the secondary level, has risen to alarming proportions. The number of candidates failing the COSC examination, for example, rose from 39.4 percent in 1970 to 73.4 percent in 1979, and the results have deterioriated in the years since then; recently,

Moshoeshoe II. Photo courtesy of David Ambrose.

Lesotho's results have been worse than those in any other country that uses the exam.

Together with the low financial returns from primary and secondary education, such factors have clearly discouraged the majority of families from sacrificing more than they already do to ensure the education of their children. Even though 75 percent of children of primary school age are enrolled in school, the drop-out rate is high, especially at the upper levels. Based on current trends, out of 100 children entering primary school today, 40 will complete their primary education, 17 will enter secondary school, 5 will complete their secondary education, and 1 will pass the COSC examination. Less than 1 in a 100 will enter the university.

This situation is the result of an education system that (1) remains heavily influenced by shortages of high-level personnel throughout the economy and therefore allows the entrance requirements of the university to dictate the curriculum at lower levels, (2) uses English as its medium from the higher primary levels up, and (3) requires that the student do well on formal written examinations and have adequate economic resources. Substantial official attempts have been made to make the primary curriculum more relevant for those who progress no further and to diversify the secondary curriculum to provide the alternative of practical vocational training (the latter with generous World Bank assistance). However, serious doubts exist as to whether the actual curriculum (what goes on in the schools) has changed much, because the population still seems to judge success by examination results and progress to higher levels within the education system. Officials associated with the World Bank secondary school project have admitted privately that the project's only economic effects may have been to secure better job gradings and pay for some migrants to South Africa. It is very hard to believe that the country receives a worthwhile economic return at present from the enormous resources devoted to education.

What can safely be assumed is that the tiny minority of students who successfully negotiate the obstacles and eventually enter the university will mainly be the children of those families with the income and influence to provide them with the best possible education. This situation serves to perpetuate Lesotho's social inequalities from one generation to the next.

NOTES

1. For a discussion, see Jerry Eckert and Ron Wykstra, "The Future of Basotho Migration to the Republic of South Africa," *Lesotho Agricultural*

Sector Analysis Project Report, no. 4 (Maseru: Ministry of Agriculture, 1979), pp. 1–24; and Colin Murray, "'Stabilization' and Structural Unemployment," South African Labour Bulletin 6, no. 4 (1980), pp. 58–61.

2. See, for example, JASPA, Options for a Dependent Economy: Development, Employment and Equity Problems in Lesotho (Addis Ababa: International Labour Office Jobs and Skills Programme for Africa, 1979), p. 87.

3. Arie van der Wiel, Migratory Wage Labour: Its Role in the Economy of Lesotho (Mazenod: Mazenod Book Centre, 1977), pp. 87–88.

4. JASPA, Options, p. 89. This idea was first expressed both strongly and explicitly by Sandra Wallman, Perceptions of Development (Cambridge: Cambridge University Press, 1977), although it is also present in earlier writers, such as E. H. Ashton, "A Sociological Sketch of Sotho Diet," Transactions of the Royal Society of South Africa 27, Part II (1939), pp. 147–214.

5. John Gray, Neil Robertson, and Michael Walton, "Lesotho: A Strategy for Survival After the Golden Seventies," South African Labour Bulletin 6, no. 4 (1980), p. 66.

6. Kingdom of Lesotho, Bridging the Gaps: The Second Lesotho National Food and Nutrition Planning Conference (Maseru: Food and Nutrition Coordinating Office, 1979), Appendix E, p. 58.

7. In addition to JASPA, Options, and van der Wiel, Migratory Wage Labour, studies at the macro level include International Bank for Reconstruction and Development (IBRD), Migration from Botswana, Lesotho and Swaziland (Washington, D.C.: International Bank for Reconstruction and Development, 1978); IBRD, Lesotho: Report of the Migrant Workers Re-Employment Mission (Washington, D.C.: International Bank for Reconstruction and Development, 1975); and E. Molapi Sebatane, "An Empirical Study of the Attitudes and Perceptions of Migrant Workers: The Case of Lesotho," World Employment Programme Working Paper, no. 42 (Geneva: International Labour Office, 1979). Those at the micro level include Colin Murray, "Keeping House in Lesotho" (Ph.D. thesis, University of Cambridge, 1976); Colin Murray, Families Divided: The Impact of Migrant Labour in Lesotho (Johannesburg: Ravan Press, and Cambridge: Cambridge University Press, 1981); Andrew Spiegel, "Migrant Labour Remittances, Rural Differentiation and the Development Cycle in a Lesotho Community" (Master's thesis, University of Cape Town, 1979); and Judy Gay, "Basotho Women's Options: A Study of Marital Careers in Rural Lesotho" (Ph.D. thesis, University of Cambridge, 1980). Unless otherwise noted, these studies are the sources for the discussion that follows.

8. IBRD, Lesotho: A Development Challenge (Washington, D.C.: International Bank for Reconstruction and Development, 1975), p. 23.

9. Kingdom of Lesotho, Second Five-Year Development Plan, 1975/76–1979/80 (Maseru: Government Printer 1976), p. 3.

10. Murray, Families Divided, p. 89.

11. van der Wiel, Migratory Wage Labour, p. 86.

12. Kingdom of Lesotho, Third Five-Year Development Plan 1980–1985 (Maseru: Government Printer 1980), p. 20.

13. For an analysis of the likely effects of the 1979 Land Act, see Andrew Spiegel, "Changing Patterns of Migrant Labour and Rural Differentiation in Lesotho," *Social Dynamics* 6, no. 2 (1981), pp. 5–8.

14. Ibid., p. 9. The concept of the developmental cycle is associated with the work of the early Soviet agricultural economist A. V. Chayanov. See his *The Theory of Peasant Economy*, edited by D. Thorner, B. Kerblay, and R.E.F. Smith (Homewood, Ill.: American Economic Association, 1966).

15. Hugh Ashton, *The Basuto: A Social Study of Traditional and Modern Lesotho*, 2nd ed. (London: Oxford University Press, 1967).

16. In Murray's survey of 105 married men in 1974, only 2.9 percent had more than one wife (Murray, *Families Divided*, p. 127); according to Gay's survey, whereas 77.8 percent of males and 82.5 percent of females over the age of 65 had undergone initiation, only 29.7 percent of males and 6.5 percent of females between 15 and 24 years old had done so (Gay, "Basotho Women's Options," p. 63).

17. For an elaboration of this argument, see Harold Wolpe, "Capitalism and Cheap Labour Power in South Africa: From Segregation to Apartheid," *Economy and Society* 1, no. 4 (1972).

18. A critique of the functionalist tendency contained within this approach can be found in Judy Kimble, "Aspects of the Penetration of Capitalism into Colonial Basutoland, c. 1890–1930," in *Class Formation and Class Struggle: Selected Proceedings of the Fourth Annual Southern African Universities Social Science Conference, 1981*, ed. John Bardill (Morija: Sesuto Book Depot, 1982), pp. 141–143.

19. See, for example, Murray, *Families Divided*, particularly Chapters 3 to 7.

20. The average size of land holdings declined from 6.2 acres in 1950 to 4.9 acres in 1970. See L. B. Monyake, "Lesotho: Land, Population and Food. The Problem of Growth in Limited Space," *Report on the National Population Symposium* (Maseru, Bureau of Statistics, 1974), p. 63.

21. Sandra Wallman, "Conditions of Non-Development: The Case of Lesotho," *The Journal of Development Studies* 8, no. 2 (1972), pp. 251–261.

22. The fullest recent study, although not mainly focused on Lesotho, is Adam Kuper, *Wives for Cattle: Bridewealth and Marriage in South Africa* (London: Routledge and Kegan Paul, 1982).

23. Sebastian Poulter, *Legal Dualism in Lesotho* (Morija: Morija Sesuto Book Depot, 1979), p. 11.

24. Both Gay and Spiegel, in their respective surveys, found that more than 90 percent of marriages, whether customary or civil, were accompanied by *bohali* transfers. Gay, "Basotho Women's Options," p. 94; and Andrew Spiegel, "Christian Marriage and Migrant Labour in a Lesotho Village" (B.A. thesis, University of Cape Town, 1975), p. 40.

25. Sebastian Poulter, *Family Law and Litigation in Basotho Society* (Oxford: Clarendon Press, 1976), p. 332.

26. Murray, "'Stabilization'" and *Families Divided*, Gay, "Basotho Women's Options," and Spiegel, "Migrant Labour Remittances" and "Christian

Marriage," have already been cited. In addition, see Elizabeth Gordon, "The Women Left Behind: A Study of the Wives of the Migrant Workers of Lesotho," *World Employment Programme Working Paper*, no. 35 (Geneva: International Labour Office, 1978).

27. The maximum permissible length of contract is two years. The proportion of Basotho migrants on the mines who served this maximum length of time increased from 7 percent in 1977 to 19 percent in 1979 and to 32 pecent by May 1980. Murray, "'Stabilization,'" p. 59; see also Table 2.5 in this book. For migrants whose homes are close to roads in lowland areas, this is offset to some extent by occasional weekend visits since the introduction of the eleven-shift fortnight in gold mining.

28. Gay, "Basotho Women's Options," p. 136.

29. For an additional critique of this view, see Murray, *Families Divided*, pp. 102–104 and p. 173. Stress is also affected, of course, by the very real difficulties of communication between migrants and their families, even when there is literacy at both ends. Letters must be collected from post offices, of which (despite expansion) there are few in rural areas. Through official channels even emergency messages—such as news of a serious injury to a migrant—on the average take more than a week to reach families.

30. For a discussion of these problems, see Kate Showers, "A Note on Women, Conflict and Migrant Labour," *South African Labour Bulletin* 6, no. 4 (1980), pp. 54–57. Husbands, of course, are not always sexually faithful while away; problems are also caused if the husband contracts a sexually transmitted disease as a migrant and then infects his wife.

31. In Gay's survey of 234 married women, 50 percent were in this category. The remaining 50 percent were divided almost equally between wives in the first and third stages of the developmental cycle (Gay, "Basotho Women's Options," p. 49).

32. Of the 54 separated and divorced women studied by Gay, only 2 were divorced (Ibid., p. 267).

33. See Judy Gay, "Wage Employment of Rural Basotho Women: A Case Study," *South African Labour Bulletin* 6, no. 4 (1980), pp. 49–50.

34. In Gay's survey, 60 percent of the women who were working in South Africa were separated or divorced (Gay, "Basotho Women's Options," p. 276).

35. Jacklyn Cock, *Maids and Madams: A Study in the Politics of Exploitation* (Johannesburg: Ravan Press, 1980), pp. 26–86.

36. IBRD, *Development Challenge*, pp. 21–22; Kingdom of Lesotho, *Second Five-Year Plan*, p. 2.

37. JASPA, *Options*, p. 239.

38. Pieter Marres and Arie van der Wiel, *Poverty Eats My Blanket: A Poverty Study—The Case of Lesotho* (Maseru: Government Printer, 1975).

39. Thabo Khaketla, "Behavioural Traits of the Poor and Underprivileged Sectors at Lower Thamae's" (B.A. thesis, National University of Lesotho, 1980), p. 37. Khaketla's estimate is consistent with the 1984 update, prepared by K. S. Nyokong of the Lesotho Bureau of Statistics.

40. JASPA, *Options,* p. 249; van der Wiel, *Migratory Wage Labour,* p. 88.

41. H. Kizilyalli, *Options for the Lesotho Economy in the Year 2000: Perspective Plan Alternatives* (Maseru: Central Planning and Development Office, 1982), p. 43.

42. Almost no published work exists on the social problems in Lesotho's urban areas. However, we are indebted to the Department of Sociology at the National University of Lesotho for allowing us to consult a number of unpublished B.A. theses written by students at the university. In addition to the work by Khaketla that has already been cited, we also found useful those by Thato Bereng (1981), Masefora Makepe (1980), Lucy Makhalanyane (1982), Margaret Mokhothu (1982), C. H. Motsoene (1982), and 'Masefinela Mphuthing (1980).

43. Kingdom of Lesotho, *Third Five-Year Plan,* p. 344.

44. Spiegel, "Migrant Labour Remittances," pp. 206–208; "Changing Patterns of Migrant Labour," p. 2; and Murray, *Families Divided,* p. 175. Compare also Jack Parson's views on the rural population in *Botswana: Liberal Democracy and the Labor Reserve in Southern Africa* (Boulder, Colo.: Westview Press, 1984).

45. Along with Cohen we define *kulaks* in this context as "a kind of agricultural petty bourgeoisie who still provide some of their own labour and consume some of their own produce, as well as holding land through non-capitalist, often kinship-based, tenure systems, but who are accumulating surpluses with which, over time, they are able to change their relations of production, economically and politically, into more capitalist ones." Dennis Cohen, "Class and the Analysis of African Politics: Problems and Prospects," in *Political Economy of Africa: Selected Readings,* ed. Dennis Cohen and John Daniel (London: Longman, 1981), p. 101.

46. See, for example, the debates that have taken place recently in the *Review of African Political Economy,* no. 17 (1980), pp. 83–105; and no. 19 (1980), pp. 48–62.

47. For a defense of the concept of the bureaucratic bourgeoisie, see Issa Shivji, *Class Struggles in Tanzania* (London: Heinemann, 1976), pp. 63–99. For a critique of this concept and particularly Shivji's use of it, see Michaela von Freyhold, "The Post-Colonial State and Its Tanzanian Version," *Review of African Political Economy,* no. 8 (1977), especially pp. 85–86.

48. For a more detailed discussion of the relationship between education and class formation in Lesotho, see James Cobbe, "The Education System, Wage and Salary Structures, and Income Distribution: Lesotho as a Case Study, Circa 1975," *Journal of Developing Areas* 17, no. 2 (1983), pp. 227–241.

49. Kingdom of Lesotho, *Report of the Education Task Force,* (Maseru: Ministry of Education, 1982), p. 31.

50. Ibid., pp. 31–33; of course, the COSC entrant would not automatically progress this far up the salary scale.

51. Ibid., p. 17. In 1979, primary school enrollment exceeded 235,000, as opposed to fewer than 1,000 students at the university.

52. James Cobbe, "A Preliminary Profile of First Year Students at the National University of Lesotho, 1975–76" (Unpublished paper, National University of Lesotho, 1976), p. 12.

53. Kingdom of Lesotho, *Education Task Force*, pp. 12–14.

4

Government and Politics

A Westminster-Style Constitution Under Strain, 1966–1970

On assuming the office of prime minister, Chief Jonathan was clearly aware that his BNP government's retention of power, under the country's Westminster-style constitution, would depend to a large extent on its ability to satisfy the popular aspirations raised during the independence struggle. "I know," he said in a speech in December 1965, "that after five years you could cast us among useless thorns. . . . But in order that you should reelect us during the next election, our duty is to fulfill the promises we have made to you."[1] Given the magnitude of the difficulties confronting his regime, this was clearly destined to be an uphill struggle. By 1970 only his most ardent supporters were prepared to claim that much headway had been made.

At the economic level, desperately short of a coherent strategy and the domestic revenue to finance one, the government adopted an essentially ad hoc policy based on the attraction of foreign investment and aid. Under the auspices of the LNDC, Lesotho was able to offer private investors an abundant supply of cheap labor and generous tax concessions. Despite this, the level of capital attracted from South Africa and elsewhere proved very disappointing, and the industrial and commercial concerns that were established succeeded in creating merely 600 new jobs between 1966 and 1970. Much of the foreign aid received during this period, especially from Britain, was used to balance the budget. The little aid that was left over for development was used mainly for infrastructural and agricultural projects in the lowlands—especially in Jonathan's home area in the northwest—and the already-disadvantaged mountain regions were left largely untouched.

At the political level, the governing party's slender parliamentary majority was enhanced by defections to its ranks from the opposition (specifically, from the MFP and the new UDP) and was sustained by Jonathan's refusal to hold by-elections in the three seats that became vacant after 1966. This facilitated the ratification of most of the legislative program. The implementation of this program was to prove far more difficult, however, not the least because of the preponderance of BCP supporters in the civil service and in the locally elected district councils. To overcome such difficulties, the district councils were suspended in 1966 and abolished in 1968. Henceforth, the organs of local government, the chieftainship included, were brought under tighter central government control, and popular participation in them was progressively reduced.

The civil service proved harder to deal with, especially as the constitutionally entrenched autonomy of the Public Service Commission prevented the arbitrary dismissal of opposition supporters. The government's attempt to neutralize their ability to obstruct its policies by moving them to "punishment" posts in the mountains merely transferred the problem from the central to the local level. The heavy concentration of BCP sympathizers within the civil service was undoubtedly a factor in persuading the government to delay its commitment to fill the upper echelons of the bureaucracy with local people; instead, the government relied on expatriate officials, particularly South Africans who were willingly seconded by Pretoria to fill such sensitive posts as chief justice, chief legal draftsman, and chief electoral officer.

An additional problem for Chief Jonathan was the threat posed by King Moshoeshoe II, who was clearly dissatisfied with the role accorded him by the constitution. After independence he continued to seek support for a revision of his constitutional position, and given his long history of friction with the prime minister, this soon provoked the government into action. Matters came to a head in December 1966 when the king and his supporters held a public gathering at Thaba-Bosiu in defiance of a government ban. After the ensuing confrontation between royalist supporters and the police, in which ten people were killed, the government moved swiftly to curtail the already-limited powers of the king. Placed under house arrest, he was forced in January 1967 to sign an agreement under which he undertook to refrain from further involvement in politics on pain of abdication.

By 1970, therefore, the ruling party had made some progress toward consolidating its control. But there were few signs that this had been accompanied by any increase in popular support and

The prime minister, Chief Leabua Jonathan, opening a brickworks at Thetsane, near Maseru. Photo courtesy of David Ambrose.

involvement or by any reduction in the cleavages that divided the nation. This has led some writers to view Lesotho as steadily moving between 1966 and 1970 toward authoritarian rule, which is characteristic of many other Third World countries.[2] Although the government's actions during the Thaba-Bosiu incident and the repeated threats to discipline the opposition unless it ceased its provocation demonstrated less than total respect for the Westminster rule book, the regime in fact put few of these threats into practice and continued to observe quite closely the constitutionally guaranteed provisions for free speech and association. The government was able to draw little comfort from this fact, because by tolerating such freedoms it exposed itself in Parliament, in the press, and at public gatherings around the country to a concerted antiregime campaign by the opposition. The limitations of the government's economic policy and its unduly obsequious relationship with South Africa were singled out for special attention.

Despite such problems, Chief Jonathan and his fellow leaders continued to approach the 1970 elections with unusual optimism. This clearly owed less to the government's positive achievements (which being few were understandably played down during the campaign) and more to its superior financial and organizational position and to confidence in its ability to manipulate the electoral machinery in its own favor.[3] Such advantages, among others, convinced most informed observers that the BNP would be returned to power. Events were soon to prove them wrong.

Lesotho's only postindependence general election took place on Tuesday, 27 January 1970. Although early returns revealed important swings to the ruling BNP in the BCP's former stronghold in the northwest, these were soon countered by even more dramatic swings to the BCP in the previously BNP-dominated mountain regions. By Thursday evening, the BCP had clearly won by a comfortable margin. The full results were never released officially, but reliable estimates gave the BCP 36 seats, the BNP 23, and the MFP 1.[4]

In explaining the BCP's victory, perhaps the most crucial factor was that dissatisfaction with government neglect in the mountain constituencies was sufficient to outweigh their ties of traditionalism, Catholicism, and anti-Communism, which had earlier bound them to the BNP. In addition, the BCP's adoption of a more moderate platform than in 1965 on issues such as South Africa and the chieftainship undoubtedly contributed to its success, as did its energetic campaigning throughout the country. Another factor was the decline of the royalist MFP, whose share of the votes dropped from 16.5 percent in 1965 to 7.3 percent in 1970.[5] Given the continuing antipathy of most ex-MFP voters to the government's policy toward the king, there seems little doubt that the BCP profited from this.

The BCP's victory celebrations were short-lived, however. Chief Jonathan's original decision to hand over power was reversed at a cabinet meeting on Friday, 30 January 1970, where the arguments for a coup were put forcibly by hardliners such as the deputy prime minister, Chief Sekhonyane 'Maseribane. Assured by the British commanders of the police and paramilitary unit (the Police Mobile Unit, or PMU) that their forces would remain loyal, the government moved swiftly into action. On Friday afternoon Chief Jonathan announced over Radio Lesotho that his government had been forced to suspend the constitution and to assume emergency powers until such time as a new constitution could be framed in line with Basotho rather than Westminster traditions of democracy. Shortly afterward, Ntsu Mokhehle and other BCP leaders were arrested and detained without trial. A curfew was imposed. Opposition publications were banned, as was the small Communist party of Lesotho. The king was placed under close house arrest and subsequently exiled to the Netherlands. Because of a rapid exodus of the country's South African judges, sittings of the High Court were suspended, and the opposition was thus prevented from testing the dubious legality of the government's actions in the courts.

On Saturday, 31 January 1970, Chief Jonathan declared that "I have seized power. I am not ashamed of it."[6] In explaining why, he focused particular attention on alleged acts of BCP violence and intimidation that had not only deprived the BNP of a rightful victory at the polls, but also posed and continued to pose a serious threat to law and order throughout the kingdom. Although satisfying Pretoria, which endorsed the coup and promised continuing support for the government, such justifications were far from convincing to any but loyal BNP supporters, as was Chief Jonathan's newly discovered concern with the defects of Westminster democracy. The argument that opposition violence had marred the elections, for example, was very much at variance with statements broadcast over the government-controlled radio earlier in the week that polling day had been remarkably peaceful, a fact substantiated by the extraordinarily high turnout (81.9 percent), which would surely have been much lower had intimidation been as widespread as the government later alleged.

To seize power is one thing; to retain it is another. The postcoup government was confronted by immediate problems, beginning with the need to eliminate all forms of resistance. This goal was accomplished, in part, by the detention and restriction of the major opposition leaders; therefore, the development of any well-organized defiance was inhibited. Resistance was also minimized by the appeals for calm addressed to the nation by Mokhehle and other opposition leaders, as well as by the country's principal churches. Although popular unrest in the weeks immediately following the coup was largely contained, some outbreaks did occur. These were ruthlessly suppressed by the police and PMU. Such strong-arm tactics served only to inflame the spirit of opposition, as did the intimidating activities of the BNP's Youth League; by March 1970 conflict began to spread throughout the country.[7] The government's response was an even greater show of force, and several hundred people died in the ensuing violence. Eventually the government's superior weapons and equipment, willingly replenished by South Africa, began to tell, and by the middle of 1970, the government reasserted its control.

The second problem was Britain's decision to withhold diplomatic recognition and aid. For a regime that depended on outside assistance for half of its recurrent and all of its capital budget, this decision was bound to have drastic consequences, especially as most other donors appeared to be waiting for a lead from Britain before committing further funds to the kingdom. In order to persuade Britain to reverse

The National University of Lesotho, Roma. Photo courtesy of David Ambrose.

its decision, Chief Jonathan realized that he would have to convince
the former colonial power that his government was not only in
effective control of the country, but that this control was based on
wider legitimacy than force alone could create. It was largely for this
reason that he entered into a series of reconciliation talks with leaders
of the three main opposition parties: the BCP, MFP, and UDP (the
United Democratic Party, formed in 1967 by Charles Mofeli after his
defection from the BCP's parliamentary ranks). Seven meetings were
held between April and June 1970. At the second of these the opposition
leaders agreed to disregard the January election results in the interest
of national unity and in the hope that this overture might serve as
a prelude to their being released from detention and house arrest to
join an all-party government of national reconciliation whose main
tasks would be to organize new elections and return the country to
normality as soon as possible. Although refusing to grant the demands
of these leaders for the restoration of the 1966 Constitution and the

reconvening of the 1965 Parliament, Chief Jonathan continued to hold out the possibility of a national government with a degree of representation for all parties. This finally satisfied the British who restored recognition and aid on 12 June 1970, a decision undoubtedly motivated in addition by concern that the denial of aid was seriously compounding the suffering caused by severe drought. Other donors soon followed suit, the United States in particular promising food aid to the value of $5 million.

Mokhehle described the British decision as politically disastrous, and for the reconciliation talks at least, this was certainly the case. They were abandoned by the prime minister as soon as the British announcement was made. In August 1970 he informed the opposition leaders that his government had decided to go it alone, and in October he felt sufficiently confident to declare a five-year holiday from politics. For his government and for the country as a whole, this holiday was to prove far from restful.

Repression, Reconciliation, and Realignments, 1970–1979

Although the use of force and the restoration of aid helped Chief Jonathan to alleviate the immediate problems resulting from his illegal seizure of power, he still held only a tenuous grip on what was still a highly volatile situation. In an effort to tighten his grip throughout the 1970s, his government sought to strengthen its control and credibility and to weaken, divide, and undercut the forces opposed to the regime. The most-criticized government policy was the continuing reliance on coercion and intimidation and the failure to reestablish effective constitutional mechanisms for the articulation of popular grievances and opinion. Although the state of emergency was lifted in July 1973, many of the arbitrary powers acquired under it by the government were retained by new legislation. The Internal Security Act of 1974, for example, gave the authorities alarming powers of detention and interrogation without trial.[8] In addition, the police and security forces were rapidly expanded and complemented by the establishment of an irregular militia of ardent BNP supporters, known euphemistically as the Peace Corps (Lebotho la Khotso).

Although the use of these forces enabled the government to coerce the opposition into a state of sullen passivity in the early 1970s, there clearly was no lasting basis for peace. With little progress being made toward constitutional reform, Mokhehle and his BCP colleagues, released eventually from detention,[9] began to show increasing signs of frustration. This was demonstrated by their refusal to participate in the interim National Assembly set up by Chief Jonathan in April 1973 on the grounds that this constituted merely a rubber stamp for the government. When the BCP leaders were harassed by the authorities into canceling their party conference later in the year, this proved the final straw. Convinced of the futility of peaceful efforts to achieve change, they switched to a violent offensive. Early in January 1974, several police stations were attacked to seize weapons for a widespread uprising against the regime. These attacks were poorly orchestrated, however, and were quickly foiled by the government's forces, which mounted a ruthless counteroffensive. Although Mokhehle and most of the BCP's executive committee fled into exile in Botswana and Zambia, nearly two hundred of their followers were detained and subjected, it was widely alleged, to ill-treatment and torture. According to an observer for the International Commission of Jurists, more than 1,000 people were killed in the reprisals launched by the security forces and the Lebotho la Khotso. Although the government claimed that such allegations were exaggerated, its own chief justice, J. T. Mapetla, directed a scathing attack on the actions of such forces, which, he argued, appeared to be acting completely above the law. He also condemned the government for abdicating its responsibility for maintaining law and order.

The flight into exile of most of the BCP's leaders impaired their ability to influence events within Lesotho and assisted the government in consolidating its control. This was reflected in the late 1970s by reduced overt repression.

The regime's reliance on force was accompanied by a sustained effort to centralize political and administrative structures more effectively in its hands. The suspension of the constitution facilitated this effort by the removal of certain constraints that had hampered earlier attempts. Of particular importance was that the autonomy of the Public Service Commission came to an end, which enabled the government to launch an attack on opposition elements within the civil service. In the months following the 1970 coup, between 600 and 800 public servants were dismissed. Their positions were filled by reliable though sometimes inexperienced BNP supporters and by expatriates. The earlier dependence on South African personnel was discontinued, however.

The official organs of local administration were also brought under tighter central control during this period. The few bodies that continued to permit some degree of local participation (district and village development committees) were increasingly politicized, membership being mainly restricted to loyal followers of the ruling party.

Similar efforts were made to politicize voluntary organizations such as cooperatives, women's groups, and trade unions. Compliant organizations received state patronage and support. Those that were less accommodating did not and were frequently harassed. An illustration of this is provided by the government's policy toward the trade union movement. In 1970 there were two main trade union federations in the country, the pro-BCP Basutoland Federation of Labour, representing about 12,000 members, and the pro-BNP Lesotho Council of Workers, reportedly representing about 3,000 (the real figure was most probably much lower—the UN and ILO mission of 1975 estimated LCW membership at about 400). Whereas the LCW could rely on government support and encouragement, the BFL, although not banned, experienced persistent harassment in the early 1970s, a fact revealed by the UN and ILO mission to investigate complaints about violations of trade union rights. According to the UN and ILO report, the detention and intimidation of BCP supporters, many of whom were also trade unionists, although not an infringement of trade union rights per se, was hardly conducive to a flourishing union movement. Nor was the dismissal at the government's behest of BCP members from public and private sector employment. The report also revealed evidence of political favoritism by the Lesotho Department of Labour in issuing employment cards almost exclusively to BNP supporters, and of the difficulties experienced by BFL-affiliated unions in obtaining government approval to hold meetings.[10]

The arbitrary nature of many of the techniques employed by the government to promote its preeminence provided ready ammunition for the regime's critics who saw in such actions clear evidence of an unrelenting trend toward authoritarian rule in the 1970s. Real as this trend was, it was nevertheless modified by certain deviations from the standard authoritarian pattern. The harassment of the opposition was accompanied neither by the banning of political parties (with the sole exception of the Communist party) nor by the declaration of a one-party state. The courts maintained a degree of independence from government interference and under Chief Justice Mapetla were not afraid to use this to critical effect. Save for a short period in 1970, the ban imposed on opposition publications was not extended to *Leselinyana*, the weekly mouthpiece of the LEC (formerly PEMS), whose columns provided an increasingly critical forum for the expression of antigovernment sentiment. The government's nationalization of the previously tripartite University of Botswana, Lesotho and Swaziland in 1975 was not accompanied, as many feared, by major encroachments on academic freedom, despite the fact that many students and staff were outspoken in their criticism of the regime.

Although these and other examples of the government's self-restraint are unlikely to provide much comfort to the innocent victims of the security forces and the Lebotho la Khotso and clearly the government's actions were no substitute for the restoration of the constitutional freedoms suspended in 1970, they do point to a somewhat paradoxical feature of Basotho political life in the period since 1970: the coexistence of repression in some areas with toleration in others. The reasons for this will be examined in more detail later, but of undoubted importance was Chief Jonathan's astuteness as a politician, which led him to the realization that might without at least some right could easily prove counterproductive. Although prepared to sanction the use of force when necessary, he was also alert to the advantages that more sophisticated techniques might confer, especially in helping to offset the declining legitimacy of his regime. This found expression over time in the adoption of a more conciliatory attitude toward the king and the opposition and of a less accommodating stance toward the Republic of South Africa.

In the aftermath of the 1970 coup, relations between the government and the king deteriorated rapidly, and governmental pressures for his abdication were only averted by intense opposition from the principal chiefs and by the king's agreement in April 1970 to go into exile in the Netherlands. But by the end of the year, Chief Jonathan was beginning to realize that the king's return might confer a welcome aura of legitimacy on the regime. Negotiations were therefore initiated, and on 4 December 1970 the King arrived home. Although his powers continued to be severely circumscribed, his return was accompanied by a noticeable reduction in tension, and his relations with the government were to prove far more cordial in the 1970s than they had been before.

In the early 1970s, this semi-rapprochement enabled Chief Jonathan to draw upon the monarch's support in his appeals for national unity and reconciliation. Although an obvious advantage, the king's backing by itself was insufficient, however, to ensure the success of such appeals, not least because many Basotho suspected that his support owed as much to duress as to consent. What was needed in addition was a tangible effort to accommodate the interests and views of the opposition parties. With this in mind, Chief Jonathan reopened negotiations with Mokhehle in 1972, having earlier prepared the way for such talks by releasing all political detainees and by purging from the government a number of hardliners opposed to reconciliation. Like the talks of 1970, however, these negotiations soon foundered. Mokhehle's demand for a genuine coalition government committed to the holding of early elections proved incompatible with Jonathan's insistence on a national government with some opposition representation but free from the divisive effects of party competition that a coalition government would inevitably entail.

To break this deadlock, the prime minister finally took unilateral action and announced plans for an interim National Assembly whose main task was to prepare a new constitution and in the meantime to serve as an interim legislature. Its 93 members were planned to include the 22 principal chiefs, 11 members nominated for distinguished service to the nation, and 60 members nominated from lists prepared by the major political parties, 34 of these from the BNP, 20 from the BCP, 4 from the MFP, and 2 from the UDP. The power of nomination, although officially vested in the king, would rest in practice with the prime minister. This would naturally enable the government to secure and maintain a comfortable majority, and it was largely for this reason that Mokhehle and his party executive denounced the assembly as a sham and refused to participate in it. Nevertheless, the MFP and UDP did accept nomination to the assembly, which first met in April 1973, as did a minority faction of the BCP led by the party's deputy leader, Gerard Ramoreboli. Although expelled by Mokhehle from the party for this action, the Ramoreboli faction refused to accept this decision and continued to claim legitimate rights to represent the BCP. The resulting confusion among the party's rank and file was exacerbated after the abortive 1974 uprising by splits within Mokhehle's external wing of the party and especially by the rift that occurred in January 1977 when Koenyama Chakela, the secretary general of the party, and other members of the executive committee attempted to oust Mokhehle from the leadership.

The participation of opposition elements in the assembly and the splits in the BCP did not lead, however, to an immediate end to criticism of the regime. On the contrary, Ramoreboli and the leaders of the MFP and UDP used the assembly in its early years as a forum for attacks on the government's shortcomings. Particular attention was focused on government corruption and nepotism, the dangers inherent in Chief Jonathan's new and hostile policy toward South Africa, and the government's failure to make satisfactory progress toward a return to constitutional rule. Although showing initial signs of overreacting to such censure, Chief Jonathan ultimately sought to counter it by co-optation rather than by confrontation. In November 1975 he announced the appointment to the Cabinet of Ramoreboli and the MFP's Patrick Lehloenya. Charles Mofeli, the outspoken leader of the UDP, was not initially included but by 1977 he too had been appointed to a ministerial position. There is little doubt that the co-optation of such leaders contributed in the period after 1975 to a reduction in the level of public criticism of the regime.

One of the most controversial aspects of government policy in the 1970s was the changing attitude of the regime toward South

Africa.[11] Although not accompanied by any fundamental reduction in Lesotho's economic dependence on the republic, the dramatic nature of the government's new stance was revealed in several directions— its increasingly hostile attacks on the system of apartheid, the suspension of its initiatives in support of dialogue between South Africa and Black Africa, its refusal to recognize the "independent" bantustans, its reduced dependence on South African personnel, its more assertive demands for the return of the Conquered Territories lost to the Free State in the wars of the 1860s, its more forthright support for the Southern African liberation movements, the hospitality provided for South African and particularly ANC refugees, and the diversification of its diplomatic ties to include the Communist bloc, much to Pretoria's displeasure.

One obvious reason for this break with past policy was Chief Jonathan's increasing appreciation of the advantages that could be obtained from a more critical stance toward Pretoria. The repeated attacks by Jonathan and other BNP leaders on the injustices of apartheid helped to undercut the BCP's previous monopoly of radical anti–South African sentiment. In addition, the government was able to use Pretoria's threatening reaction to such criticism as a convincing weapon in its appeals for national unity and as a means for diverting attention away from pressing domestic problems. Moreover, the regime's defiant stance toward South Africa was largely responsible for the dramatic increase in international recognition and assistance that was forthcoming in the 1970s. The rapid growth in foreign aid enabled the government to initiate a far more ambitious program of social and economic development than in the 1960s and by so doing to partially offset its declining level of popular support.

By the late 1970s, therefore, the government had clearly achieved some success in strengthening its control and credibility at the expense of the opposition. The prospects for the future were still far from certain, however. In the first place, although the rapid growth in foreign aid and Customs Union revenue had helped to facilitate a much faster rate of growth in certain sectors of the economy than had occurred hitherto, it had done little to alter Lesotho's fundmental position as an underdeveloped labor reserve or to alleviate many of the serious problems, economic and social, that resulted from this. With the population rising, agriculture remaining stagnant, and South African employers showing signs of reducing their demand for Basotho labor, the economic "boom" of the 1970s had every appearance of being a transient phenomenon.

Second, despite the many promises that were made, the government failed to take advantage of the relative calm that characterized the closing years of the 1970s to return the country to constitutional rule and to hold elections that, given the opposition's disarray, it had every chance of winning. The government also failed to respond favorably to the peace feelers put out by the exiled wing of the BCP. In summary, the government missed two obvious opportunities to resolve some of the bitter divisions that continued to plague Basotho politics.

Third, in the 1970s, disunity within the ranks of the ruling party was growing because of, among other complaints, dissatisfaction with what some regarded as Chief Jonathan's nepotism and autocratic control of the party and state apparatuses. Others felt antagonism toward his changing policy on South Africa and the Communist bloc. Although the prime minister managed to maintain his authority through a combination of purges and reshuffles,[12] there was little doubt that this internal dissension would continue to compound the already-onerous tasks with which he was confronted.

Fourth, in 1971, despite constant assurances by the Lesotho government that its more militant stance against apartheid need not necessarily threaten its close economic cooperation with South Africa, Chief Jonathan was warned by South African Prime Minister Vorster not to "tempt me too far."[13] This statement served as an early notice of the dangers inherent in the regime's new policy toward Pretoria— dangers that were made vividly clear in 1982 and 1983.

And finally, although the BCP had certainly been weakened by divisions within its ranks, it clearly remained a powerful force in the land, and Mokhehle continued to command the support of many Basotho. With its overtures for negotiation spurned by the government, there were signs that the exiled wing of the party was preparing once again for armed confrontation. In May 1979 these signs became reality when explosions rocked Maseru. Shattering more than the windows of the town's main post office, they also destroyed the calm that had prevailed for the past few years and inaugurated a new era of turbulence in the political life of the kingdom.

Destabilization and Dissension, 1979–1984

Responsibility for the explosions was claimed by the Lesotho Liberation Army (LLA), the military arm of Mokhehle's wing of the exiled BCP. The escalation of violent conflict by the LLA, together with Pretoria's related efforts to destabilize Chief Jonathan's regime, has come to dominate the political life of Lesotho in the period since 1979.[14]

Despite divisions within its ranks and defections from them,[15] the LLA has mounted a concerted campaign aimed at the violent overthrow of the Jonathan government. Bombings have become an everyday part of life in the kingdom, with targets including the airport and abattoir, the Hilton (now Lesotho Sun) and Holiday Inn hotels, fuel depots and electricity substations, and diplomatic agencies such as the U.S. Cultural Centre. Such attacks have been accompanied by military raids on police stations and border posts, by mortar attacks on the barracks of the Lesotho Paramilitary Force (LPF), and by attempts to assassinate leading members of both the ruling party and BCP factions opposed to Mokhehle. The most prominent figures to have been murdered so far, both in mid-1982, were the BNP Minister of Works, Jobo Rampeta, and the BCP Secretary-General, Koenyama Chakela, who had earlier returned to the country under the government's 1980 amnesty offer.

Although the LLA claims to be operating from mountain bases within Lesotho itself with arms captured from the security forces, the government's own assertion that the organization is based in South Africa and its bantustans has far more credibility. This version is supported not only by LLA defectors but also by numerous eye-witness accounts from both sides of the border of LLA movements into and out of the kingdom. It also seems certain that Mokhehle has been directing operations from the Republic since 1981 when he was expelled from Botswana and Zambia.

If the LLA is based in the Republic, then obviously the question of South African collusion is raised. Although such collusion has been denied by both the LLA and Pretoria, it seems inconceivable that a guerrilla force, equipped with sophisticated arms and explosives, could operate from South African territory without at least the passive complicity of the authorities. Chief Jonathan has charged that South African involvement has been more than passive and that Pretoria has in fact armed, trained, and directed the LLA, which "is nothing other than a code name for South Africa's war operations against Lesotho." Such a charge is difficult to substantiate conclusively, but there certainly is considerable evidence that Pretoria has at least armed if not orchestrated the LLA.

Equally important as determining the degree of complicity is determining an explanation for it. This is not too hard to find. South Africa's support for the LLA in Lesotho, as well as for movements such as the MNR (also known as Renamo—Résistance nacional mocambicana; Mozambique National Resistance) in Mozambique and UNITA (União nacional de Independência total de Angola; National Union for Total Independence of Angola) in Angola, reflects a move-ment away from its disappointing détente initiatives of the early 1970s to more forceful actions aimed at securing its interests in the subcontinent through the destabilization of the economic and political systems of its neighbors. Destabilization, of course, if pushed too far, might result in chaos rather than instability, which could well prove counterproductive to South Africa's designs. Probably for this reason, collusion with the LLA has fallen short of total support for that organization's prime objective of toppling the present Lesotho government from power. Pretoria's aim has not been the replacement of Jonathan by Mokhehle per se. Rather Pretoria is trying to force Jonathan's government to withdraw its support of the ANC, to reverse its policy toward the Communist bloc, and to adopt a more favorable attitude toward South Africa's homelands policy and proposal for a Constellation of Southern African States (CONSAS).

In an effort to realize these objectives, the South African government has not only provided a degree of controlled support for the LLA, it has also pursued its own initiatives. These culminated in the brutal raid on Maseru on 9 December 1982 in which twenty-seven ANC refugees, three South African visitors, and twelve Lesotho citizens died. This raid was allegedly undertaken to destroy ANC bases in Lesotho from which terrorist attacks could be launched against South Africa. As there was no evidence for the existence of such bases, however, the real purpose of the raid and of the massive propaganda campaign in the South African media that accompanied it was to warn the government and people of Lesotho, and of other nearby states, of the costs of defying Pretoria's wishes.

Although the raid provoked widespread international protest, reflected in the rare unanimity of the UN Security Council's condemnation, South African threats against Lesotho continued unabated. Pretoria refused to rule out the possibility of further raids and warned that economic reprisals might also be forthcoming. They followed in May 1983 when the South African authorities began to impose serious delays on the transit of people and goods at its borders with the kingdom.

The actions of the LLA and South Africa have succeeded in destabilizing Chief Jonathan's regime, not only by presenting it with the most serious challenge yet to its security but also by exacerbating the intractable problems already confronting it. Economically, the LLA and South Africa have inflicted infrastructural damage, discouraged tourism and investment, and compelled the Lesotho government to divert scarce resources from urgent development tasks to defense and security, whose share of the budget has risen from 8.4 percent in 1980 to 22 percent in 1983 and 1984. Politically, they have served to enhance the level of popular frustration directed against the Jonathan regime. For although the government has been able to exploit South

African and LLA aggression by using it to foster national unity and to accentuate the divisions already prevalent within the BCP, these points in Chief Jonathan's favor have been offset by a growing feeling among many Basotho that they are being asked to pay too high a price (in terms of the disruption of their daily lives) for national pride, the protection of refugees, and the ability to pursue an independent foreign policy. Such frustrations have found expression in the increasing domestic criticism of the government's policy toward South Africa and the Communist bloc not only from opposition leaders such as the UDP's Charles Mofeli, who returned to the attack with renewed vengeance after his dismissal from the Cabinet in 1981, but also from within the ranks of the ruling party itself. One of the most prominent critics has been C. D. Molapo, the former and influential minister of information and foreign affairs, whose well-known opposition to Chief Jonathan's foreign policy culminated in his resignation from the Cabinet in June 1983. This did little to dispel rumors of a major Cabinet split that had circulated for some time and were especially rife at the time of the Prime Minister's month-long visit to China, North Korea, and Eastern Europe in May and June 1983. The increasing antagonism shown by the Catholic Church to Jonathan's relations with the Communist bloc accentuated dissension within the predominantly Catholic ranks of the ruling party.

The Lesotho government's response to these problems, as in the past, was based on a somewhat vacillating combination of repression and reconciliation toward its domestic opponents and a similar combination of defiance and accommodation toward Pretoria. The regime's renewed recourse to force was reflected in the rapid expansion of the country's defense and security forces, spearheaded by the Lesotho Paramilitary Force (established in 1980 to replace the PMU), and their increasing use to counter the activities of LLA guerrillas and to intimidate their sympathizers within the kingdom. In addition, the country's security laws were tightened and extended, most notably by the Internal Security Act of 1982, which conferred even greater powers on the authorities than its 1974 predecessor. The government claimed with some justification that such measures were necessary to deal with the challenge posed by the LLA and South Africa. Nevertheless, growing internal and international concern was expressed that the government frequently went further than the interests of national security demanded. Abuses of the security laws—most notably the ill-treatment and torture of detainees—were sharply criticized, for example, in the reports of a working party of the University Senate in 1982 and of an Amnesty International mission that visited Lesotho in 1981.

Equally disturbing were the activities of a death squad, known as the Koeoko, which was held responsible for a number of assassination attempts on prominent critics of the regime. The squad's most notable victim so far has been Edgar Motuba, the outspoken editor of the antigovernment publication *Leselinyana*, who was murdered in September 1982. The government's denials of complicity, accompanied as they have been so far by a total failure to bring any Koeoko members to justice, did little to allay popular suspicion that the death squad is in fact a secret unit of the security forces.

Recognizing, as in the past, that the unrestrained use of force could easily result in a crucial reduction in the level of internal and external support for the regime, Chief Jonathan attempted to offset these excesses by extending his efforts at reconciliation. Opposition parties and publications like *Leselinyana*, although clearly harassed, were not suppressed and continued to provide an important forum for dissent. In addition, through its 1980 Amnesty Act, the government reversed its former refusal to allow members of the exiled BCP to return home. Chakela and other BCP exiles who were opposed to Mokhehle and the LLA took advantage of this act to return to the kingdom.

Such tactics, although useful, were by no means sufficient to curtail LLA activity, to enhance significantly the popularity and legitimacy of the regime, or to assuage the misgivings of foreign aid donors concerning human rights violations. More determined efforts would have to be made if the situation was not to get out of hand, and these were eventually forthcoming. In May 1983, after years of unfulfilled promises, the government introduced in the National Assembly proposals for elections and a new constitution.[16] These proposals were paralleled by plans for increased popular participation in a reorganized and decentralized system of local government, a move undoubtedly prompted by the need to reverse the common alienation from the existing centralized system that had rendered many local communities fertile breeding grounds for LLA activity and support.

Whether these changes will succeed in leading the country toward a peaceful return to democratic rule is far from certain, especially as Mokhehle and the LLA have so far responded negatively to the government's invitation to cease hostilities and return to Lesotho to contest the elections.[17] On the contrary, they have declared their intention of stepping up their campaign and of disrupting the elections if they do take place. If this happens, one strong possibility is that the government will postpone the return to constitutional rule, and the instability so prevalent in recent years will continue unabated.

One other possibility, however, is that Chief Jonathan might agree to some form of rapprochement with South Africa under which his government will concede to some of Pretoria's demands if South Africa will assist in curbing the LLA and neutralizing its threat to disrupt the elections. Such a move might realize additional advantages by helping to heal the divisions within the ruling party and to promote closer economic cooperation between the two countries on such projects as the Highlands Water Scheme.

Rapprochement, however, clearly involves costs as well as benefits. The government would inevitably risk losing face and, perhaps more important, the international respectability and material support that its assertive policy toward South Africa has earned it over the past decade. It has been the awareness of such costs that has undoubtedly restrained Chief Jonathan from capitulating to Pretoria's pressure since 1979. Such defiance reached its peak in the aftermath of the South African raid of 9 December 1982 and was rewarded by even greater international sympathy and support, reflected in the UN's approval of a M50 million program of economic assistance to be devoted to projects—such as the new International Airport—that might lessen the country's dependence on her powerful neighbor.

By mid-1983, however, with South Africa's economic blockade of the country's borders beginning to tell, the pendulum began to swing from defiance to accommodation. In August the Lesotho government began to place pressure on about 500 ANC refugees, regarded by Pretoria as "politically active," to submit to "voluntary" evacuation under the auspices of the UN. By mid-September about 40 had left Lesotho, and a further 200 were expected to follow shortly.[18] This action paved the way for a closer understanding between Lesotho and South Africa, evidenced in December 1983 by the arrest of eight suspected members of the LLA by the South African authorities, and by the visit to Lesotho of a delegation of South African officials for talks with their Lesotho counterparts about closer cooperation in both the economic and security fields.

Although undoubtedly contributing to a reduction in tension between the two countries, such developments should not be seen as heralding a return to the harmonious relations of the 1960s. For although Chief Jonathan has been prepared under pressure to make concessions on the refugee issue, it is likely that he will not go much further to meet Pretoria's demands for a reversal of opposition to the bantustans and CONSAS and of efforts to extend ties with the Communist bloc. Such policies have become so inextricably linked with his own reputation, with the government's international standing, and with plans for economic development that they could be abandoned with only the greatest difficulty.

Exactly how far Pretoria will press such demands and how resolutely Chief Jonathan will resist them cannot be predicted with any degree of certainty, of course. But what is likely is that South Africa will refuse either to take steps to curb the LLA completely or to desist entirely from its own destabilization efforts until more concessions have been wrung. If Jonathan proves reluctant to yield to such pressure, as he undoubtedly will, the suspicion and hostility that has marked the relations between the two countries in the past will almost inevitably recur, with obvious implications for the regime's stability.

One final and by no means implausible possibility is that Chief Jonathan may be ousted from power in a palace coup staged by right-wing elements within the ruling party with support from South Africa. Rumors of such a coup have circulated freely for some time in Lesotho, and barely two weeks after the visit of the South African delegation in December 1983 the government announced that it had uncovered a plot, involving South African mercenaries, aimed at toppling the prime minister.

The prime minister's chances of surviving such plots will depend to a considerable extent on his ability to retain the loyalty of the armed forces, which are rumored to be split into pro-Jonathan and anti-Jonathan factions. Should he survive, the suspicion of South African involvement will almost inevitably lead to a deterioration in relations. If, however, a coup succeeds in removing him from power, his replacement will probably prove more accommodating to Pretoria's demands. But as this in turn would undoubtedly result in a loss of internal and international credibility, the prospects for a return to democratic rule, as well as for an end to the cleavages that have divided the nation, could well prove just as inauspicious as under the present leadership.

CHANGING PATTERNS OF POLITICAL CLEAVAGE

During a speech in 1970, Chief Jonathan observed that "one of the greatest advantages we have as a nation is the possession of one culture, one language, and the absence of tribalism."[19] Such assets, however, have clearly failed to prevent the emergence of serious cleavages that divide the nation. The cleavages result from growing social stratification, regional disparities, differential access to education, religious rivalries, divergent attitudes toward Lesotho's apartheid neighbor, as well as a variety of personal and dynastic disputes. The differing ideologies and social composition of the two major nationalist parties, the BCP and BNP, that contested the struggle for independence reflect the cleavages in Lesotho's milieu. Since 1966, the rivalry between these two parties—or more precisely between the dominant factions within them associated with Mokhehle and Jonathan, respectively— has grown deeper and more acrimonious. Yet the premises on which this rivalry has been based have undoubtedly undergone considerable modification, and a number of cleavages have clearly lost much of their former salience in explaining the persistence of interparty strife.

In the first place, although polarization along religious lines has far from disappeared, the divisive effects of religious competition have been reduced since independence. Alarmed by the damaging consequences of continuing party conflict, the country's main churches have shown increasing signs of burying past differences in favor of joint appeals for moderation and restraint. Such interdenominational cooperation has been further encouraged by the establishment of a number of ecumenical organizations, such as the Lesotho Christian Council, which in Richard Weisfelder's words has "drawn the major Churches together in mutual efforts to provide a Christian input towards economic and social progress."[20] In addition, the growing hostility demonstrated by the Catholic Church, particularly in the columns of its weekly publication *Moeletsi oa Basotho*, toward the government's extension of diplomatic links with the Communist bloc has seriously weakened the harmony of interest that formerly prevailed between the ruling party and the Catholic hierarchy. Moreover, although many BCP supporters feel that they are still subjected to discrimination on religious grounds, the evidence suggests that a Protestant background alone is no longer such an impediment to political and economic advancement as it was in the past.

Second, with the gradual transformation of the BNP's rural outlook and traditional base, the earlier distinction between the class and regional composition of the two main parties has become increasingly blurred. Although the BCP is still very much a party of the urban middle class, the same is true to a considerable extent nowadays of the BNP. Eighteen years of managing the modern, largely urban-based institutions of the state, of exposing themselves and their children to the advantages of Western education, and of realizing the possibilities for private accumulation that their privileged political and bureaucratic positions have conferred have given many of the BNP's leaders the same middle-class aspirations and tastes that were once the exclusive prerogative of their political adversaries. This transformation has been most noticeable among commoners, but the BNP's chiefly elements have also been affected. As we saw earlier, their political and economic power rests far less today on their traditional status and far more on their position as salaried functionaries of the state, as well as on their agricultural and commercial ventures. One result of these developments is that the chieftainship in general no longer provides the same source of interparty friction as it did in the past. Nor does the position of the paramount chief, King Moshoeshoe II. With the gradual acceptance of his limited role as head of state and the consequent improvement in his relations with the government, the Monarchy has ceased to be such a contentious issue as it was in the past, a fact which undoubtedly helps to explain the declining significance of the royalist party, the MFP.

Third, with the possible exceptions of South Africa and the Communist bloc, toward which the divergent attitudes of the two parties have undergone a total and somewhat opportunistic reversal since 1966, it is difficult today to identify major ideological points of difference between Mokhehle's BCP and Jonathan's BNP. Although the BNP has succeeded in a number of ways in modernizing its image, it still remains committed to a rather conservative belief in the advantages of evolutionary change, a philosophy that not surprisingly has led to few fundamental alterations in the structures of external dependency and internal inequality. As a result of this Mokhehle and his wing of the BCP continue to retain considerable support among the ranks of the underprivileged, who correctly feel that the ruling party has done very little for them since 1966. What seems clear, however, is that this continuing support rests to a large extent on an unrealistic, though undoubtedly genuine, belief in the BCP's capacity to represent a viable and more radical alternative.

Had the BCP taken its rightful place as the governing party in 1970, it would have been faced with the same formidable constraints that confronted the BNP. More important perhaps, the accession to power of a BCP government would have undoubtedly revealed the serious ideological limitations that have always characterized the party. For although its manifestos showed greater concern than those of the BNP for the plight of the underprivileged, there was little evidence that this concern was matched by any coherent strategy for tackling the root causes of poverty, a fact belatedly acknowledged by Koenyama Chakela, the party's secretary-general, in an interview in 1980.[21] One of the clearest illustrations of this point, as well as of the narrow ideological gap between the two parties, is contained in Mokhehle's 1972 statement of the party's objectives:

> We are, to a certain extent, socialist, but we are definitely not in favour of a drastic shake-up of the present order of things. We would insist

on an evolutionary socialism and because Lesotho is already largely socialist, this change wouldn't be so drastic as is feared. Although our social structure and even, to a certain extent, the policies of the present Government are socialistically inclined, we would want to move towards a true socialism which would not necessarily mean the abolition of private property and free enterprise.[22]

This ambiguous understanding of socialism was partly responsible for the split in the late 1950s and early 1960s between Mokhehle and ANC elements within the BCP. The increasing antagonism toward the ANC's more militant insistence on a fundamental socialist transformation of society has proved one of the few consistent threads in Mokhehle's ideological worldview, rendering his subsequent collusion with Pretoria less paradoxical than it might appear at first sight.

If cleavages due to religion, regions, rural or urban base, class base, and ideology no longer provide an adequate explanation for the bitter rivalry that continues to characterize relations between the two parties, then the question that arises is what does? Perhaps the most satisfactory explanation lies in the dynamics of the competitive struggle for power. Since 1970, the BCP leaders' resentment and frustration have resulted less from their concern with the shortcomings of the BNP's policies and more from the fact that they were deprived of their rightful opportunity to assume the reins of government by Jonathan's unconstitutional usurpation of power. With the government's reluctance to contemplate fresh elections or genuine constitutional change and with its frequent use of strong-arm tactics against BCP supporters, this frustration intensified and led ultimately to the abortive coup attempt of 1974 and more recently to the LLA's violent campaign to overthrow the regime. At the same time the ruling party has demonstrated an equally strong determination to hold on to power at almost any cost. Always fearful of the loss of the political and economic privileges that the transfer of power to the BCP would necessarily entail, the BNP leaders have become increasingly concerned that this would probably be accompanied by reprisals inflicted in retaliation for their own past excesses.

This somewhat Machiavellian interpretation is not intended to imply that deep-seated ideological differences based on religion, class, and other social divisions are no longer of any significance in understanding the complexities of political life in Lesotho. Although losing much of their former salience in accounting for the persistence of interparty strife, such factors continue to help explain the growth of intraparty factionalism. Divergent attitudes toward South Africa, for example, have not only been responsible for splitting the ruling party in recent years but were also a factor in the serious rift that occurred within the external wing of the BCP in January 1977, when Chakela's faction disassociated itself from Mokhehle's policy of accommodation with Pretoria.

What the above analysis does suggest, however, is that new political organizations may be required if the current divisions within Basotho society are to be reflected more accurately than seems possible within the existing party framework. There are signs that such organizations may soon be forthcoming. Since the early 1980s there has been speculation that a third force might be established to offer a more radical alternative to that provided by the established parties. This would be constituted through an alliance between sections of the intelligentsia (disillusioned with the lack of commitment shown by both the BCP and BNP to genuine social and economic reform) and working class organizations, such as the Lesotho Mineworkers Union, that had remained unaffiliated to either of the two partisan trade union federations.[23]

A fourth force of the extreme right emerged in February 1984 in the shape of the Basotho Democratic Alliance (BDA). Led by Phoka Chaolane, a disaffected member of Ramoreboli's internal BCP faction, this party is a rather ill-defined amalgamation of cliques within other parties who oppose the "Communist" inclinations of the government and favor a more accommodating policy toward South Africa. The first president of the BDA was C. D. Molapo, who had resigned his ministerial post in 1983 in disagreement with the government's policy toward South Africa. The BDA was formed after visits by Chaolane, Molapo, and others to South Africa for talks with Pik Botha, the foreign minister, and obviously can count on Pretoria's support. The Catholic Church may also lend some backing.

The impact of the BDA cannot yet be assessed but is unlikely to be substantial until its organizational aims are clarified more effectively. The BDA will undoubtedly have to face the government-controlled media's accusations that it is little more than a South African creation, designed to further divide and destabilize the kingdom. In addition, with the possible exception of the UDP, all existing parties have disowned the new organization. The internal wing of Mokhehle's faction, for example, has vigorously denied that Chaolane in any way represents their interests. The UDP's Charles Mofeli is already showing signs of distancing himself and the UDP from the BDA and instead is cultivating his own independent and well-known links with Pretoria.

POLITICAL CONSTRAINTS ON DEVELOPMENT

Although Chief Jonathan's government has made more determined efforts in recent years in the development field, these have done little so far to overcome the low levels of agricultural productivity, industrial growth, and domestic employment creation; to offset the continuing reliance on migrant labor and the economic dependence on South Africa; or to alleviate many of the social problems associated with Lesotho's position as an underdeveloped labor reserve. That this is so is not altogether surprising, given the magnitude of the problems that have confronted the regime and over which it has had little or no control. Nevertheless, the evidence suggests that the government's disappointing record can also be attributed in part to important political and administrative shortcomings of its own making that have constrained its ability to frame and implement an effective program of social and economic development.[24]

In a speech in the Lesotho National Assembly in 1968, Ntsu Mokhehle accused the government of failing to develop a coherent philosophy and likened it to a ship without a compass. At that time the country's leaders could have legitimately claimed that this was inevitable, given their own inexperience in office, the acute shortage of qualified personnel, the lack of an effective planning machinery, and the paucity of statistics on which to base their development programs. Today they would have no such excuse. Eighteen years in power have enabled the ruling party to increase its own expertise and to train personnel for development tasks. In addition, a well-staffed planning office has been established (the Central Planning and Development Office, CPDO), whose numerous reports, together with those of ministerial planning units, the Bureau of Statistics, and the various aid agencies, have supplied a steadily expanding stream of information on which to base policy. Even so, Mokhehle's observation is in many ways as accurate today as it was fifteen years ago. Although having identified the broad objectives of development (stated in the Second Five-Year Development Plan as economic growth, social justice, maximum domestic employment, and economic independence), the government has failed to provide a comprehensive and systematic strategy through which these might be realized. Instead, development initiatives have tended to be piecemeal and haphazard; therefore, it is not surprising that they have been able to do little more than ameliorate some of the symptoms of Lesotho's contemporary malaise and have left the underlying causes largely unresolved.

The development planning that has taken place has also been characterized by a number of limitations. Of particular importance has been the lack of direction and coordination. The obvious body to have assumed these functions would have been the CPDO. But as David Hirschmann has shown, it has been prevented from doing so by a combination of its own internal defects and rivalry from other ministries involved in development. Instead, the CPDO's main functions continue to be those of eliciting aid and preparing five-year plans rather than controlling or even influencing policy.[25] Major projects have been introduced by individual ministries or the Cabinet without any reference to the CPDO; some projects have even been initiated in defiance of strong CPDO reservations concerning the projects' viability.[26] As a result, the planning process has been characterized more by interdepartmental competition than by collaboration, and the one body able to exercise a degree of coordination—the Cabinet— has had neither the time nor the expertise to coordinate effectively.

Equally important has been the lack of popular involvement. Few mechanisms exist for soliciting the needs or the views of the supposed beneficiaries of the government's development efforts. And the few institutions that might have contributed in this direction (District and Village Development Committees, or local BNP branches, for example) have been used far more often to convey official policy to the people than to transmit popular opinion to the authorities.

The lack of a coherent and coordinated development strategy has been dramatized by the growth in foreign aid that has occurred during the 1970s, premised more on Lesotho's unique geopolitical situation than on criteria of absolute economic need. The seemingly inexhaustible supply of external assistance has undoubtedly fostered a sense of complacency on the part of Lesotho's policymakers by allowing them to escape from the hard choices and serious thinking that a smaller volume of aid might have necessitated. Further, the aid agencies have assumed much of the responsibility for establishing Lesotho's development priorities, because the government's role has been confined largely to providing lists of projects from which the donors make their selections. When such shopping lists fail to meet with donor approval, they have been hurriedly replaced, for example, as when the agricultural chapter of the Third Five-Year Development Plan was redrafted with explicit donor participation.

This is not to say that Lesotho would have been better off without any aid at all. But in the absence of a locally framed and popularly sanctioned strategy into which foreign assistance could be dovetailed, what does seem evident is that many externally funded projects, particularly the ambitious area-based agricultural projects of the 1970s, have yielded minimal long-term returns from the large amounts of aid invested in them.[27] During the US$15 million Thaba-

Bosiu project, for example, production per acre actually decreased between 1973 and 1977. Meanwhile, production costs rose and incomes stagnated, despite rising prices for the main crops produced.[28]

Problems of policy formation have been paralleled by a number of major drawbacks in the implementation of the government's development schemes. In the first place, although the introduction of officially sponsored training programs has helped to alleviate the critical shortage of qualified personnel their effective utilization continues to be impeded by high turnover of staff and by the government's inability to provide sufficient incentives to attract personnel away from Maseru to the more remote districts where their skills are urgently needed. Perhaps the worst obstacle to effective utilization of personnel, however, has been the government's tendency to subordinate professionalism to political loyalty. The most extreme manifestation of this occurred in the early 1970s when hundreds of BCP supporters were removed from the civil service. Although some of these were subsequently reinstated, their chances of promotion, especially to the higher ranks of the administration, have continued to be limited on political grounds. But so too have the promotion prospects of many able and qualified Basotho who, although not opposition supporters, have nevertheless lacked the political connections or the willingness to display the necessary degree of uncritical support for the ruling party that in many ways remain the keys to rapid bureaucratic advancement in Lesotho. The effects on civil service morale and performance have clearly been very serious.[29]

Second, the absence of coordination in the framing of development policies has been matched by a similar deficiency in their execution. Responsibility for coordination at the local level was vested until recently in the district administrators (DAs), who were normally too preoccupied with routine administrative duties to devote sufficient time to this function. It was for this reason that the position of district development secretary was created in 1970 to assist the DAs in coordinating development programs at the district level. But despite the CPDO's suggestion that qualified graduates be appointed to these positions, the Cabinet ultimately opted for reliable party stalwarts who lacked the necessary training and experience to fulfill their role effectively, a fact belatedly acknowledged by the government itself in its Second Five-Year Development Plan.[30] Even so, had the CPDO's advice been heeded, the situation probably would not have improved dramatically. For although the district administrators and development secretaries, as well as the District Development Committees that were established to assist them, were given the responsibility for coordination, they were not provided with the necessary authority to ensure that it actually took place. Instead, the local officials of the ministries involved in development (Agriculture, Education, Finance, Health, Interior, and Rural Development) have continued to be accountable to their ministerial headquarters in Maseru rather than to any local coordinating person or group. In the absence of any insistence by the Cabinet to integrate their activities, these ministries have largely acted independently of each other.

Of late, the government has taken some steps to try and remedy this situation. In 1980, district administrators were replaced by district coordinators who, on paper at least, were given greater powers and status. In addition, the Ministry of Rural Development has been assigned a leading role in what is planned to be a more effective integrated approach to development efforts in the rural areas. Although it is too early to assess the outcome of these changes, most informed opinion suggests that by themselves they are unlikely to overcome the long history of ministerial resistance to collaboration.

Third, through the ruling party's efforts to consolidate its power by politicizing local government organs and voluntary associations and bringing them under tighter central control, it has discouraged the popular participation that is so vital to the implementation of any effective program of social and economic development. Although the recent emphasis on decentralization suggests a commitment to the reversal of this trend, the government's numerous references to this issue have as yet been accompanied by only a few institutional changes through which popular involvement might be increased, and these are proving difficult to implement. An illustration of the difficulties is the lack of progress in establishing locally elected land committees (to which land allocation powers were transferred under the 1979 Land Act) because of opposition from the chiefs.

Finally, the problems of implementation have been seriously compounded by financial mismanagement and corruption. In 1964 the British Colonial Office observed that the standards of accounting in Basutoland were the worst it had come across in any territory for many years.[31] If anything, the period since independence has witnessed a deterioration in this respect. According to the *Report of the Auditor-General on the Public Accounts of Lesotho* for the three years ending 31 March 1978, the decade from 1968 to 1978

has witnessed a progressive decline and laxity in the management of the financial affairs of the Government. . . . Widescale financial indiscipline has led to disregard of financial regulations and instructions and has culminated in the breakdown of accounting controls that has reached catastrophic dimensions in recent years. Inbuilt safeguards against financial irregularities have been vitiated, and this has presented opportunities for the perpetuation of peculation [embezzlement] and fraud which have escaped early detection.[32]

The report was not completed until 1982 owing to considerable and not altogether surprising delays experienced by the auditor-general in obtaining submissions from the various government departments. Its 118 pages present a scathing indictment of the government's financial ineptitude and of the extensive misuse and embezzlement of public funds. As the misappropriation of those funds tied to foreign aid received particular attention, the report must have caused the aid agencies to reflect seriously on the continuing value of their development assistance.

The constraints on development outlined above are not unique to Lesotho, of course, and exist in varying degrees in most if not all developing countries. Their very pervasiveness has in turn led scholars such as Samuel P. Huntington to view them as independent variables, reflecting a general administrative malaise and capable of explaining phenomena such as the political instability prevalent in so many Third World countries.[33] However, such a view overlooks the fact that these constraints themselves require further explanation. Such an explanation should be rooted in the nature and role of the postcolonial state in Lesotho, and it is to this question that we can now turn our attention.

THE NATURE AND ROLE OF THE STATE

Interest in the concept of the state[34] has experienced a major revival in recent years, especially among scholars of a Marxist persuasion. Attention has been focused on the dynamics of the capitalist state in general and of its postcolonial or neocolonial variant in particular.[35] Few studies have been conducted, however, on the Lesotho state, and the one major attempt to explore this issue, that made by John D. Holm,[36] has been offered as an explicit alternative to both Marxist and liberal-pluralist paradigms.

In his detailed account of the state and rural development in Botswana and Lesotho, Holm contends that, far from being responsible to dominant internal or external classes (the Marxist view) or swamped by a plurality of vested interests, based on both class and nonclass forces (the pluralist view), the state in Lesotho has in many ways become the dominant force in society, pursuing objectives that are independent of and frequently at variance with those of other groups and classes. The principal objective has been the self-aggrandizement of the holders of state power, whether motivated simply by political ambition and economic greed, or by more complex desires to leave a mark on posterity. This goal has been realized through the rapid expansion of state and parastatal institutions and their increasing penetration into all areas of social, economic, and political life.

In the process, alternative sources of power have been steadily eroded. The churches have been forced to yield much of their control over education to the state. The chiefs have been stripped of most of their former privileges. So too have the European and Indian traders. And voluntary associations, from cooperatives to trade unions, have been increasingly politicized and subjected to state direction. Far from controlling the state or making successful demands on it, such groups have come to depend on state sufferance and support for their very existence and for whatever influence they continue to wield. Even external interests, particularly those represented by the principal aid donors, have been able to exert little pressure. In the absence of any clear idea of what to do with all the money they have to spend, the aid agencies have largely fallen in with the government's plans, irrespective of any reservations they might secretly hold concerning the utility and viability of the plans.

Holm's analysis is rooted, of course, in a long and diverse tradition of scholarship (from Weber to Friedman) that has come to view the state as an exploitative agency in its own right. Such a view presents problems for pluralists and Marxists alike. The pluralist notion of the state as a mediator of the struggles that arise between competing interest groups loses much of its relevance in situations like that in Lesotho where the state itself has become the major interest group in society. At the same time, once it is acknowledged that state power can exist independently of and at variance with class power, serious questions are directed to Marxist theory, which has long regarded classes as the only effective source of economic and political power.

Marxist scholars do not acknowledge this, but their explanations of the continuing importance of class determination in situations where the state has clearly become an overriding force in society, although providing undoubted insights at times, have frequently raised more problems than they have resolved. The argument, for example, that the state, or those persons it consists of, in such circumstances has in fact become the ruling class—i.e., the argument that the bureaucratic bourgeoisie is the dominant class—applies only if this class is in a position to determine the process of economic reproduction in society, a condition that is rare in most Third World countries, where this process continues to lie in many ways in the hands of external interests.

Slightly more revealing, at first sight, is the concept of relative autonomy, popularized in the writings of Nicos Poulantzas and his rapidly growing band of disciples.[37] This argues that the independence of the state from control by any single section or fraction of the economically ruling class is in fact essential to the state's primary function—namely, maintaining the necessary social cohesion for unimpeded continuation of capital accumulation and class domination by the ruling class as a whole. So long as such cohesion is apparent in any given society, the state (irrespective of its own class interests and composition) must by definition be acting in the interests of the economically ruling class, however inimical some of its actions might be to the interests of individual fractions of it. Although superficially appealing, this view is revealed on closer inspection to be in many ways tautological and devoid of real explanatory power.[38]

In spite of this, it would be unwise in the Lesotho case, if not more generally, to overestimate the value of statist conceptions such as that advocated by Holm or to discard Marxist interpretations entirely. Although in many ways enlightening, Holm's study quite clearly exaggerates the extent to which social groups and classes in Lesotho have been subordinated to state power. According to his own evidence, the chiefs, for example, have frequently been able to frustrate various legislative attempts to curtail their powers, particularly over land allocation. Nevertheless, he fails to modify his conclusions accordingly. In addition, his argument that the growing volume of aid has not been accompanied by a commensurate increase in the leverage exerted by the aid donors fails to square not only with the picture presented earlier in this chapter, but also with some of his own data. His case study of the Cooperative Crop Production Program (the predecessor of the present and much-vaunted Food Self-Sufficiency Program) shows that although this project was assigned major priority by the government, not a single donor could be found to fund it. Moreover, his unsubstantiated assertion that European trading groups have been deprived by the state of much of their former power is also belied by the evidence, not least by the sacking in 1975 of Joel Moitse, the Cabinet minister responsible for commerce and industry, for his specific advocacy of a more aggressive stance toward such groups.

This last point leads to one of the most important limitations of Holm's analysis, especially as a viable alternative to Marxist approaches, which is his silence on the question of the relationship between the state and foreign capital. Given that the crucial role assigned to the continuing dominance of the latter forms one of the few common themes in Marxist interpretations of the neocolonial state, this is clearly an important omission. Had Holm focused on this issue, he could have mentioned that the Lesotho state has made efforts since independence to reduce its reliance on South African capital and to create greater flexibility by diversifying its links with countries farther afield. Whatever autonomy this has afforded the state should not be exaggerated, however, especially as a number of efforts to attract more diverse forms of foreign investment—a Japanese motor assembly plant, an Italian shoe factory, and a West German television assembly plant—were ultimately abandoned in the face of pressure from Pretoria.[39]

What is required to better understand the Lesotho state is an integrated analysis that acknowledges the importance of the social composition, motivations, and methods of the holders of state power. Further, such an analysis must acknowledge that the class interests of those controlling the state are formed and realized not in a vacuum, but subject to shaping and constraints because of objective conditions that result from Lesotho's position as an underdeveloped and dependent labor reserve within the regional political economy of southern Africa.[40]

The starting point for such an analysis would be the weak position, in relation to both internal and external forces, of the governing class (to borrow Poulantzas's terminology if not his theoretical framework as a whole) that assumed control of the state apparatus at independence. Of particular importance was its lack of access to the limited but nevertheless crucial opportunities for indigenous capitalist accumulation that were largely monopolized by the BCP opposition. Unable to do battle immediately with foreign capital, the governing class could at least try to strengthen its position with respect to the BCP's educated and commercial supporters. This it has attempted to do both by consolidating its own power and by neutralizing the ability of its opponents to challenge and disrupt its hegemony. We have already examined some of the techniques used to achieve these twin objectives: the politicization and centralization of state institutions and voluntary organizations, the denial of effective constitutional mechanisms for the articulation of opposition interests and grievances, and the somewhat paradoxical combination of intimidation and co-optation of opposition leaders.

At the same time, the rapid expansion of state institutions and the ability to offer increasingly attractive bureaucratic salaries have enabled the governing class to broaden its basis of support by incorporating what Michaela von Freyhold has called "supportive classes": groups that do not control the state but which benefit from it.[41] In the Lesotho context these have been drawn largely from sections of the heterogeneous petty bourgeoisie and from the lower ranks of the chieftainship. In maintaining the loyalty of such groups and in sustaining its own cohesion, the governing class has also been able to utilize additional weapons. Its control over the educational system, particularly over grants and loans for higher education, has obviously been vital in a situation where access to post-secondary education is one of the main keys to economic and political advancement. Similarly, its ability to channel state funds through parastatal bodies such as BEDCO to indigenous commercial and industrial accumulators has strengthened its control over such groups and weakened their former attachment to the BCP.

The expansion of state power has depended to a considerable extent on a corresponding growth in state revenue, which in turn has been premised largely on the rapid increase in foreign aid and Customs Union revenue. Although the increase in aid has obviously accentuated the state's reliance on the international aid community, it has nevertheless been defended as a way of reducing the more debilitating dependence on South Africa. No such reduction has taken place in practice, however, not least because much of the aid has been devoted to the expansion of state infrastructure and to the satisfaction of the rising consumption needs of the governing class rather than to genuine efforts to create a more independent economy. Given the increasing dependence on Customs Union revenue, an equally important factor has been the lack of incentive to lessen the reliance on migrant labor. As the growth in revenue has resulted largely from the rise in migrant remittances, the governing class has had a positive incentive to do exactly the reverse. At the same time, it has shown unwillingness to share the revenue with those who helped to contribute to its generation—the migrants and their families. Instead, the governing class has attempted to deprive these and other members of Lesotho's subordinate classes of channels through which they might stake an effective claim to a share of the state's expanding resources.

The subjugation of local groups and classes is far from complete, as shown clearly by the present challenge posed by the LLA's armed struggle and by dissension within the governing class's own ranks, prompted in particular by the continuing influence of the Catholic Church. The governing class's scope for maneuver has been limited in many other ways as well. Its ability to avert the damaging consequences of South Africa's campaign of destabilization by capitulating to Pretoria's demands has been constrained by the knowledge that such accommodation could well lead to a reduction in international recognition and aid. In the light of the auditor-general's report, aid could well be curtailed in any case, unless an effort is made to improve the level of honesty and efficiency in the state institutions. If such an effort were made, it could lead, however, to further disunity within the ranks of the governing and supportive classes by alienating those members whose loyalty has depended on the possibilities for accumulation, both legal and illegal, that membership in the state apparatus has so far conferred. If aid is reduced, the governing class might be tempted to compensate for the loss of revenue by imposing income tax on migrants (long recommended by the World Bank, for example). But this could well result in a storm of protest that would make the clearly unsettling disturbances that followed the introduction of the government's compulsory deferred pay scheme in 1974 appear pale by comparison. However, Pretoria's intention to subject all earners in South Africa to a unified income tax from April 1984 and Lesotho's reaction—that Lesotho citizens in South Africa should be taxed by Lesotho—may presage an attempt to impose income tax on migrants.[42]

In the light of such contradictions, as well as many others, it is hardly surprising that the actions of Lesotho's governing class have been characterized by so much indecision and inconsistency. This analysis helps one to understand, although not approve or condone, the regime's disappointing record in the fields of constitutional reform, human rights, and socioeconomic development.

NOTES

1. Cited in Richard Weisfelder, "Defining National Purpose: The Roots of Factionalism in Lesotho" (Ph.D. thesis, Harvard University, 1974), pp. 363–364.

2. See, for example, Lawrence Frank, *The Basutoland National Party: Traditional Authority and Neo-Colonialism in Lesotho* (Denver: Center on International Race Relations, 1971), pp. 26–29; and B. M. Khaketla, *Lesotho 1970: An African Coup Under the Microscope* (London: C. Hurst, and Berkeley: University of California Press, 1971), pp. 171–192.

3. The BNP's superior financial position was of special importance given the government's unpopular decision in its 1968 Electoral Act to raise candidates' deposits from R50 to R200, which hurt the opposition parties much more than the BNP. For a discussion of this and of the ways in which the ruling party attempted to manipulate in its favor the delimitation of constituencies, the registration of voters, and the nomination of candidates, see Khaketla, pp. 193–206.

4. W.J.A. Macartney, "Case Study: The Lesotho General Election of 1970," *Government and Opposition* 8, no. 4 (1973), p. 485. According to

Macartney's calculations, the details were BCP, 152,907 votes (49.8 percent of the turnout) for 36 seats; BNP, 129,434 votes (42.2 percent) for 23 seats; and MFP (in alliance with MTP), 22,279 votes (7.3 percent) for 1 seat. Other parties that received too few votes to hold any seats included the Independent Royalists, 772 votes (0.2 percent), the Independent Nationalists, 724 votes (0.2 percent); the United Democratic Party, 345 votes (0.1 percent); and the Communist Party of Lesotho, 68 votes (0.02 percent). The election turnout was 81.9 percent. Macartney's article provides a useful analysis of the background to the 1970 election and the coup that followed it.

5. A fact that was not really surprising given the half-hearted campaign mounted by the MFP. See Khaketla, *Lesotho 1970*, pp. 172–174.

6. Colin Legum, ed., *Africa Contemporary Record: Annual Survey and Documents 1970–71* (London: Rex Collings, 1971), p. B480. (Henceforth cited as ACR.)

7. One of the fiercest conflicts, in which more than 200 people were killed, took place in April 1970 at the Kao diamond diggings in the mountains. The already-strong anti-BNP sentiments of the independent diggers erupted into violent confrontation with the security forces after the government announced that they were to be removed from the Kao area to make way for two multinational mining companies, Lonrho and Newmont Mining, who had been granted prospecting rights by the LNDC. See Gabriele Winai-Strom, *Development and Dependence in Lesotho: The Enclave of South Africa* (Uppsala: The Scandinavian Institute of African Studies, 1978), p. 134.

8. This act, which replaced the Internal Security Act of 1967, extended the period of detention without trial from 2 to 60 days, extendable indefinitely.

9. Mokhehle was released from detention in June 1971 and from restriction (house arrest) in January 1972. By January 1972 all political prisoners detained in the aftermath of the 1970 coup had been released.

10. For a more detailed discussion of these points, see Wogu Ananaba, *The Trade Union Movement in Africa: Promise and Performance* (London: C. Hurst, 1979), pp. 89–101.

11. For a well-argued analysis of this question, see David Hirschmann, "Changes in Lesotho's Policy Towards South Africa," *African Affairs* 78, no. 311 (1979), pp. 177–196.

12. Influential party leaders dismissed or forced to resign from the government included Justice Mokotso and A. C. Manyeli (1972), Matete Majara and Selbourne Letsie (1974), Peete Peete (1975), and Sekhonyane 'Maseribane (1976). Majara, Peete, and 'Maseribane were later reappointed to Cabinet rank. Of the numerous Cabinet reshuffles that took place during this period, perhaps the most drastic occurred in July 1974 when all but two of the eleven Cabinet portfolios changed hands (the two exceptions being Prime Minister Jonathan and the Finance Minister E. R. Sekhonyana).

13. *ACR 1971-72*, p. B315.

14. By far the most detailed and useful source material on LLA activity, South African efforts at destabilization, and other aspects of the contemporary political and economic situation in Lesotho can be found in *Lesotho Clippings*,

published since January 1982 by the Documentation and Publication Division of the Institute of Southern African Studies, National University of Lesotho, Roma, Lesotho. Much of the material in this section has been taken from these clippings.

15. According to the government there are at present three factions within the LLA. The Marabele faction, which is loyal to Mokhehle; the High Command, which is opposed to him; and the Lesotho Settlement Army, which is trying to heal the rift between these two groups. *Lesotho Weekly*, 3 June 1983.

16. These proposals were contained in the Parliament Bill, which was passed by the assembly in June 1983. Under the new Constitution there will be a Senate, consisting of the 22 principal and ward chiefs, and a House of Representatives, consisting of 60 elected members and 20 members nominated by the king. Although this power of nomination might help to satisfy the monarch's continuing ambition for a greater constitutional role, it could also prove the source of future constitutional deadlock and serve as a prelude, therefore, to renewed friction between king and government. *Africa Research Bulletin* 20, no. 5 (1983), pp. 6836–6837. In April 1984, it was announced that elections would be held in November 1984, but they have since been repeatedly postponed. On 14 August 1985, BNP candidates were ruled to have been returned unopposed in all constituencies and the election scheduled for September was canceled.

17. Except on the condition that the elections are held under UN or Commonwealth supervision, a condition unacceptable to the government.

18. *Africa Resarch Bulletin* 20, no. 9 (1983), pp. 6967–6968.

19. Prime minister's speech on Moshoeshoe Day, 12 March 1970.

20. Richard Weisfelder, "The Basotho Nation-State: What Legacy for the Future?" *Journal of Modern African Studies* 19, no. 2 (1981), p. 243. This article provides an incisive analysis of some of the major cleavages that continue to impede the achievement of national unity.

21. *The Vanguard* 3, no. 7 (1980), p. 10.

22. *To the Point*, 15 September 1972.

23. It has also been rumored that the king, who appears to have curtailed his former links with the MFP, might sympathize with the objectives of such an organization. It is unlikely, however, that he would be prepared to risk renewed confrontation with the government by translating such sympathy into open support. The government has also sought to lessen the threat from unaffiliated unions by coercing them into the new merged federation.

24. For two detailed, useful, and balanced accounts of such shortcomings, see David Hirschmann, *Administration of Planning in Lesotho: A History and Assessment* (Manchester: Manchester University Papers on Development, no. 2, 1981); and Roeland van de Geer and Malcolm Wallis, *Government and Development in Rural Lesotho*, Public Administration Research and Curriculum Development Project, National University of Lesotho (Morija: Sesuto Book Depot, 1982).

25. Hirschmann, *Planning in Lesotho*, p. 70.

26. Major projects introduced without reference to the CPDO include the Thaba-T'seka and Mantsa-Tlala (Self-Sufficiency in Food) projects; those initiated despite CPDO reservations include the new airport and the ill-fated and ultimately aborted Phuthiatsana Irrigation Project.

27. For a convincing survey of the limited achievements of foreign aid in Lesotho, see Calvin Woodward, "Not a Complete Solution: Assessing the Long Years of Foreign Aid to Lesotho," *Africa Insight* 12, no. 3 (1982), pp. 167–179.

28. Henk Huisman and Jan Sterkenburg, "The Spatial Organization for Development in Lesotho" (Research Report 1, Urban and Regional Planning Programme, Department of Geography, National University of Lesotho, 1981), pp. 24–26.

29. van de Geer and Wallis, *Government and Development*, pp. 28–30 and 151–152.

30. Ibid., p. 36.

31. Woodward, "Not a Complete Solution," p. 168.

32. Kingdom of Lesotho, *Report of the Auditor-General on the Public Accounts of Lesotho for the Three Years Ended 31st March 1978* (Maseru: Government Printer, 1982), p. 5. For an extended discussion of this report, see Paul Wellings, "Making a Fast Buck: Capital Leakage and the Public Accounts of Lesotho," *African Affairs* 82, no. 329, October 1983, pp. 495–508.

33. Samuel P. Huntington, *Political Order in Changing Societies* (New Haven, Conn.: Yale University Press, 1972), pp. 1–92.

34. By the term *state* we refer to the cluster of political, administrative, judicial, military, ideological, and coercive institutions that the term *government* does not adequately embrace, as well as to the personnel that control such institutions.

35. For a useful discussion of Marxist theories of the capitalist state in general, see Bob Jessop, "Recent Theories of the Capitalist State," *Cambridge Journal of Economics*, no. 1 (1977). Divergent Marxist interpretations of the postcolonial state can be found, for example, in the works of Hamza Alavi, "The State in Post-Colonial Societies: Pakistan and Bangladesh," *New Left Review*, no. 74 (1972); Colin Leys, "The 'Overdeveloped' Post-Colonial State; A Re-evaluation," *Review of African Political Economy*, no. 5 (1976); John Saul, "The State in Post-Colonial Societies: Tanzania," in *The Socialist Register*, ed. R. Miliband and J. Savage (London: Merlin Press, 1974), pp. 349–372; Issa Shivji, *Class Struggles in Tanzania* (London: Heinemann, 1976), pp. 61–99; and Michaela von Freyhold, "The Post-Colonial State and Its Tanzanian Version," *Review of African Political Economy*, no. 8 (1977).

36. John D. Holm, "The State and Rural Development in Botswana and Lesotho," (Unpublished paper, Department of Political Science, Cleveland State University, 1979).

37. For a detailed critique of the Poulantzian theory of the state see Simon Clarke, "Marxism, Sociology and Poulantzas' Theory of the State," *Capital and Class*, no. 2 (1977).

38. Some of Nicos Poulantzas's works are *State, Power, Socialism* (1978); *Classes in Contemporary Capitalism* (1975), and *Political Power and Social Classes* (1973), all published in London by New Left Books.

39. Winai-Strom, *Development and Dependence,* p. 115.

40. A useful model for this kind of analysis, although in the different context of Tanzania, is provided by von Freyhold, "Post-Colonial State."

41. von Freyhold, "Post-Colonial State," p. 77.

42. "No Income Tax for Lesotho Citizens," *Lesotho Weekly,* Friday, 9 March 1984, p. 3.

5

Lesotho and the World

Lesotho's international relations are dominated by its history and its geography. Accordingly, relations with South Africa and with the United Kingdom (UK) are the most all-embracing and influential. Indeed, until independence, these were the only international relations the country had, except for some interactions with the other High Commission Territories. Since independence, Lesotho has had more interaction with other African states and at least some interaction with other Third World countries; greatly diversified relations with developed market economies to the extent that both the United States and West Germany have overtaken the UK as aid donors (if not in general influence); and, most recently, the beginnings of formal relations with the Eastern bloc following diplomatic recognition of the People's Republic of China, North Korea, the Soviet Union, Yugoslavia, and several other East European countries.

In chronological terms, the initial changes in Lesotho's international relations are easy to explain. In the immediate aftermath of independence, there were strong political, emotional, and economic reasons to try to lessen dependence on South Africa, to strengthen ties with other African countries, and to diversify sources of foreign aid and possible foreign investment. The opening to the Eastern bloc is harder to explain, because in the past Chief Jonathan and his government were virulently anti-Communist. Probably the most plausible explanation is the simplest. At independence, the BNP had no direct experience of international relations or the Eastern bloc and was relatively uncritical of Pretoria. Over time, official antiapartheid vehemence increased, relations with Pretoria deteriorated and those with liberation movements improved, and participation in international organizations increased. Greater exposure to representatives of Communist regimes convinced Jonathan and his colleagues that a Communist label was not necessarily a sign of the devil. Further, Lesotho came to see that there were potential advantages—politically, in international forums; as an alternative source of security equipment and training; and possibly economically, especially for technical assistance and training—in recognition of Eastern bloc nations. This move also to some extent undercut the opposition BCP, which historically presented itself as more open to the whole world than the firmly capitalist and Western-oriented BNP. At the same time, however, the move alienated the more conservative, deeply anti-Communist elements in the Catholic Church, traditionally staunch supporters of the BNP and the government.[1]

RELATIONS WITH SOUTH AFRICA

As has already been pointed out, Lesotho's whole society and economy, as well as its culture and politics, are dominated by the powerful influences of the country that surrounds it. It is difficult to find any aspect of life in Lesotho that is not in some way influenced by South Africa. This situation stems from four main factors. First, until shortly before independence, although juridically a separate unit, for all practical purposes Basutoland simply was just another South African "native reserve." Second, Lesotho's economic dependence on South Africa is colossal, and that dependence involves a substantial proportion of Lesotho's citizens' working in South Africa and also very close commercial, transport, and financial links. Third are the ethnic and cultural links. Many people from Lesotho settled permanently in the Republic, and the Republic has a "South Sotho" community larger than the population of Lesotho. Many personal and family links exist across the border. Unsurprisingly given its wealth, the Republic and its media exert a strong influence on Lesotho's culture, consumption, fashion, and aspiration patterns as well as ideas in both the vernacular and English. Last is the inevitable influence of geography. Quite apart from any other consideration, a country that is a relatively small enclave within a larger country is bound to be influenced by and to have significant relations with the surrounding country.

In Lesotho's case, of course, relations with South Africa are made tremendously more complex by the two countries' ideological and systemic differences. South Africa has a long history of white domination and racial discrimination, under which Basotho within the Republic have suffered and continue to suffer indignities, repression, discrimination, and punitive control. Nowadays, South Africa's ruling Nationalist party in its officially disseminated ideology claims to be moving away from discrimination based on race alone, but this change is purely cosmetic because it is coupled with the intention that "there will be no Black South Africans." Discrimination on the basis of race is thereby replaced by discrimination on the basis of "citizenship." Those Blacks who accept the internationally worthless bantustan "citizenship" thrust upon them by Pretoria are intended by Pretoria to be marginally better off than the Blacks who have so far evaded it or who carry a "local passport" from a neighboring state.[2]

Apartheid is, of course, anathema to Basotho. Lesotho's elites historically had strong links with Black South African elites, who were the articulators of Black opposition to the system. Younger elites in Lesotho have been exposed to expatriate teachers from Europe, North America, South Asia, and elsewhere in Africa, who overwhelmingly oppose apartheid, and also to the literature of the South African liberation movements, the Organization of African Unity (OAU), and the UN, both in original form and as reinterpreted by teachers, politicians, the churches, and the Lesotho media. The masses in Lesotho generally have personal experience of apartheid as migrant workers, shoppers, or visitors or have heard stories from close relatives or friends. Among those without much education, the Republic may often be viewed quite positively in some respects (because wages are perceived as high and the amenities of modernity are more abundant),[3] but this attitude is normally coupled with a well-developed sense of and opposition to the civil, economic, and political disenfranchisement that a Black skin carries with it in that country.

Any Lesotho government will inevitably reflect some hostility to the policies of the South African government and sympathy for the aspirations and organizations of the South African Black majority, even though at the same time, the Lesotho government is linked institutionally with South Africa and cooperates with it on a day-to-day functional basis. What varies from time to time and might change if the political complexion of Lesotho changed is the degree of vitriol in public statements exchanged and the number and intensity of hostile acts as opposed to statements. Although there has been fluctuation around the trend, it seems that since independence, when in some quarters Jonathan was almost regarded as a puppet of Pretoria, the tendency has been for public exchanges to become more and more vitriolic and for overt hostile acts to become more frequent and more significant.

One of the major peculiarities of Lesotho's relations with South Africa is the complete absence of diplomatic representation of each in the other's country, despite their recognition of each other, the frequent occasions to communicate with each other, and the fact that both in principle expressed willingness to exchange consular officials in the 1960s. However, that never happened and is now unlikely to. Diplomatic exchanges are in practice mainly handled by telex. Ministers meet on occasion, and officials more frequently. Lesotho has its Labour Representative in the Republic, but the closest thing to a South African official presence in Maseru is the South African Transport Services office at Maseru railroad station. Cooperation obviously exists between parastatals (e.g., LEC [Lesotho Electricity Corporation] and ESCOM, posts and telephones, LMA and the SA Reserve Bank) and also to some extent between government departments. The Lesotho Mounted Police (LMP) for a long period cooperated with the South African Police in a stock-theft unit, and for the 1970s there is convincing anecdotal evidence of exchange of information, at the very least, between the LMP's Special Branch and the South African Security Police.[4]

The major formal institutional links between Lesotho and South Africa have already been discussed. They include the Customs Union, the Rand Monetary Area, and the Labour Agreement. The first two involve institutionalized consultation mechanisms, in the form of commissions and committees that meet at regular intervals. However, although these mechanisms are essential for administering the agreements, the provisions with respect to consultation have proved far from satisfactory from the point of view of Lesotho. The agreements cede to South Africa full control over customs and excise duties and exchange rate policy, although consultation with the other parties is also called for to the extent possible. South Africa has, perhaps understandably, interpreted this requirement for consultation as being satisfied by notification slightly (sometimes minutes) in advance of public announcement. Put bluntly, advance knowledge of tax or exchange rate changes is information that can be exploited for gain, and the South African authorities neither trust their partners to keep such information confidential nor have any intention of altering their decisions in light of their partners' interests, which often differ from South Africa's.

Apart from the political offensiveness of this attitude on the part of the South African authorities, the differences in economic structure and objectives between South Africa and Lesotho imply that the indirect tax policy and exchange rate and monetary policies set by South Africa will often be very far from optimal for Lesotho, and unexpected changes can cause problems. Examples are easy to provide. The introduction of sales duty in the early 1970s was regressive and lowered Customs Union revenues, but no advance warning was given. In 1982, LNDC focused its efforts to attract foreign investment on the advantages available to investors who used the financial rand market to bring in capital at an advantageous exchange rate; in early 1983, without advance warning, South Africa unified its foreign exchange markets, abolished the financial rand, and destroyed totally this investment incentive for foreign companies.

In recent years, relations between Lesotho and South Africa have deteriorated considerably. Lesotho politicians have made their antiapartheid, pro-ANC, and pro-UN rhetoric very much sharper. South Africa has connived in the activities of the LLA, which has engaged in a series of acts of violence in Lesotho, often striking from or returning to South Africa. The South African policy is viewed widely as being part of the general policy of destabilization aimed at all those neighboring territories that it perceives as acting hostilely to its interests (they include Botswana, Angola, Zimbabwe, and Mozambique in addition to Lesotho, but apparently not Swaziland).

It is not entirely clear what South Africa regards as the minimal behavior "hostile" to its interests that warrants destabilization by it. The alleged justification for overt cross-border military raids, such as that on Maseru in December 1982, is always harboring "terrorists," South Africa's term for ANC guerrillas. However, Lesotho government policy has always been that ANC members in Lesotho should refrain from launching attacks on South African targets from Lesotho, and there is no evidence that this policy has ever been violated. The closest Lesotho can ever be said to have come to complicity in an ANC action in South Africa was the occasion when certain ANC members believed to have been involved in the sabotage of a power station in Durban were arrested in May 1981 on charges of illegal entry into Lesotho and carrying firearms without permission. South Africa requested extradition, but Lesotho argued that there was no extradition treaty. The men were given small fines and allowed to leave by air for Maputo. This disposition of the case did not please South Africa.

South Africa is also believed to have offered an explicit deal—under which it would prevent LLA violence against Lesotho from South Africa in return for Lesotho expelling ANC members—at a meeting between the two countries' foreign ministers in August 1981. Lesotho rejected the offer. Afterward the incidence of LLA and South African violence against Lesotho and the exchange of accusations between government spokesmen tended to increase.[5] However, by 1984 it would appear the offer had been accepted, implicitly if not explicitly.

The Lesotho view is that there are distinct limits to how far government can go to accommodate South African concerns, and that South Africa's method of dealing with its security concerns in particular is damaging to overall relations. Prime Minister Jonathan has said "our future relations with SA will remain marred by this unfortunate episode (the December 1982 Maseru raid)—unless they can themselves succeed in acting to improve relations. I don't see how I can trust them, and I cannot compromise over my stand on apartheid." Referring to an intergovernmental consultative committee of Lesotho and South African officials, Jonathan further expressed surprise that "issues relating to the ANC were never raised in the consultative committee although it met only a month or so before the attack."[6]

There are two important issues here about relations between Lesotho and South Africa, one fairly self-evident and the other involving some probable tension between what can be said openly and what is the underlying issue. First, Lesotho cannot, if it wishes to retain its self-respect in international circles, embrace Pretoria, refuse asylum to South African refugees, or, perhaps, totally forbid an ANC (and Pan-Africanist Congress [PAC] and Black Consciousness, for that matter) presence in Lesotho. Second, however, there is nothing really surprising about Pretoria's violent tactics and apparent lack of use of less violent channels to achieve its ends. Put bluntly, it is reasonable to assume that the South African authorities do not believe that the Lesotho government is able to prevent what South Africa regards as subversive activities by South African exiles in Lesotho. Therefore, the most effective way to prevent such activities, from the South African point of view, is counter-terror, which emphasizes to the South African exiles their vulnerability in Lesotho and thus induces them to leave.[7] Alternatively, the total absence of South African exiles in Lesotho might be achieved by strong economic pressure on Lesotho by the South African government.

Similarly, although Pretoria and Maseru officials may meet to discuss matters, it still makes sense for Pretoria, from its point of view, to continue to use diplomatically unconventional forms of pressure on Lesotho. Thus there is no contradiction in the events of June 1983, when the foreign ministers of the two countries met and agreed to prevent raids across the border in both directions, and yet a large raid occurred from South African territory shortly thereafter— particularly because in the interim Lesotho officials escalated further their rhetorical attacks on the South African government.

In mid-1983, South Africa seemed to have concluded that the only way satisfactory to it to deal with the security problem posed by Lesotho was to ensure that no possible guerrillas were resident in Lesotho. The South African government sought to pressure economically the Lesotho government into repatriating or expelling South African exiles—estimated by the UN to number 11,500, of whom

2,000 are officially registered refugees. Border controls were tightened in early July, and again in mid-August, at which time only Lesotho citizens with multiple-entry visas for South Africa (a tiny minority) were permitted to cross. In addition, at a meeting of officials in Pretoria in August, South Africa was reported to have threatened to ban Basotho migrants from the mines unless its demands were met. A statement from the Lesotho Foreign Ministry on August 15, 1983, referring to "no alternative but to put the interests of its own nationals above those of the refugees," strongly suggested that Lesotho would expel South African exiles (by air to Mozambique), despite the fact that at the beginning of August the Lesotho Parliament had passed a new Refugee Bill giving more formal status to refugees.[8]

However, it is important to realize that the use of South Africa's major economic weapon against Lesotho—reductions in the numbers of migrant mine workers—tends to be opposed by the mining companies. Reportedly, several mining executives expressed public alarm about a South African radio commentary in April 1984 suggesting that tight restrictions on border crossings might be reintroduced if Lesotho continued to be "obstructionist." The mining industry has a substantial investment in the skills of miners from Lesotho, which the industry does not wish to lose. When later in 1984 a threat was reportedly made to reduce the number of miners from Lesotho to 65,000 unless Lesotho signed a nonaggression pact similar to the Nkomati Accords, mining houses reacted by immediately requesting *more* Basotho workers from TEBA.[9]

It is very difficult to summarize relations between Lesotho and South Africa. Such relations permeate all aspects of life in Lesotho, and the broad social and cultural impact of South Africa on Lesotho is very powerful. The intergovernmental situation is one of apparent paradoxes and coexisting contradictions—no formal diplomatic representation; frequent, widely based, and often relatively uncontentious cooperation at the functional and technical levels; highly negative, even vicious, public exchanges of rhetoric at the highest levels; and sympathy for and at least occasional active support to groups attempting to overthrow the other's government by force. Regrettably, in the Southern African context, there is nothing truly paradoxical or unusual about this. It is the way that White-ruled South Africa interacts with its Black neighbors; because of their dependence on South Africa and the tremendous disparities of power between them and South Africa, countries like Lesotho have no choice in the matter unless they wish to become satellites of Pretoria.

Even more difficult to understand are Lesotho's relations, or nonrelations, with the South African bantustans, particularly those

labeled by Pretoria "Independent National States." Lesotho has steadfastly maintained the standard international opinion on this matter,
that the units in question are not independent states but merely
administrative units within South Africa. This produces some practical
difficulties, since Transkei and Qwa Qwa have borders with Lesotho.
For example, at the time of Transkei's supposed "independence,"
Lesotho maintained that when the border posts on the South African
side of the affected portion of the frontier were transferred to
Transkeian jurisdiction, the border had been closed in violation of
agreement with South Africa.[10] Confusion arose because traffic was
still physically crossing the border, although a UN fact-finding commission agreed with Lesotho's "closing" contention and recommended
additional international aid to assist Lesotho to improve internal
communications to the affected regions. Some such aid, for road
building in particular, did materialize.

In practice, the bantustans are denied anything that could be
interpreted as signifying official recognition by Lesotho, but normal
commercial intercourse and movements of individuals are permitted.
Vehicles with bantustan license plates are frequently seen in Lesotho,
and even ministers in bantustan governments occasionally make private
visits to relatives or for vacations in Lesotho. In practice, all concerned
connive implicitly to preserve the illusion of their preferred interpretation of the situation, with the pragmatic forces of necessity
normally overcoming symbolic concerns about recognition.

However, the refusal to recognize the bantustans, quite apart
from the fact that refusing is contrary to South Africa's desires, does
introduce a further point of friction with the South African authorities.
Whenever some substantive issue arises concerning a bantustan (e.g.,
a civil dispute, a car theft), Lesotho communicates with the South
African authorities as, in its view, the recognized and responsible
authorities. The South Africans can either cooperate, by forwarding
the communication and encouraging and transmitting on to Lesotho
the reply, or they can obstruct by denying responsibility and referring
Lesotho to the bantustan authorities. The latter produces an impasse
because Lesotho refuses to take actions implying recognition, and the
former means delay and can also result in an impasse if the bantustan
decides to refuse to use the South African authorities as an intermediary.
The end result is greater uncertainty and slowness about the conduct
of relations when they involve bantustans and irritation for individuals
concerned.

Despite the many and varied disputes between South Africa
and Lesotho, it is important to stress that in terms of economics the
two countries are still intimately connected. Moreover, notwithstanding

official policy in Lesotho to lessen dependence and support SADCC moves in support of reduced economic reliance on South Africa, Lesotho also continues to encourage investment in Lesotho by private South African firms, stressing the advantages it can offer in terms of access to markets in Black Africa and the European Community (under the Lomé Convention). Lesotho has also claimed that such investment is favored by the South African government.[11] Hence, the paradox of negative political relations but positive and pragmatic economic ones continues.

LESOTHO AND AFRICA

Historically, Lesotho was frequently grouped with Botswana and Swaziland as the (former) High Commission Territories. However, strong economic and political differences now exist among the three countries. In fact, they have little in common except their self-government by Blacks in proximity to white-ruled South Africa, their economic integration with South Africa, and some relics of British administrative convenience. Virtually all the institutions established to serve all three countries have collapsed since independence and have been replaced by individual national ones. Common institutions now are of three types: (1) new ones created to formalize links with South Africa, such as the Customs Union Commission; (2) a few survivors of the general break-up of regional institutions fostered by the British, such as the Institute of Development Management (initiated as part of the now defunct University of Botswana, Lesotho and Swaziland) or the Schools Examination Council; and (3) new institutions with broader memberships, such as the Southern African Development Coordination Conference (SADCC), of which more will be said below.

Botswana is a functioning multi-party democracy, which has held elections regularly and also has enjoyed for most of its independence extraordinarily rapid economic growth. By 1982, the World Bank estimated Botswana's GNP per capita as $900, and Swaziland's as $940, almost double Lesotho's $510. Batswana and Basotho are ethnically close, and their languages, Setswana and Sesotho, although recognizably different, are largely mutually intelligible. Thus, relations between Botswana and Lesotho can to some extent be regarded as similar to relations within family, with jealousy and something akin to sibling rivalry clearly present. Basotho tend to be jealous of Botswana's economic success, which they see as relatively undeserved, deriving largely as it does from minerals, and to resent what they interpret as hubris on the part of Botswana with respect to relative political freedom and institutional success. Basotho also tend to be critical of income and wealth disparities in Botswana, which are more pronounced than in Lesotho, and of Botswana's heavy reliance on foreign aid and personnel, but again, this critical attitude may be partly jealousy, because Botswana receives very much more foreign aid in per capita terms than does Lesotho, despite Botswana's greater wealth (in 1979, $116 per capita in Botswana as opposed to $49 in Lesotho—and $98 in Swaziland—according to the World Bank).

One factor that probably explains much of the occasional acrimony and bitterness in intergovernmental relations is that Gaberone, the capital of Botswana, has frequently been the preferred residence for Basotho exiles, self-styled refugees from Chief Jonathan's government. Because of ethnic affinities, Gaberone is a not unpleasant place for Basotho; until recently, Botswana's rapid economic growth and subsequent persistent shortages of skilled personnel have meant educated Basotho can usually find employment. The Botswana government officially enjoins such exiles from political activity, but in Gaberone they have had good access to both South African and international media (such as the British Broadcasting Corporation). Much of the most vocal criticism of the Lesotho regime originates from Gaberone-based Basotho, and this is a definite irritant in Lesotho-Botswana relations.

Swaziland is a rather different case. Swaziland is smaller than Lesotho, but has a much richer and more diversified resource base. It also has a very conservative and autocratic regime, far less inclined to conflict with South Africa than either Botswana or Lesotho. Economically, the contrasts with Lesotho are also extreme. Whereas Lesotho probably has a higher percentage of its labor force employed as migrants outside its borders than any other country in Africa, Swaziland has more workers as a percentage of its labor force regularly employed for cash wages within its borders than any other country in Africa. Swaziland has flourishing industrial and commercial sectors, as well as a very large plantation agriculture and forestry sector based largely on foreign ownership of land.

The most obvious source of conflict between Lesotho and Swaziland is relations with South Africa. On the surface, all three former High Commission Territories try to maintain an image of friendliness and general agreement. However, Botswana and Lesotho, although they may disagree on specific points, generally agree on opposing South African policies openly and vocally while recognizing the need to cooperate with the Republic for reasons of economic necessity (Botswana is heavily dependent on South Africa for transport, for technical skills, and for employment of migrants). Swaziland tends to be much more compliant to South African pressure and circumspect in its criticism of South Africa's policy. In the view of most educated Basotho, a view privately reflected within the Lesotho government, the ruling class in Swaziland is far too willing to publicly sup with the apartheid devil. The most celebrated instances of this relationship are the proposed land deal with Swaziland—under which Swaziland would accept a very large number of former Black South Africans (most from urban areas) as its citizens in return for a relatively small border adjustment—the alleged manipulation of Customs Union data to sweeten it, and the initially secret 1982 nonaggression treaty, revealed in 1984 after the similar Mozambique–South Africa agreement.

Since independence, Lesotho has made substantial efforts to expand and strengthen its ties with other Black African states. These ties take a number of forms, of which actual physical exchange of diplomatic representatives is almost the least frequent. Lesotho only has two diplomatic offices on the continent, in Nairobi and Maputo (Mozambique). Since the fall of Idi Amin in Uganda, no African country has a permanent diplomatic mission in Lesotho, although in 1982 Botswana, Egypt, Ethiopia, Ghana, Guinea, Kenya, Liberia, Malawi, Nigeria, Swaziland, Tanzania, Zambia, and Zaire all had nonresident accredited diplomatic missions to Lesotho (mostly resident in Gaberone, Lusaka, Maputo, or Nairobi).[12] This situation reflects the high cost of maintaining diplomatic missions abroad in Africa and Lesotho's small size.

Lesotho has, however, been very active in the OAU. Lesotho's diplomatic representatives at the OAU and in Nairobi, London, New York, Washington, and elsewhere, as well as the country's representatives at international conferences or traveling on missions, have been fairly successful in explaining Lesotho's geopolitical and economic position and the Lesotho government's political position, particularly with respect to South Africa. Lesotho in recent years has received virtually no criticism from elsewhere in Africa for its dealings with South Africa, and the government has managed to obtain both considerable empathy and rhetorical support for its plight and positions, and some small amounts of material assistance (most notably, in the late 1970s, from Nigeria).

Lesotho has been an active member of the OAU, and representatives from Lesotho have served on several important OAU committees. Although continent-wide relations and opinions have some symbolic importance at the rarefied level of international conferences, elsewhere, with the exception of Nigeria (because of its wealth and size), what governments in West, East, and North Africa think of the Lesotho government is not of much practical importance.

Relations with the other countries of Southern Africa are another matter.

Lesotho is not a member of the Front Line States, which is perhaps not surprising since it neither has a border with Zimbabwe nor had yet adopted such an uncompromising attitude toward white government in the region when the Front Line States came together and named themselves. However, Lesotho does belong to the larger organization that grew out of the Front Line States' desire to widen their concerns from the political to the economic—the Southern Africa Development Coordination Conference (SADCC)—and government seems to be placing considerable emphasis on its membership.[13] The members of SADCC are Angola, Botswana, Lesotho, Malawi, Mozambique, Swaziland, Tanzania, Zambia, and Zimbabwe. The objectives of the organization are to promote development on a regionally coordinated basis and to reduce dependence, particularly, but not only, on South Africa. This initiative has received on the whole a very positive response from Western donor countries and the international community in general, but a very negative response from South Africa. The South African government and much of the South African news media see SADCC as an "anti–South Africa" organization, rather than one whose main objective is the positive goal of accelerating the SADCC's members' development and promoting regional cooperation.[14]

Although at the political and rhetorical level the Lesotho government strongly endorses SADCC and its aims, in practical terms SADCC is not likely in the short run to offer Lesotho much material assistance. Nor, despite Lesotho's expressed willingness, is there likely to be all that much Lesotho can do for SADCC. SADCC is trying very hard to avoid the bureaucratic excesses and ineffectiveness of many regional organizations. It has only a tiny secretariat, and its programs are developed on functional lines with a particular country having responsibility for development of each program. Thus, for example, Mozambique has responsibility for transportation, and Maputo is the site of the Transport Commission. Lesotho suffers from not having land borders with other members and not having any functional area of regional concern in which it can offer special leadership. However, its situation is not unique, and in a fashion that has been said to have characterized the allocation of sectoral responsibilities to some other countries, Lesotho has responsibility within SADCC for regional coordination of activities concerned with soil conservation and land utilization—an area in which Lesotho has clear problems, if not expertise.

The SADCC organization and in particular its meetings have been an important factor in promoting regional solidarity among its member countries. This solidarity, coupled with Lesotho's escalated level of rhetorical criticism of South Africa and South Africa's clear program of destabilization and crude pressure on Chief Jonathan's regime, has done much to enhance the acceptability of the Lesotho government to other governments in the region. As most observers recognize, the facile labels of "left" and "right" applied to African regimes by Western politicians and media are often extreme simplifications and grossly misleading. Nevertheless, it is on the surface perhaps a little surprising that Lesotho has an ambassador resident in Maputo, has regularly scheduled flights to Maputo, has a formal trade agreement with Mozambique, and seems in most respects to be as close to the government of Machel in Mozambique as to any government in the region. The surprise, however, arises from the confusion over misleading labels, i.e., that Jonathan's regime is conservative and Machel's strongly leftist. In Southern Africa, ideological inclinations of governments are of far less importance in their interrelations than structural positions and constraints within the regional system, the core of which is the South African economy. From that perspective, one can more readily understand the "simpatico" between Machel and Jonathan. Both Lesotho and Mozambique are heavily dependent on South Africa, have many migrants there, have been attacked and destabilized by South Africa, and yet are forced on a day-to-day basis to deal with South Africa. Any pair of regimes in Lesotho and Mozambique, so long as they disapproved of apartheid, would be likely to understand the difficulties of, and hence to sympathize with, each other.

LESOTHO AND THE WEST

For almost a hundred years, Lesotho was a British colony, and relations with the UK and to a lesser extent other Commonwealth countries remain extremely important. In the early days of independence, Britain was by far the most important aid donor, especially of technical assistance. This has long since ceased to be the case; now West Germany and the United States are both larger bilateral donors, and Lesotho also has a greatly expanded list of other donors. However, the British connection is still of considerable importance.

When the former colonial power was the dominant aid donor, and also undoubtedly felt some guilt about previous neglect of the country, it was not surprising that Lesotho felt able to request aid from the UK for projects that most donors, in most countries, would have rejected out of hand—for example, the construction of prisons, police stations, and sewage systems. The UK in effect became the donor of last resort and to some extent has retained this role. It also has remained a very important source of technical assistance personnel in routine, technical types of activity, such as public works, telecommunications, and education. Further, the British High Commission remains the most imposing diplomatic mission in Maseru, and it is widely believed (even if with little concrete evidence to back the belief) that as a result of inertia, personal links, and similar factors, the British know better what is happening in the Lesotho government and have a little better ability to influence it than do the representatives of other countries.

The only other Western countries with ambassadors resident in Maseru are the United States and West Germany. This is significant because although many other countries have ambassadors accredited to Lesotho, if they are resident elsewhere, the intensity of relations is qualitatively different.

Lesotho's relations with West Germany probably rank second or third in overall importance after Lesotho's relations with South Africa and perhaps the UK, but are hard to accurately characterize and to explain. In several recent years, West Germany has been the largest single bilateral donor to Lesotho. West German aid has not only financed fairly standard projects such as rural development, but also has provided key technical assistance advisors in agencies such as the CPDO, and training and equipment for the LMP and paramilitary force. It is widely believed that in some fashion West Germany played a role in the 1970 coup, and a proposed West German–financed project on election methods caused substantial controversy (and was dropped). In many circles, West Germany is regarded as the foreign country that is closest to, and gives most support to, the Jonathan regime. The West German mission has been the target of a violent attack in Lesotho, presumably by the LLA. Why West Germany is so generous to, and supportive of, Jonathan remains a puzzle. Two hypotheses that may have some validity are current. One explains the behavior in terms of public relations, both in West Germany and elsewhere, as a counterweight to West Germany's relatively acquiescent behavior toward the Pretoria regime. The reasoning here runs as follows: trade with and investment in South Africa are economically important to West Germany, and for various reasons the government of the Federal Republic of Germany (FRG) takes a relatively inactive line of criticism and opposition toward apartheid. But antiapartheid sentiment in the FRG is vocal, and the government of the FRG is, for obvious historical reasons, sensitive to charges of racism in the international community. Hence, generous aid to Lesotho is something positive the FRG does in Southern Africa that can be used to help deflect criticism of the FRG's South Africa policy.

The second hypothesis concerns Lesotho's links with Maputo and the issue of relations between the two Germanys. Mozambique recognizes the German Democratic Republic (GDR), and Mozambique's refusal to acknowledge West Berlin as part of the FRG has been an obstacle to Mozambique's accession to the Lomé Convention with the European Community (EC). This has caused some difficulties for EC support of SADCC, which is substantial. This line of reasoning argues that strong support for Lesotho from West Germany may help to advance the FRG's position on such subjects as West Berlin and the GDR with other countries in the region, Mozambique in particular.

The United States was the first country to open an embassy in Lesotho, joining the British High Commission soon after independence. Initially, there was one U.S. ambassador for all three former High Commission Territories, resident in Gaberone, but more recently Lesotho has had its own U.S. ambassador. Unfortunately, the U.S. ambassadors have tended recently to be political appointees of dubious qualifications and suitability (President Ronald Reagan's first appointee was a Republican party supporter, a banker from Colorado, a pleasant and affable man with no prior knowledge or experience of Southern Africa). The quality of U.S. representatives in Lesotho has tended to be questioned almost as much as the genuineness of official U.S. commitment to change in Southern Africa.

The U.S. aid program in Lesotho has also fluctuated greatly from year to year with changes in the political climate in Washington. Recently, the program has benefited from special allocations for the whole Southern African region and from an attempt to compensate for criticism of the Reagan policy of "constructive engagement" with South Africa by greater material assistance to the poorer countries of the region. U.S. aid suffers from some problems, however. Despite a good deal of experience with it now, officials in Lesotho still find some of its bureaucratic and paperwork requirements cumbersome and strange. Problems also can arise from the unfamiliarity of U.S. contractors with the region and the enormous gaps between individual compensation levels considered normal by the United States and those prevalent in Lesotho.[15] Aid from the United States has been largely concentrated in three areas, rural development, road construction, and education. All are useful and can be made to seem consistent with the legislated mandate of the U.S. Agency for International Development (AID) to direct assistance to the "poorest of the poor." However, U.S. AID's priorities often do not coincide with Lesotho's, and U.S. AID is seen as relatively costly to Lesotho and inflexible. U.S. AID and its staff are, therefore, not perhaps as influential as less generous donors, such as Canada, the Netherlands, and the Nordic countries, who are seen as more flexible (especially, for example, about procurement-tying), more willing to listen to Lesotho's wishes rather than following their own agenda, less bureaucratic, and quicker to make decisions.

It is very hard to assess either the influence of the United States in Lesotho or the state of U.S.-Lesotho relations. Despite the size of the U.S. AID program, a large Peace Corps presence, and a well-equipped U.S. International Communications Agency library and operation, the general impression is that the Americans are neither as influential nor as well-regarded as, say, the British. Much of this is probably connected with a general lack of understanding of the structure of the U.S. government and, hence, with confusion about what U.S. policy is and why it seems to change so often. Very few Basotho have a good grasp of the U.S. concept of separate executive and legislative branches and thus have difficulty in understanding how supposedly powerful members of Congress can say things that seem totally at variance with pronouncements of the executive branch.

However, in recent years, two aspects of actual U.S. policy have perhaps been much more important. First, U.S. policy toward South Africa has been seen as implicitly or explicitly supporting apartheid, even when the rhetoric is critical. This is obviously more serious under Reagan than before, but the general opinion of the Carter administration was that although Andrew Young may have said the right things, usually the United States actually did the wrong ones. There is an interesting contrast with the UK here. The British are not seen as a reliable ally against apartheid either, of course, but in their case it is thought of as understandable—40 percent of the whites in South Africa are, after all, of British descent, and it is appreciated in Lesotho that South Africa is economically important to the UK. Further, the UK has rarely made verbal commitments about South Africa not supported by behavior, and it has supported Lesotho's positions with respect to South Africa with some consistency and vigor.[16] This British semihypocrisy is seen as being in the British self-interest and understandable: perfidious Albion is at least pre-dictable and reliable in a fashion. But U.S. behavior to most Basotho is just inexplicable. White South Africans are not Americans. South Africa is not *economically* important to the United States. Why then does the United States act the way it does, unless the explanation is racism? The only alternative explanations that seem valid to many Basotho are the crude Marxist ones, which see U.S. behavior in terms of maintaining the dominance of the capitalist system. Neither view is very helpful to U.S. influence or interests, and both are negative consequences of U.S. policy toward South Africa.

Second, to a large extent the United States simply has not had a policy toward Lesotho. Lesotho is an afterthought, a small and unimportant country. In Southern Africa, U.S. policy—particularly under Reagan—has focused on South Africa, the Namibia question, Cuban troops in Angola, and the alleged Marxism of Mozambique. Policy toward Lesotho has basically been "be helpful within the limits of available resources according to standard U.S. AID guidelines." Nobody likes being ignored and considered unimportant. Worse still, nobody likes being insulted by being sent an ambassador who knows nothing about the country, the region, or diplomacy, especially when his career service support is also widely viewed as second rate. The size of the United States and its power, and the size of the U.S. AID budget and the possibilities of the portion going to Lesotho being raised, of course imply that the United States has some influence. Nevertheless, that influence is very limited, and it is dubious whether the U.S. State Department has much of an appreciation of the realities of Lesotho and its government.[17]

Of course, Lesotho as such really does not matter much to U.S. interests. But Southern Africa does matter, and Lesotho is gaining in stature and influence in the region with each year the Jonathan regime survives and as the government improves understanding of its plight both in the region and in the wider international community.

Beyond the "big three" of the UK, the United States, and the FRG, Lesotho has been very active in widening the scope of its bilateral relations, especially with actual or potential donors. The government has managed to attract considerable attention from the aid agencies of some of the smaller European countries, notably Ireland, the Netherlands, Denmark, and the Nordic countries. In many cases, the driving force is essentially antiapartheid sentiment in the donor country overcoming some distaste for the authoritarian style of Jonathan's government. In a few cases, skillful individuals have been able to make much of particular affinities. For example, Lesotho is one of a very few countries in which Irish aid is concentrated. Partly this is a result of identifying Lesotho needs in areas where Ireland has real expertise—improving the quality of the Basotho pony, horses being an important form of transport in rural Lesotho, and assessing the possibilities of exploiting peat deposits.[18] In other cases other factors play a role. Church interests play some role in both Canadian and French behavior; many Roman Catholic missionaries in Lesotho are Canadian, and the LEC derives from the Paris Evangelical Mission Society. Lesotho has tried to cultivate alternative sources of aid and maintains embassies or high commissions in Brussels (also accredited to the European Community [EC]), Ottawa, Denmark, and Italy as well as London, Washington, and Bonn.

Before the fall of the shah, Lesotho also had extensive bilateral relations with Iran, maintained an embassy in Tehran, and received substantial Iranian aid, both civil and paramilitary. Since the change of regime in Iran, this relationship has essentially ceased to exist. Bilateral relations with Asian and Latin American countries to a large extent do not exist, except for those involving China, Taiwan, the Koreas, and Cuba discussed below.

Lesotho regards the various international organizations as very important to it. Probably the two most important are the United Nations and the EC, but the Commonwealth and the World Bank group also deserve mention. The UN and its specialized agencies are important in several ways. First, they represent a useful and usually sympathetic set of forums for expressing Lesotho's point of view and explaining its position. Second, they are in themselves a source of aid, especially technical assistance. Third, they help to legitimize and propagate Lesotho's case for additional assistance because of its situation with respect to South Africa. UN missions were sent to evaluate the effects of both the 1976 Transkei border closure and the 1982 Maseru raid, and on both occasions their reports appealed to the international community to provide Lesotho with more aid.

The EC is, nowadays, an important source of aid in itself. It also maintains a well-staffed office in Maseru, and some observers informally would rank the EC resident staff as among the best-informed diplomats in Lesotho. The EC is also important as, via the ACP group (that is, African, Caribbean, and Pacific members of Lomé Convention), an important forum for putting Lesotho's case, and because of EC interest in and support for SADCC, the most involved economic power bloc from outside interested in the Southern African region. Lesotho has hopes of promoting exports to EC markets under the Lomé Convention, and has been active in ACP activities.

The Commonwealth is a loose organization, but one which offers several useful minor opportunities to Lesotho. The forum is again useful, and many specialized conferences are offered under Commonwealth auspices. It is a source of certain specialized kinds of technical assistance. The secretariat is very strongly antiapartheid, pro-SADCC, and sympathetic to Lesotho's plight.

The World Bank group is a source of low-cost loans through the International Development Association and of reputedly high-quality technical expertise. It has funded several large Lesotho projects in road construction, rural development, and education. It is enormously influential in the general aid donor community. However, Lesotho's experience with the World Bank has been very disappointing. The Thaba Bosiu rural development project was, to a large extent, an unmitigated disaster, as acknowledged by the Bank itself.[19] The education projects are of dubious quality. Bank expertise in Lesotho has also been questionable. The only World Bank economic report on Lesotho to have been formally published was fatally flawed by a totally misconceived assumption about the nature of the economy.[20] The technical assistance personnel made available by the World Bank have not been of uniformly high quality and are widely believed to have had little if any impact on policy. Again, as with the United States, the problem is probably largely that Lesotho is not very important and therefore does not get the attention required to produce good results.

LESOTHO AND THE EAST

Traditionally, Jonathan and the BNP were regarded as virulently anti-Communist. But in recent years, this perception has clashed more and more with actual behavior. Links were developed with Mozambique. Partly through the Non-Aligned Movement (another forum in which Lesotho tries hard to put its case), delegations from Lesotho visited Cuba. It was announced that relations would be established with the Soviet Union. Students started to be sent on scholarships to the GDR and the Soviet Union by the government, not the BCP. Aid was accepted from Yugoslavia. Finally, in early 1983, Jonathan made a Far East tour that included China and North Korea, and relations with Taiwan were broken.

This process has caused considerable controversy within Lesotho, heavy criticism from conservative elements in the Catholic church, and virulent (and usually factually inaccurate) criticism from South Africa. Neither the motivations nor the expected benefits are clear, although it seems very likely they involve pragmatic politics, not ideological changes. The material impact is likely to be somewhat negative, because Taiwan had provided some aid and it is unlikely that China will be as generous.[21] In addition, there has been significant private investment by firms based in Taiwan, and it is not clear how this will be affected by the switch in recognition to China.

The significance of this opening to the Eastern bloc by the Lesotho government is probably not very great. The South African government and media have made much of it, often with more imagination than credibility.[22] It serves the current purposes of the

South African government to portray Lesotho as a dangerous sanctuary for ANC guerrillas. Further, because in the mythology of Pretoria all antiapartheid sentiment is merely an expression of the Soviet and Communist scheme to take over all of Southern Africa via a "total onslaught," and thus weaken the "free world," the fact that Lesotho now recognizes and has dealings with the Soviet Union, mainland China, and other Eastern bloc nations is corroboration of its anti–South African and mistaken ways.

One can never tell how much of their own propaganda South African elites actually believe. In this case, their propaganda encompasses a half truth by reversing the order of causation. Lesotho is not becoming anti–South African because of Soviet or Communist influence; Lesotho *is* antiapartheid, and that is part of the reason for broadening international contacts to include the Eastern bloc, which (for whatever reasons) tends to be more supportively antiapartheid than governments in the West.[23] It seems likely that this is understood by the South African government. Nevertheless, in order to justify its behavior toward Lesotho to the South African public and to western governments and public opinion, it is useful to present the distortions that communism is gaining strength in Lesotho, that Lesotho harbors anti–South African "terrorists" (which it does not) and that strong measures (such as the Maseru raid, border closures, and threatening to expel miners) by South Africa are therefore justified.

Viewed in this light, one can see Lesotho's developing relations with the Eastern bloc as just one more thing that has to viewed in the Southern African regional context, to be understood. The dominant fact of life in Lesotho is South Africa. Lesotho is dependent on South Africa, but Lesotho cannot go very far in appearing to acquiesce to the perpetuation of the apartheid system. A dilemma arises: Lesotho needs all the help and support it can find to lessen its dependence on South Africa and to strengthen its resolve to oppose apartheid, at least rhetorically. But some of the sources most willing to offer strong support, including the possibility of military and security aid, are Eastern bloc countries that are anathema to the Pretoria regime. Relations with them run the risk of provoking ever more overt destabilizing, hostile actions by South Africa. There is the danger of a terrible escalation: South Africa destabilizes, acts violently and hostilely; the Lesotho government feels even more insecure and isolated and turns increasingly to the Eastern bloc, which is more willing to provide security equipment and assistance than the West; this action by Lesotho provokes Pretoria into further escalation, and so on.

This scenario is not yet being played out in Lesotho, but the possibility is clearly there. Because of concerns about human rights, most Western donors are relatively reluctant to aid the Lesotho government militarily; in the past, the security forces have primarily been used for internal repression. West Germany is the major exception. In Southern Africa, it is dangerously misleading to see bilateral relations in East-West, Cold War terms. All questions of international relations must be interpreted in terms of how they affect the regional configuration of forces and South Africa's position. Small, weak countries like Lesotho do need all the international recognition and support they can obtain. It is absurd to imagine Chief Jonathan or his government as either sympathizing with the aims of Marxist-Leninist regimes or permitting such regimes to act within Lesotho in ways likely to undermine the existing ruling groups. Unfortunately, the Lesotho government is authoritarian, and security assistance can be used for internal repression to bolster such authoritarianism as well as to counter South African threats. One of the most depressing aspects of Lesotho's international relations in recent years is that, intentionally or otherwise, South Africa's hostility to Jonathan's regime has made it easier for that regime to obtain aid, sympathy, and respectability from both East and West, despite the regime's considerable shortcomings.

NOTES

1. See, for example, "Ties with Mainland China: Hard Facts of Life Forced on Us," *Lesotho Weekly* 27 May 1983, p. 8.

2. Lesotho, in common with some other countries that send migrants to South Africa, issues two types of passport. The "local passport" is good for travel in Southern Africa, is accepted by South Africa, and is the normal document held by migrant workers. The "international passport," considerably more expensive and harder to get, is good worldwide but normally only carried by civil servants and others who have to travel outside Southern Africa. Its holders tend to be viewed with deep suspicion by South African passport control officers and police, because its possession indicates that the holder probably has more education, wealth, and travel experience than the inspecting South African official—a situation that runs deeply counter to the racial stereotypes and expectations of such functionaries.

3. See Cobbe, "Emigration and Development in Southern Africa, with Special Reference to Lesotho," *International Migration Review* 16, no. 4 (Winter 1982).

4. A Zimbabwean known to one of the authors was questioned in the 1970s by the LMP Special Branch and shown reports of his alleged activities originating from the Rhodesian Special Branch and forwarded to the LMP by the South African Security Police. Such links presumably originated before independence; how long they persisted is not known.

5. Much of this is chronicled in Deon Geldenhuys, "Recrossing the Matola Threshold: the 'Terrorist Factor' in South Africa's Regional Relations," *South Africa International* 13, no. 3 (January 1983), pp. 152–171. Because Geldenhuys is generally sympathetic to the Pretoria government's objectives, his allegations of their complicity in LLA activity carry considerable weight.

6. Both quotes from "Lesotho: Posers over Peking," *Financial Mail* (Johannesburg), 13 May 1983, p. 781.

7. Press reports indicated that many ANC members and other exiles did leave Lesotho for Mozambique after the Maseru raid.

8. See, for example, "S. Africa Pressures Lesotho To Expel Refugees," *Boston Globe*, 17 August 1983, p. 10; "S. Africa Tightens Screws on Lesotho," *Africa News* 21, no. 6, 8 August 1983, p. 9; and "No SA 'Enemies' here—Peete," *Lesotho Weekly* 7, no. 19, 5 August 1983, pp. 1, 6 [Peete Peete, a prominant BNP minister, was speaking on behalf of the government]. Some press reports have suggested that the whole ANC issue is a smokescreen and that the real intention behind Pretoria's pressures is "to get us to join the constellation of states, to recognize the bantustans, and to force us to sell them water [from the Highlands scheme] at a cheaper rate" and also incidentally to leave the Southern African Development Coordination Conference (SADCC). "SADCC 1: Acrimony at Maputo" *Financial Mail* (Johannesburg), 15 July 1983, pp. 46–47, quoting an anonymous "senior Lesotho source." Although the South African government would no doubt like to achieve all the aims cited, later events suggest that the ANC issue is not just a pretext.

9. Allegedly, TEBA managed to process 4,000 novices within three weeks. Both incidents are described in Fion de Vletter, "Recent Trends and Prospects of Black Migration to South Africa," International Migration for Employment Working Paper no. 20 (Geneva: ILO [International Labour Office], 1985), pp. 17, 30, 33, 39.

10. See discussion in Roger Southall, *South Africa's Transkei* (New York: Monthly Review Press, 1983), p. 250.

11. For example, Mooki Molopo, foreign minister of Lesotho, is reported to have claimed that both countries want to see more South African factories in Lesotho, despite the "formally cool relations" between them. *Africa News* 21, no. 2, 11 July 1983, p. 12.

12. Kingdom of Lesotho, Ministry of Foreign Affairs, *Diplomatic List* (Maseru: Ministry of Foreign Affairs, 1982).

13. This may be partly for publicity reasons. The third annual conference of SADCC was held in Maseru in January 1983, barely six weeks after the SADF raid on Maseru. Many statements were made highly critical of the South African government, especially by European and international organization representatives (see, e.g., the statement by E. Pisani, member of the Commission of the European Community in response to the opening address, referring to South Africa as "a threat to peace," and by the Danish foreign minister, who referred to "South African soldiers . . . in Maseru spreading death and horror. This [was a] flagrant violation of Lesotho's sovereignty

and South Africa's breach of the principles of international law"). Major documents of the meeting were collated in *SADCC: Maseru* (3 volumes, Roma, Lesotho, Institute of Southern African Studies [ISAS], National University of Lesotho [NUL], Photocopied); press reports are collated in "SADCC Supplement," *Lesotho Clippings* January–March 1983 (Roma, ISAS, NUL, Photocopied), pp. 47–72.

14. The Johannesburg *Sunday Times*, for example, headlined its first story on the Maseru conference "Lesotho to Host Anti-SA Summit" (9 January 1983). Mr. Peter Musi, Vice-President of Botswana, and chairman of SADCC, responded by calling such reports "nonsense and small-minded," emphasizing the distinction that is often not grasped in the Republic, namely that SADCC members "are not enemies of South Africa, but we hate the apartheid system of that country." *The Citizen* (Johannesburg), 26 January 1983. Both newspaper reports are reproduced in "SADCC Supplement," *Lesotho Clippings*.

15. For example, a U.S. company responsible for AID-financed road construction hired as cook for its road camp the chef of the best restaurant in Maseru, by offering him roughly double his former salary.

16. Contrast, for example, responses to the SADF raid on Maseru in December 1982 in London and Washington: The South African ambassador in London was summoned to the Foreign Office and given a strong protest; in Washington, a State Department spokesman deplored the tragic loss of innocent life, but also condemned violence by all sides and implied that the appropriate response was "constructive engagement" and peaceful resolution of disputes.

17. An indication that the U.S. embassy is a little out of touch with reality was provided by a circular sent, over the ambassador's signature, to all U.S. citizens resident in the country in 1982, when the internal security situation was not very good. It advised that people should not try to drive through government roadblocks without stopping, especially at night, and that U.S. citizens should avoid as much as possible government offices, because they were likely to be targets of attack. Apart from antagonizing the Lesotho government, the latter piece of advice seemed to show an astonishing ignorance of the fact that many U.S. citizens in the country worked in government offices!

18. Irish aid is not confined to these activities, but also includes extensive technical assistance to the Ministry of Works and Lesotho Airways.

19. IBRD, *World Development Report 1983* (New York: Oxford University Press, 1983), p. 98, and Chapter 4 of this book.

20. IBRD, *Lesotho: A Development Challenge* (Washington, D.C.: IBRD, 1975); for a critique, see J. H. Cobbe, "Growth and Change in Lesotho," *South African Journal of Economics* 46, no. 2 (June 1978), pp. 135–153.

21. However, North Korea has sent a mission to examine irrigation projects previously assisted by Taiwan, supposedly with the intention of replacing Taiwan's technical assistance. "N. Korean Delegation Tours Irrig. Schemes," *Lesotho Weekly* 7, no. 19, 5 August 1983, p. 2. China provided M800,000 in aid by April 1984. *Lesotho Weekly* 8, no. 1, 6 April 1984, p. 1.

22. A famous incident concerned a reference to the large staff of the Soviet embassy in Maseru—before diplomatic recognition by Lesotho of the Soviet Union, let alone exchange of ambassadors!

23. This is not to suggest that the Eastern bloc is any less pragmatic in its dealings with South Africa than any other group of countries. Despite official denials, there is conclusive evidence of trade between South Africa and both the Soviet Union and other East European countries when mutually advantageous. The differences, of course, are in terms of state control (of trade and individual movement), official state hostility, and the willingness of governments in the Eastern bloc to provide South African liberation movements with arms and munitions.

6

Prospects for the Future

It is extremely unwise to try to forecast the future in Southern Africa. In the case of Lesotho, surrounded by South Africa, on which it is so extremely dependent, forecasting is particularly difficult because developments in South Africa so obviously will affect what happens in Lesotho but are themselves impossible to predict with much confidence.

Recognizing these difficulties, the approach adopted here attempts to circumvent rather than overcome them. We begin with a review of the major difficulties and constraints that limit to a large extent what can happen in Lesotho. Next, we identify what we believe to be reasonably clear trends from recent years that are likely to continue. Last, we frankly speculate about some of the possible consequences of events that we do not predict *will* happen, but do believe *could* happen: namely, forced repatriation of migrants; change in political regime; and radical change in South Africa.

LIMITED OPTIONS

The major limitations on what can happen in Lesotho should be evident from earlier chapters. We will discuss them under three headings: economic, political, and administrative.

Economic Constraints

Lesotho does not at present possess the natural resources, the physical capital—either infrastructural or productive—or the human capital to support its population at the consumption levels to which it has become accustomed, without massive export of labor. This then is the fundamental economic constraint—that in the short to medium term, continued access to migration is simply necessary for national economic survival.

The past also places constraints on what attempts can be made to change the economic situation. Because so much of the population

189

is rural and the land tenure system and rural economic interactions play such a large part in ensuring some income for so many, attempts to increase agricultural production are constrained by the need to take care not to displace too many workers, nor to remove income sources from too many rural residents, too fast. Attempts to generate nonagricultural sources of income for the population, especially in manufacturing, are constrained by physical infrastructure, transport costs and uncertainty, and the difficulties of competing with South African bantustans.

Fiscal considerations make it risky to consider leaving either the Customs Union or the monetary area, which in turn greatly constrain policy options and make it very difficult to enhance the attractiveness of Lesotho as a site for productive activity compared to South Africa and its bantustans. Finally, the continued possibilities of employment elsewhere in Southern Africa for those with skills in short supply constrain the possibilities of reducing domestic income inequalities without incurring high costs from low-quality personnel or vacant posts.

Political Constraints

Again, these have been made clear. On the international side, the Lesotho government is in danger of suffering substantial damage if it misjudges its stance vis-à-vis South Africa. If it appears too compliant with South African government wishes, it risks other governments' condemnation and withdrawal of moral support, plus possibly some loss of material aid from multilateral sources and the more politically sensitive bilateral donors. If it resists Pretoria too resolutely, it stands to suffer continued political, military, and economic destabilization, with the Damocles Sword of repatriation of migrants always dangling over its collective head.

But there are domestic political constraints as well. The churches remain powerful and influential, and they are clearly unhappy about both the flirtation with Communist governments and the human rights violations involved in domestic repression. Migrants, the salariat of the civil service and parastatals, the education establishment, traders, and the larger farmers are all groups with the potential to cause government considerable difficulty if they feel too threatened or damaged by government action or inaction. More crudely, so are the police and the military. Potentially, the young—especially the educated urban underemployed and unemployed, who are likely to grow rapidly in numbers—could also cause trouble for the government if their futures seem too bleak.

Politically, the country remains divided, and the government insecure. Thus, the government must tread with care in terms of adopting policies that will have differential effects on different groups. Some governments in such situations gamble with bold policy initiatives. In terms of domestic policy, Leabua Jonathan has in the past always combined shrewdness with caution, and it is unlikely that this will be reversed.

Administrative Constraints

Despite enormous expansion in the size and cost of government since independence, the final set of constraints on what may happen are set by the relative administrative ineffectiveness of the Lesotho government. Government machinery remains weak and unreliable. Hence, the government is forced to act somewhat cautiously in terms of policy initiatives since its ability to actually implement new policy effectively is severely limited. This has many dimensions and many sources. A very few examples may help to give the flavor. The income tax law, like much other legislation, has never been translated into Sesotho. When a prominent and successful entrepreneur visited a university class and was asked if he had any problems with the (quite complex) English language tax returns, his response was simply "What tax returns? I have never seen one." Morale and discipline in the civil service are poor. Dismissal for political reasons, although less frequent today than in the past, is by no means uncommon; yet dismissal for theft, corruption, or dereliction of duty is extremely rare. Corruption, according to the latest auditor-general's report, is endemic throughout the public service. Many posts in the higher grades of the civil service remain vacant, and the incumbents of other posts are not always effective in their jobs. For technical and professional posts, the government apparatus is still heavily dependent on expatriates, whose absolute numbers have tended to grow. Most are technical assistance personnel, and although some are very effective, others are either inappropriate for their posts or never able to establish good relations with their local counterparts and subordinates.[1]

Add to this situation the inevitable difficulties of administration in a poor country with few roads, high transport costs, unreliable telephones and electricity, and much civil dissension, and it is obvious that the government's ability to implement policy will be limited. Consider in addition the extreme openness of the economy, the legal-tender status of the surrounding country's currency, and the permeability of the borders, and there is an obvious danger that many attempts at policy changes may be simply ineffective. For example, there is no way of knowing how many individuals and companies maintain bank accounts in South Africa, and no way to monitor or prevent use of such accounts. There is no way of knowing the true money supply, because the amount of rand currency in circulation within the country can only be estimated. Export and import data are inevitably very approximate, because most are recorded by means of very loosely monitored self-reporting. At one point in the early 1970s, possibly the most valuable commodity export was a wholly unrecorded and illegal one, cannabis destined for South Africa's urban areas.[2] Thus one must always keep in mind that in Lesotho, it is often hard even now to be confident quantitatively about what was happening in the past, let alone now. In the British context, a prime minister once compared formulating economic policy to planning a complex rail journey with last year's timetable; to adapt the analogy to Lesotho, formulating all policy is akin to planning such a journey with a copy of last year's timetable that has half the pages missing, the others blurred, and a good chance that some of the stations have been closed.

PROBABLE TRENDS

Inertia of Context and Policy

To take past trends and project them into the future can easily lead to absurd predictions. However, this is often truer of quantitative trends than of qualitative ones, and in the Lesotho context there have been few sharp breaks in trends since 1970, and a great deal of continuity both in the kinds of change taking place and in government policy. Here, we identify some trends that we believe to be important and likely to continue.

The general situation is likely to continue to drift without major change. This prediction implies that South Africa will continue to be dominated by the Nationalist Party, that South Africa will continue to experience conflict between White and Black, that South Africa's economy will not grow fast enough to absorb all indigenous Black work seekers or to fulfill the economic aspirations of its Black population, and that hostility between South Africa and its neighbors will also continue—the present coerced agreements with neighbors, such as the Nkomati accords, notwithstanding. Domestically, unity and consensus will not be achieved within Lesotho, and political dissension will continue extraparliamentarily as well as, possibly, through the ballot box. The fundamental dilemmas of the structural situation will not be resolved. Short-term considerations will encourage continuation of the status quo with minor adjustments, implying continued pragmatic cooperation and accommodation with South Africa. Long-term objectives will suggest the need for radical breaks with the past and with South Africa, but the short-term costs will prevent adoption of any radical policy initiatives. In these circumstances, we do not expect any major changes in government policy soon.

Growing Inequality and Dissension

The implication, however, is that trends that have become apparent in the last decade toward greater differentiation domestically will continue and become more apparent. The gaps between rural households with access to migrant earnings and those without such access will widen. The differences in economic status between those with large agricultural assets (land, livestock, capital) and those without them and between the young with sufficient education to secure formal sector employment and those with less education will also widen and become more stark. These latter two differentials will be made stronger by the operation of policy. The progressive implementation of the 1979 Land Act and the range management policies, intended to increase commercialization of arable and stock farming respectively, will widen rural inequalities and foster the growth of the rural landless and stockless. Recent policies on education provision and finance and the interaction of political, economic, and fiscal realities imply that although the number of secondary-school graduates will grow rapidly (in 1983, 5,511 candidates sat the Junior Certificate exam and 3,736 passed; in 1979, only 4,077 sat and 2,954 passed), the vast majority of young people will not enter secondary school and only a minority of those holding a Junior Certificate can hope for formal sector employment.

The economic dimension is not the only one on which inequality exists. At least as important is inequality of access to political power, government, and the administrative machinery. Clearly the political experience since 1970 has led to severe polarization, with much of the population totally alienated from the government and regarding themselves as having no legitimate channels through which to make their views known. If growing inequality is coupled with deepened impoverishment of the poorest sections of the population—and indications are that it will be—this could result in the economic and political cleavages at least partly coalescing. It is entirely possible that this could lead to an increase in extralegal protest and a further deterioration of the internal security situation. On the basis of past experience, the government would meet this by some cosmetic concessions, an increase in spending on security forces, and more severe internal repression. The prospects of a peaceful rapprochement between the conflicting groups domestically seem unlikely without dramatic change either in external conditions or in economic prospects.

Declining Migrant Opportunities

South Africa faces a serious problem of Black unemployment and underemployment within its own borders. Since the early 1970s, it has reduced the foreign component in the mine labor force from more than 77 percent to less than 40 percent. The South African government has made it almost impossible for new Black migrants from outside South Africa to legally enter or find employment outside mining. Penalties and policies against illegal migrants have been increased and strengthened. The mine labor force has been stabilized in terms of employment, so that now fewer than 5 percent of contracts are with novices.

At first, Lesotho benefited from the changes in mine labor policy, because real wages grew rapidly, and the numbers of Lesotho migrants also grew, replacing Malawians and Mozambicans. But by the beginning of the 1980s, severe restrictions on recruitment were enforced, total numbers of mineworkers apparently stabilized, and fears expressed earlier of falling demand from the mines for Basotho labor seemed more and more justified. What the future will hold is very uncertain. Some points are clear, however. First, there will be few if any new opportunities for migrants outside mining, and the number of migrants employed outside mining will dwindle to zero as the present holders of the jobs are squeezed out, retire, or lose Section 10 rights to residency. Second, mining employers not affiliated with the Chamber of Mines stopped hiring novices in Lesotho about 1980; such employers probably have been treating and will continue to treat Lesotho as a residual, last resort source of labor. Hence, numbers of migrants that these mines employ, which have been falling, will also probably fall to zero. The Chamber of Mines, through TEBA, appears to have a formal or informal quota of about 100,000 migrants from Lesotho. The chamber is probably willing to maintain that level for many years, but cannot act wholly independently of the South African government.

Overall, therefore, a reasonable prediction is that the tendency for the next ten years or so is that migrant labor flows will become more concentrated on chamber mines, there will be very few opportunities for new migrants, and that total numbers will fall slowly. Numbers could fall much faster, or even precipitously, if either the chamber was to change its policy or Pretoria was to decree a change.

This process is already having marked consequences in Lesotho. These consequences will tend to become more extreme and to accelerate over the next few years. The most important are (1) the progressive widening of income differentials in rural areas between those with access to migrant earnings and those without; (2) a growing crisis of unemployment and underemployment, particularly among the young, leading to grave social problems especially in the urban areas (mainly Maseru); and (3) increased insecurity of income for all (since TEBA will be the monopsonistic, and selective, employer of migrants), leading to tension at the level of individual families and quite possibly greater proclivities for extreme and violent behavior socially and politically. Political power, because of its patronage possibilities, will become more important, and the consequences of losing a job more horrific. Given the impossibility of surviving solely from agricultural activities for most families and the political tensions in the country, the outlook for the future is indeed very grim.

SPECULATIONS AND POSSIBILITIES

No More Migrant Labor

It is within the power of South Africa's government to bring to an end the employment of Lesotho citizens in South Africa. Botha's regime has threatened to do just that at least once in recent years. Suppose the threat became reality; what would it mean for Lesotho?

Immediately, the end of migrant labor would be an economic disaster of major magnitude. Disposable income in Lesotho would fall by about half. Foreign exchange receipts would fall even more. With assistance from the World Bank, the International Labour Organisation (ILO), the UK, Sweden, and other donors, the Lesotho government has done some contingency planning for this possibility since 1974. However, this planning has mainly been viewed in terms of "reemployment" and is quantitatively inadequate. The main vehicle of the publicly known planning is labor-intensive public works schemes, to be implemented through rapid expansion of the existing Labour Construction Unit (LCU). However, in December 1983, after six years' operation, LCU employed only 863 laborers, with plans for expansion to 2,000 during 1984. It is extraordinarily unlikely that LCU has the administrative or logistic capacity, or a stockpile of potential projects, to employ 100,000 to 150,000 workers in a matter of months.

This, however, is probably irrelevant. The LCU is the nucleus for a massive public works job program; but the immediate problem in the aftermath of a mass repatriation of migrants would not be jobs, it would be income support. Few migrant households have the assets to maintain consumption at acceptable levels for more than a few months without remittances. In early 1984, after two years of drought, Catholic Relief Services estimated that 30,000 children in Lesotho were likely to die unless emergency food aid deliveries were increased.[3] Recalling how low a proportion of total rural incomes come from cultivation and how high a proportion from migrant earnings, one can see that a sudden mass repatriation of migrants would produce widespread famine conditions quite quickly. LCU in practice, therefore, would be a mix of window-dressing and a vehicle for relief to a favored few.

The consequences of a total and sudden halt to migration would be so severe it is doubtful whether it would be enforced by South Africa more than temporarily. Donors would be appealed to for assistance, and many would probably respond, although logistically they could do nothing significant without South African cooperation for transport. The Lesotho government machinery would almost certainly be incapable of administering relief efficiently and fairly, and there would be serious political trouble within Lesotho. Realistically, the sanction is only likely to be applied if the Lesotho government is being intransigent about something the South African government considers important to its interests, and then only temporarily until either the Lesotho government gives in or is changed. However, even a brief interruption would cause havoc within the country and could have long-run political implications.

Regime Change in Lesotho

There has been no change of government in Lesotho since independence. Eventually, change must occur; interest centers on whether it might happen before Leabua Jonathan would like it to. This could come about either by elections or by violence.

Although it was announced in April 1984 that elections would be held in November 1984, the date has been repeatedly postponed. In January 1985 the National Assembly was dissolved, and a delimitation commission to establish constituency boundaries was set up. The commission submitted a provisional report in April 1985, which was the subject of much criticism at later public hearings. Speculation has continued that the elections may not take place and that the promise to hold them is little more than a sham designed to confuse the opposition and appease Western aid donors. However, registration of voters was well under way by May 1985, and elections in late 1985 seem very likely, not least because the ruling party has an excellent chance of winning them. The five opposition parties, MFP,

UDP, National Independence Party, BDA, and United Fatherland Front, that had emerged by August 1985, apparently judged the situation similarly. All five declined to put forward candidates to the nomination courts held on 14 August 1985, for the election scheduled for 17 and 18 September 1985, on the grounds that they had been denied access to the voters' roll. As a result, BNP candidates were declared to have been unopposed in all 60 constituencies and the elections were canceled because they were said to be no longer needed by the government's electoral office. This owes less to its intrinsic popularity, however, than to the opposition's disarray and the electoral advantages of the BNP.

The BCP must still be considered the major opposition party. However, it is badly fragmented. Mokhehle's external wing refuses to participate in elections without international supervision. The internal BCP is split into some four factions, and it is unlikely that they will be able to unite and mount an effective campaign for a single slate of candidates. The MFP continues to lose both leaders and followers to the BNP. The new Basotho Democratic Alliance (BDA) has no clear program, and the UDP has only very small support; both are heavily compromised by their close connections with Pretoria. The possible "third force" has not emerged and is unlikely to be a factor.

Against this probably disorganized and fragmented opposition, the BNP can bring to bear all the advantages of control of the government and electoral apparatus, notably broadcasting and the official media, transport, finance, and organization. For example, to participate, migrants must return to Lesotho to register. Of course, not all of them can or will return for this purpose, and migrants are believed in general to oppose the government. Furthermore, the BNP is unlikely to repeat the errors of 1970 and appear overconfident. Indeed, throughout 1984 and early 1985 the government made efforts to bring under tighter party control all those organizations and institutions that might act as a focus for opposition activity if elections were to be held. Increasing interference by the ruling party has been particularly noticeable at the university and within the trade union movement.[4] Thus, elections, if and when they are held, are unlikely in our opinion to remove the BNP from power. However, in January 1985 it was alleged that Godfrey Kolisang's faction of the BCP would form a "common front" with the UDP, the BDA, and the National Freedom Party for the elections and would field a single common candidate in each constituency. If this front materializes, the election might be closer than anticipated.

Violent overthrow of the government could arise in principle from three sources: the LLA, a right-wing coup by the security forces (higher ranks), or a left-wing coup by the security forces (lower ranks). None is likely, but all are possible.

Although the LLA does have some internal support, it is hard to envisage Mokhehle achieving power through the LLA without active South African assistance, and by late 1983 this appeared to have been withdrawn, with the South African authorities arresting LLA militants. This is scarcely surprising because once Jonathan had acquiesced to Pretoria's demands concerning the ANC, South Africa had little or nothing to gain from replacing him with Mokhehle.

Similarly, although there have been suggestions that right-wing senior officers in the security forces had considered a coup because of dissatisfaction with Jonathan's intransigence toward South Africa, the settlement of the ANC matter and the recent changes in relations between South Africa's government and its neighbors make this eventuality unlikely in the short run. Pretoria's support for the BDA and its impatience with Jonathan's continuing refusal to sign a formal Nkomati-style agreement do suggest, however, that an attempt at such a coup, with or without Pretoria's support, is not impossible.

Very little is known about the lower ranks of the police and military, although it is widely believed that most are BNP supporters and that chiefly families and Jonathan's relatives are well represented among junior and noncommissioned officers. However, in Southern Africa, politics are in perpetual ferment, and it is always possible that a group of junior officers, NCOs, or other ranks could become sufficiently disturbed by acquiescence to South African pressure and denigration of Lesotho's sovereignty and pride to mount a coup with nationalistic but relatively left-wing objectives. A coup of this kind would imply greater conflict with South Africa, and would probably be followed by attempts at a countercoup from the right with South African backing.

Overall, a change of regime, whether peaceful or violent, seems unlikely in the near future. But if it were to happen, what new implications would it have for government policy in Lesotho? Probably very few, because any new regime would still face the same constraints as the Jonathan government.

Despite the more socialist rhetorical tinge to the BCP in the past, if it came to power, it probably would not act much differently from the BNP. Beneath the rhetoric the BCP was never very radical and recently has been strongly anti-Communist. A further restraint on BCP behavior would be the party's recent reliance on South African support.

An extreme right-wing government, of a type the South African government might help to bring to power, would no doubt be more accommodating to South African wishes and in return might gain concessions on access for migrants to South Africa. However, this would probably be offset at least in part by losses of moral and material aid from international organizations and governments sensitive to the South African issue.

Similarly, a left-wing military regime might wish to sever ties with South Africa and institute radical changes in policy, but would find itself subject to the same constraints of dependence on migrant earnings and vulnerability to South African destabilization as Jonathan's regime has. Whatever government were to replace Jonathan's, the basic constraint of economic dependence and insecurity and the need to balance national self-interest between acquiescence and antagonism to South Africa would remain and would make major change in policy unlikely.

One consequence of a change of regime is likely, however. Despite the many shortcomings of Jonathan's government, and although it is autocratic, that government has shown commendable tolerance of its opponents for substantial stretches of time. Although human rights violations have occurred, they have not been widespread and cannot be said to be a systematic feature of policy. Daily and political life in Lesotho is several orders of magnitude more civil than in, say, the Uganda of recent years. However, massive tensions exist under the surface, and if Jonathan were to lose power, especially by a coup, violence might well be unleashed on a massive scale with extensive settling of scores, reprisals, and counterreprisals. Jonathan's human rights record is not good, but it is very plausible that the human rights situation under any successor regime might be very much worse.

A wholly domestically generated change of regime, therefore, seems unlikely. If it was to happen, furthermore, it would probably have little if any positive effect on the lives of most Basotho and quite probably would have negative ones. The most probable source of major change in internal conditions thus remains the possibility of major change in external conditions, i.e., in South Africa.

Radical Change in South Africa

Suppose the South African regime no longer followed an apartheid policy. How would this affect Lesotho? Obviously, much would depend on how South Africa reached such a situation and on the nature of the Lesotho government at the time. But there are three major possibilities. One is no real change, but a major cosmetic facelift for apartheid and much more cordial and closer cooperation. Migration and economic integration would continue, but in a friendlier atmosphere. Temporary migration would probably decline for standard labor market reasons, but illegal migration would probably expand and the educated and skilled from Lesotho would probably flock to South Africa. This could lead to the second possibility, namely that a racially color-blind or pro-Black government in South Africa might well also be highly nationalist, very concerned about domestic employment and income, and therefore more willing than the present government to cut off migration from Lesotho. The ensuing impoverishment and chaos in Lesotho could then precipitate the third possibility, namely that Lesotho would cease to exist as a sovereign state, becoming absorbed (by coup or military might) into the new South Africa. It is worth recalling that the ANC subscribes to the Freedom Charter, which states, "the people of the Protectorates . . . [including Lesotho] . . . shall be free to decide for themselves their own future," and that BCP leaders are on record as saying that when South Africa is liberated, there will be no reason for Lesotho to exist as a separate state. In practice, however, members of any future government in Lesotho, a BCP one included, would undoubtedly appreciate that they as individuals would have much to lose if Lesotho ceased to be a sovereign state, and their resistance to incorporation would receive considerable international support, especially in Africa, where the OAU considers independence frontiers sacrosanct. Possibly some sort of federal or confederal arrangement might emerge, but at this point speculation is in danger of becoming absurd, especially as a multiracial South Africa does not seem likely in the foreseeable future without a substantial escalation of violence, the outcome of which, for South Africa and Lesotho alike, is impossible to predict.

CONCLUSION

Finally, let us step back from these speculations about possible futures and reiterate what we see as the most likely future. It is, regrettably, grim for the bulk of the Basotho. Lesotho will continue to be governed by autocratic and sporadically repressive regimes, with domestic politics characterized by sharp dissension and occasional violence. The country will remain heavily dependent economically on South Africa, with migrant earnings the mainstay of the economy. Inequalities of income and wealth will become more severe, and the poor—especially those without access to migrant earnings or local cash wage jobs—will become more impoverished. Industrial development will be slow and halting, and tourism stagnant and discouraged by political instability and the symptoms of growing urban poverty. This is a bleak prognosis, and we hope the Basotho will find a way to avoid it. It is difficult, however, to see what that way might be.

NOTES

1. This difficulty is sometimes exacerbated by resentment by Basotho over income differentials and/or real or imagined racial attitudes.

2. This possibility was based on an estimate of volume given by the last British Police Chief and an estimate of the South African retail price. It was probably a gross overestimate because the wholesale price in Lesotho was no doubt substantially lower. South Africa rigorously attempts to prevent dagga (cannabis or marijuana) trafficking and destroy crops; Lesotho has similar legislation but normally acts only against individuals driving loaded vehicles with foreign plates.

3. *Africa News* 22, no. 9, 27 February 1984, p. 4.

4. One obvious example of increasing official interference in university affairs was the introduction in July 1984 of legislation that removed the powers hitherto held by the University Council over the selection and appointment of the vice-chancellor and vested these powers solely in the hands of the government. This enabled Jonathan to ignore the council's recommendation for the post (which had become vacant at the end of June 1984) and to impose his own candidate for the position, B. A. Tlelase, the former minister of education and staunch BNP stalwart. With reference to the trade union movement, the government has been attempting to secure the merger of the two major trade union federations, the Lesotho Federation of Trade Unions (formerly the BFL) and the Lesotho Council of Workers, undoubtedly in the expectation that a single federation would be more susceptible to official control. The two federations merged voluntarily in January 1983 but subsequently split again in November 1983. The government during 1984 coerced another merger with the threat of legislation to enforce it.

Selected Bibliography

In compiling this bibliography, we have attempted to balance a desire to give credit to our sources against both the needs of our readers and space limitations. Our solution has been to list *only* formally published books and journal articles, which should be accessible through a university library, and to omit all mimeographed materials, theses and dissertations, documents of international organizations, government documents published in Africa, and specialized references already cited in notes. It will be obvious to those familiar with Lesotho that we have relied heavily on some of these omitted items, even though on occasion for the sake of brevity we have not made reference to them. Even within the included categories, we have been highly selective and have listed the items that we feel are most likely to be useful to the reader. Those who would like more detail are referred to Shelagh M. Willet and David P. Ambrose *Lesotho: A Comprehensive Bibliography*, World Bibliographical Series, Vol. 3, Oxford and Santa Barbara: Clio Press, 1980.

Agency for Industrial Mission (AIM). *Another Blanket: Report on an Investigation into the Migrant Situation.* Horison, South Africa: Agency for Industrial Mission, 1976.

Ambrose, David; Campbell, Alec; and Johnson, David. *The Guide to Botswana, Lesotho and Swaziland.* Saxonwold: Winchester Press, 1983.

Bardill, John. "Dependence and Development in Lesotho: A Critique of Winai Strom." *South African Labour Bulletin* 6(4): 79–90, November 1980.

Breytenbach, W. J. *Crocodiles and Commoners in Lesotho: Continuity and Change in the Rulemaking System of Lesotho.* Pretoria: Africa Institute, 1975.

Burman, Sandra. *The Justice of the Queen's Government: The Cape's Administration of Basutoland, 1871–1884.* Cambridge: African Studies Centre, 1976.

——— . *Chiefdom Politics and Alien Law: Basutoland Under Cape Rule, 1871–1884.* London: Macmillan, 1981.

Coates, Austin. *Basutoland.* London: Her Majesty's Stationery Office, 1966.

Cobbe, James. "Wage Policy Problems in the Small Peripheral Countries of Southern Africa, 1967–76." *Journal of Southern African Affairs* 2(4):441–468, October 1977.

———. "Growth and Change in Lesotho," *South African Journal of Economics* 46(2):135–153, June 1978.

———. "Planning in Lesotho." In *Development of Urban Systems in Africa*, edited by R. A. Obudho and S. S. El-Shakhs. New York: Praeger, 1979.

———. "Integration Among Unequals: The Southern African Customs Union and Development." *World Development* 8:(4):329–336, April 1980.

———. "Emigration and Development in Southern Africa, with Special Reference to Lesotho." *International Migration Review* 16(4):837–868, Winter 1982.

———. "The Education System, Wage and Salary Structures, and Income Distribution: Lesotho as a Case Study, Circa 1975." *Journal of Developing Areas* 17(2):227–241, January 1983.

———. "The Changing Nature of Dependence: Economic Problems in Lesotho." *Journal of Modern African Studies* 21(2):293–310, June 1983.

Duncan, Patrick. *Sotho Laws and Customs*. Cape Town: Oxford University Press, 1960.

Eckert, J. B. "The Employment Challenge Facing Lesotho." *Development Studies Southern Africa* 5(2):248–261, January 1983.

Ellenberger, D. F. *History of the Basuto: Ancient and Modern*. Translated by J. C. Macgregor. London: Caxton, 1912; New York: Negro Universities Press, 1969.

Frank, Lawrence. *The Basutoland National Party: Traditional Authority and Neo-Colonialism in Lesotho*. Denver: Center on International Race Relations, 1971.

———. "Khama and Jonathan: Leadership Strategies in Contemporary Southern Africa." *Journal of Developing Areas* 15(2):173–198, January 1981.

Gay, Judy. "Basotho Women Migrants: A Case Study." *Institute of Development Studies Bulletin* 11(4):19–28, October 1980.

———. "Wage Employment of Rural Basotho Women: A Case Study." *South African Labour Bulletin* 6(4):40–53, November 1980.

Germond, R. C. *Chronicles of Basutoland*. Morija: Sesuto Book Depot, 1967.

Gordon, E. "An Analysis of the Impact of Labor Migration on the Lives of Women in Lesotho." *Journal of Development Studies* 17(3):59–76, April 1981.

Gray, John; Robertson, Neil; and Walton, Michael. "Lesotho: A Strategy for Survival After the Golden Seventies." *South African Labour Bulletin* 6(4):62–78, November 1980.

Haliburton, Gordon. *Historical Dictionary of Lesotho*. Metuchen, N.J.: Scarecrow Press, 1977.

Halpern, Jack. *South Africa's Hostages: Basutoland, Bechuanaland and Swaziland*. Harmondsworth: Penguin, 1965.

Hamnett, Ian. *Chieftainship and Legitimacy: An Anthropological Study of Executive Law in Lesotho*. London: Routledge & Kegan Paul, 1975.

Hirschmann, David. "Changes in Lesotho's Policy Towards South Africa." *African Affairs* 78(311):177–196, April 1979.

———. *Administration of Planning in Lesotho: A History and Assessment.* Manchester: Manchester University Papers on Development (2), November 1981.

Holm, John D. "Political Stability in Lesotho." *Africa Today* 19(4):3–16, Fall 1972.

Jingoes, Stimela Jason. *A Chief Is a Chief by the People.* London: Oxford University Press, 1975.

Jobs and Skills Programme for Africa (JASPA). *Options for a Dependent Economy: Development, Employment and Equity Problems in Lesotho.* Addis Ababa: International Labour Office Jobs and Skills Programme for Africa, 1979.

Khaketla, B. M. *Lesotho 1970: An African Coup Under the Microscope.* London: C. Hurst, 1971; Berkeley: University of California Press, 1972.

Kimble, Judy. "Aspects of the Penetration of Capitalism into Colonial Basutoland, 1890–1930." In *Class Formation and Class Struggle: Selected Proceedings of the Fourth Annual Southern African Universities Social Science Conference, 1981,* edited by John Bardill. Morija: Sesuto Book Depot, 1982.

———. "Labour Migration in Basutoland, c. 1870–1885." In *Industrialization and Social Change in Southern Africa: African Class Formation, Culture and Consciousness, 1870-1930,* edited by Shula Marks and Richard Rathbone. London and New York: Longman, 1982.

Knight, J. B., and Lenta, G. "Has Capitalism Underdeveloped the Labour Reserves of South Africa?" *Oxford Bulletin of Economics and Statistics* 42(3):157–201, August 1980.

Kowet, Donald Kalinde. *Land, Labour Migration and Politics in Southern Africa: Botswana, Lesotho and Swaziland.* Uppsala: The Scandinavian Institute for African Studies, 1978.

Legassick, Martin. "The Sotho-Tswana Peoples Before 1800." In *African Societies in Southern Africa,* edited by Leonard Thompson. London: Heinemann, 1972.

Leistner, G.M.E. *Lesotho: Economic Structure and Growth.* Pretoria: Africa Institute, 1966.

Leys, Roger. "Lesotho: Non-Development or Underdevelopment: Towards an Analysis of the Political Economy of the Labour Reserve." In *The Politics of Africa: Dependence and Development,* edited by T. Shaw and K. Heard. Halifax, N.S., African Studies Series, 1978.

Lye, William F., and Murray, Colin. *Transformations on the High Veld: The Tswana and the Southern Sotho.* Totowa, N.J.: Barnes and Noble, 1979.

Macartney, W.J.A. "African Westminster? The Parliament of Lesotho." *Parliamentary Affairs* 23(2):121–140, 1970.

———. "Case Study: The Lesotho General Election of 1970." *Government and Opposition* 8(4):473–494, Autumn 1973.

Marres, Pieter, and van der Wiel, Arie. *Poverty Eats My Blanket: A Poverty Study—The Case of Lesotho.* Maseru: Government Printer, 1975.

Murray, Colin. "Marital Strategy in Lesotho: The Redistribution of Migrant Earnings." *African Studies* 35:99–121, April 1976.

──── . "High Bridewealth, Migrant Labour and the Position of Women in Lesotho." *Journal of African Law* 21(1):79–96, 1977.

──── . "Migration, Differentiation, and the Developmental Cycle in Lesotho." In *Migration and the Transformation of Modern African Society*, edited by W.M.J. van Binsbergen and H. Meilink. Leiden: Afrikastudiecentrum, 1978.

──── . "The Work of Men, Women, and the Ancestors: Social Reproduction in the Periphery of Southern Africa." In *Social Anthropology of Work*, edited by Sandra Wallman. London: Academic Press, 1979.

──── . "Migrant Labour and Changing Family Structure in the Rural Periphery of Southern Africa." *Journal of Southern African Studies* 6(2):139–156, April 1980.

──── . "From Granary to Labour Reserve: An Economic History of Lesotho." *South African Labour Bulletin* 6(4):3–20, November 1980.

──── . "The Effects of Migrant Labour: A Review of the Evidence from Lesotho." *South African Labour Bulletin* 6(4):21–39, November 1980.

──── . "'Stabilization' and Structural Unemployment." *South African Labour Bulletin* 6(4):58–61, November 1980.

──── . *Families Divided: The Impact of Migrant Labour in Lesotho.* Johannesburg: Ravan Press; and Cambridge: Cambridge University Press, 1981.

Palmer, Vernon, and Poulter, Sebastian. *The Legal System of Lesotho.* Charlottesville, Va.: Michie Company, 1972.

Perry, J.A.G. "Land and Politics in Lesotho." *African Studies* 42(1):57–66, 1983.

Poulter, Sebastian. *Family Law and Litigation in Basotho Society.* Oxford: Clarendon Press, 1976.

──── . *Legal Dualism in Lesotho.* Morija: Morija Sesuto Book Depot, 1981.

Safilios-Rothschild, Constantina. "The Persistence of Women's Invisibility in Agriculture: Theoretical and Policy Lessons from Lesotho and Sierra Leone." *Economic Development and Cultural Change* 33(2):299–318, January 1985.

Sanders, Peter. *Moshoeshoe: Chief of the Sotho.* London: Heinemann, 1975.

Sheddick, V.G.J. *Land Tenure in Basutoland.* Colonial Research Studies, No. 13. London: Her Majesty's Stationery Office, 1954.

Showers, Kate. "A Note on Women, Conflict and Migrant Labour." *South African Labour Bulletin* 6(4):54–57, November 1980.

Singh, A. "Foreign Aid for Structural Change: Lesotho." In *Industry and Accumulation in Africa*, edited by Martin Fransman. London: Heinemann, 1982.

Spence, Jack. "British Policy Towards the High Commission Territories." *Journal of Modern African Studies* 2(2):221–246, July 1964.

──── . *Lesotho: The Politics of Dependence.* London: Oxford University Press, 1968.

Spiegel, Andrew. "Rural Differentiation and the Diffusion of Migrant Labour Remittances in Lesotho." In *Black Villagers in an Industrial Society,* edited by P. Mayer. Cape Town: Oxford University Press, 1980.

————. "Changing Patterns of Migrant Labour and Rural Differentiation in Lesotho." *Social Dynamics* 6(2):1–13, December 1981.

Stevens, Richard P. *Lesotho, Botswana, and Swaziland: The Former High Commission Territories in Southern Africa.* London: Pall Mall Press, 1967.

Theal, George McCall. *Basutoland Records.* 4 Vols. Facsimile Reproduction of 1883 Edition. Cape Town: Struik, 1964.

Thompson, Leonard. *Survival in Two Worlds: Moshoeshoe of Lesotho 1786–1870.* Oxford: Oxford University Press, 1975.

Turner, Stephen D. "Soil Conservation: Administrative and Extension Approaches in Lesotho." *Agricultural Administration* 9(2):147–162, 1982.

van de Geer, Roeland, and Wallis, Malcolm. *Government and Development in Rural Lesotho.* Public Administration Research and Curriculum Development Project, National University of Lesotho. Morija: Sesuto Book Depot, 1982.

van der Wiel, Arie. *Migratory Wage Labour: Its Role in the Economy of Lesotho.* Mazenod: Mazenod Book Centre, 1977.

Wallis, Malcolm, and Henderson, Robert D'A. "Lesotho 1983: Year of the Election?" *The World Today* 39(5):185–193. May 1983.

Wallman, Sandra. *Take Out Hunger: Two Case Studies of Rural Development in Basutoland.* London: London School of Economics Monographs on Social Anthropology, No. 39, 1969.

————. *Perceptions of Development.* Cambridge: Cambridge University Press, 1977.

Ward, Michael. "Economic Independence for Lesotho?" *Journal of Modern African Studies* 5(3):355–368, September 1967.

Weisfelder, Richard. "Defining National Purpose in Lesotho." *Papers in International Studies, Africa Series No. 3.* Athens, Ohio: 1969.

————. "Lesotho and South Africa: Diverse Linkages." *Africa Today* 18(2):48–55, Spring 1971.

————. "Lesotho." In *Southern Africa in Perspective: Essays in Regional Politics,* edited by Christian Potholm and Richard Dale. London: Collier-Macmillan; New York: Free Press, 1972.

————. "The Basotho Monarchy: A Spent Force or a Dynamic Political Factor?" *Papers in International Studies, Africa Series No. 16.* Athens, Ohio: 11–29, 1973.

————. "Early Voices of Protest in Basutoland: The Progressive Association and the Lekhotla la Bafo." *African Studies Review* 17(2):397–410, September 1974.

————. "The Decline of Human Rights in Lesotho: An Evaluation of Domestic and External Determinants." *Issue: A Quarterly Journal of Africanist Opinion* 6(4):22–23, Winter 1976.

————. "Lesotho: Changing Patterns of Dependence." In *Southern Africa: The Continuing Crisis,* edited by Gwendolen Carter and Patrick O'Meara. Bloomington: Indiana University Press, 1979.

———. "The Basotho Nation-State: What Legacy for the Future?" *Journal of Modern African Studies* 19(2):221–256, June 1981.

———. "Human Rights Under Majority Rule in Southern Africa: The Mote in Thy Brother's Eye." In *Human Rights and Development in Africa: Domestic, Regional and International Dilemmas,* edited by Claude E. Welch, Jr., and Ronald I. Meltzer. Albany: State University of New York Press, 1983.

Wellings, P. A. "Aid to the Southern African Periphery: The Case of Lesotho." *Applied Geography* 2:267–290, 1982.

———. "Making a Fast Buck: Capital Leakage and the Public Accounts of Lesotho." *African Affairs* 82(329):495–508, October 1983.

Wellings, P. A., and Crush, J. S. "Tourism and Dependency in Southern Africa: The Prospects and Planning of Tourism in Lesotho." *Applied Geography* 3:205–223, 1983.

Williams, J. C. *Lesotho: Three Manpower Problems—Education, Health, Population Growth.* Pretoria: Africa Institute, 1971.

———. *Lesotho: Land Tenure and Economic Development.* Pretoria: Africa Institute, 1972.

Winai-Strom, Gabriele. *Development and Dependence in Lesotho: The Enclave of South Africa.* Uppsala: Scandinavian Institute of African Studies, 1978.

Woodward, Calvin. "Not a Complete Solution: Assessing the Long Years of Foreign Aid to Lesotho." *Africa Insight* 12(3):167–179, 1982.

Index